Linking Windows™ 3.1

Jenna Christen

Bryan Pfaffenberger

que

Linking Windows 3.1

Copyright © 1992 by Que® Corporation.

All rights reserved. Printed in the United States of America. No part of this book may be used or reproduced in any form or by any means, or stored in a database or retrieval system, without prior written permission of the publisher except in the case of brief quotations embodied in critical articles and reviews. Making copies of any part of this book for any purpose other than your own personal use is a violation of United States copyright laws. For information, address Que Corporation, 11711 N. College Ave., Carmel, IN 46032.

Library of Congress Catalog No.: 92-64355

ISBN: 1-56529-051-8

This book is sold *as is*, without warranty of any kind, either express or implied, respecting the contents of this book, including but not limited to implied warranties for the book's quality, performance, merchantability, or fitness for any particular purpose. Neither Que Corporation nor its dealers or distributors shall be liable to the purchaser or any other person or entity with respect to any liability, loss, or damage caused or alleged to be caused directly or indirectly by this book.

94 93   5 4 3 2

Interpretation of the printing code: the rightmost double-digit number is the year of the book's printing; the rightmost single-digit number, the number of the book's printing. For example, a printing code of 92-1 shows that the first printing of the book occurred in 1992.

Screen reproductions in this book were created using Collage Plus from Inner Media, Inc., Hollis, NH.

Excerpts and/or screen captures from Harvard Graphics™ 1.0 for Windows, including text material, are used with the permission of Software Publishing Corporation, which owns the copyright to such product. This program has no connection with Harvard University.

Publisher: Lloyd J. Short

Associate Publisher: Rick Ranucci

Product Development Manager: Thomas H. Bennett

Book Designer: Scott Cook

Production Team: Jeff Baker, Claudia Bell, Jodie Cantwell, Paula Carroll, Brook Farling, Bob LaRoche, Jay Lesandrini, Cindy L. Phipps, Caroline Roop, Sandra Shay, Linda Seifert, Lisa Wilson, Phil Worthington

Product Director
Timothy S. Stanley

Acquisitions Editor
Tim Ryan

Production Editor
Lori A. Lyons

Editor
Barb Colter

Technical Editor
John Tyler Fosdick III

Composed in ITC Garamond and MCPdigital
by Que Corporation.

Dedication

To my lovely mother: you were always there for me and I will always be there for you — JC

To Suzanne — BP

About the Authors

JENNA CHRISTEN

Jenna Christen is an independent consultant and computer software writer based in Portland, Oregon. She has written several computer applications books and instructor's manuals for four major publishers, including Que Corporation. Jenna formerly worked as a technical editor and corporate trainer. She has a degree in English from the University of California at Berkeley and also studied at the Sorbonne, the College of William and Mary, and Tulane University.

BRYAN PFAFFENBERGER

A professional writer on computer-related subjects, Bryan Pfaffenberger, Ph.D., teaches technology studies and technical writing at the University of Virginia (School of Engineering and Applied Science), where he is Associate Professor of Humanities. Bryan has written more than 30 books on computer-related subjects, including Que's *Computerizing Your Small Business*, *Que's Computer User's Dictionary*, and *Using Word 5 for the Mac*, Special Edition. Very happily married to his wife of 16 years, Suzanne, he is the father of two children (Michael and Julia). Bryan's hobbies and interests include space and New Age music, folk guitar, model aeronautics, and hiking.

Trademark Acknowledgments

Que Corporation has made every effort to supply trademark information about company names, products, and services mentioned in this book. Trademarks indicated below were derived from various sources. Que Corporation cannot attest to the accuracy of this information.

1-2-3 and Lotus are registered trademarks of Lotus Development Corporation.

Ami Pro is a trademark of Samna Corporation, a wholly owned subsidiary of Lotus Development Corporation.

Harvard Graphics is a registered trademark of Software Publishing Corporation.

IBM and IBM PS/2 are registered trademarks of International Business Machines Corporation.

Microsoft, Microsoft Excel, Microsoft Word for Windows, Microsoft Windows, and MS-DOS are registered trademarks of Microsoft Corporation.

Quattro Pro is a registered trademark of Borland International, Inc.

WordPerfect is a registered trademark of WordPerfect Corporation.

Trademarks of other products mentioned in this book are held by the companies producing them.

Acknowledgments

Our gratitude to family and friends who supported us during the writing process. We also want to thank everyone who made this book possible: the product teams at Lotus, Microsoft, Borland, WordPerfect, and Software Publishing Corporation; and at Que, Tim Stanley who pulled the project together; Lori Lyons and Barb Colter for their superb editing; and most of all Tim Ryan, whose unique mixture of efficiency, humor, and understanding made it a true pleasure to work on the project.

Contents at a Glance

Introduction 1

Part I: Understanding Linking and Embedding Basics 7

1 Understanding Linking and Embedding 9
2 Creating and Managing Links 21
3 Embedding Objects 41
4 Packaging Objects 59
5 Understanding Dynamic Data Exchange (DDE) 83

Part II: Exploring Linking and Embedding Techniques 111

6 Linking between 1-2-3 and Ami Pro 113
7 Linking a Named Range in 1-2-3 to WordPerfect 131
8 Linking between Ami Pro and WordPerfect 153
9 Linking an Embedded Excel Chart to a Word Memo 177
10 Embedding Word in an Excel Worksheet 195
11 Embedding a Harvard Graphics Presentation in Quattro Pro 213

Index 227

Table of Contents

Introduction 1

Why Integrate Windows Applications? 2
Why a Book on Linking? 3
Who Should Read This Book? 4

Part I: Understanding Linking and Embedding Basics

1 Understanding Linking and Embedding 9

Understanding the Need for Linking and Embedding 9
Learning the Basic Terms 10
Understanding Linking 12
Understanding Embedding 14
Choosing between Linking and Embedding 16
Understanding Packaging 18
Understanding DDE 19
Summary 20

2 Creating and Managing Links 21

Linking to Other Applications 23
Understanding How Linking Works 26
Editing Linked Documents 27
Opening Documents That Contain Links 30
Editing Multiple Links 31
Controlling Link Settings 31
    Choosing the Data Type 32
    Controlling Update Frequency 34
    Updating Manual Links 36
Breaking the Link 36

ix

Restoring a Broken Link 37
Troubleshooting Links 38
Summary 40

3 Embedding Objects 41

Understanding When To Use Embedding 42
Choosing the Correct Embedding Procedure 45
Creating an Embedded Object 46
    Starting from the Server Application 47
    Starting from the Client Application 49
Editing Embedded Objects 52
Deleting an Embedded Object 52
Canceling Embedding without Deleting the Object 53
Using Microsoft's OLE Servers 54
Troubleshooting Embedding Problems 56
Summary 58

4 Packaging Objects 59

Packaging Options 62
    Packaging an Entire Document 63
        Packaging with the Clipboard 63
        Packaging with Drag-and-Drop 65
        Packaging an Entire Document
            Using Object Packager 67
    Packaging Part of a Document 70
Activating the Packaged Object 72
Editing the Package
    with Object Packager 72
Choosing Manual Updating 74
Creating Your Own Icons 76
Packaging a DOS Command 78
Putting It All Together: Creating
    Interactive Documents 80
Using Other Object Packager Commands 81
Summary 82

5 Understanding Dynamic Data Exchange (DDE) 83

Understanding the Purpose of DDE 85
Understanding the Structure of DDE Messages 87
Understanding Windows' DDE Message Set 91
Using Advanced DDE Capabilities 93
   Accessing Bookmarks in Word
     Processing Documents..93
   Accessing Spreadsheet Ranges 95
   Accessing Databases 95
Using DDE Commands in Macros 97
   Understanding DDE Macro Commands.....................98
   Looking at a DDE Macro 99
   Using the SYSTEM Topic 100
   Sending Data to the Server Application 102
   Executing Commands 104
Putting It All Together: An Automated
   DDE Application 105
Troubleshooting DDE Commands 109
Summary 110

Part II: Exploring Linking and Embedding Techniques

6 Linking between 1-2-3 and Ami Pro 113

Linking Portions of an Ami Pro Document to
   a 1-2-3 Spreadsheet File 114
   Preparing the Ami Pro Document 115
   Preparing the 1-2-3 Spreadsheet 117
   Creating the Link 118
   Changing the Linked Bookmark 121
   Deactivating versus Deleting Text 124
Linking a 1-2-3 Spreadsheet to
   an Ami Pro Document 125
   Copying the Spreadsheet To Be Linked 125

xi

Creating the Link 126
Editing the Link 126
Making Format Changes 129
Deactivating the Link 129
Summary 130

7 Linking a Named Range in 1-2-3 to WordPerfect 131

Using the Edit Link Create Command 134
    Setting Up the 1-2-3 Spreadsheet
       and Named Range 135
    Setting Up the WordPerfect Document 137
    Creating the DDE Link 137
    Changing the Format of the Linked Data 139
    Editing the DDE Link 140
Using the Spreadsheet Link Command 142
    Creating the Spreadsheet Link 144
    Setting Link Options 146
    Editing the Spreadsheet Link 148
    Updating the Spreadsheet Link 149
    Deleting the Spreadsheet Link 151
Summary 152

8 Linking between Ami Pro and WordPerfect 153

Linking an Ami Pro Agenda to a WordPerfect Memo 155
    Using DDE Linking 156
    Creating the Agenda and Copying It
       to the Clipboard 158
    Opening and Preparing the
       WordPerfect Document 159
    Creating the Link and Modifying
       the Source File 160
    Unwanted Coding 162
    Editing the Link 163
    Updating the Link 165
Linking a WordPerfect Table to an Ami Pro Report 166

Using OLE Linking 167
Preparing the WordPerfect Table 167
Using the File Manager and Object Packager 168
Pasting the Package into Ami Pro 171
Opening the Package 172
Editing the Link 174
Summary 176

9 Linking an Embedded Excel Chart to a Word Memo 177

Linking a Chart Embedded in a Worksheet 178
Setting Up the Data To Be Charted 179
Creating an Embedded Chart 180
Saving the Chart and Copying It
  to the Clipboard 184
Setting Up the Word Memo 185
Creating the Link from Excel to Word 186
Choosing Manual Updating 187
Reconnecting a Broken Link 189
Cancelling the Link 190
Editing the Appearance of the Chart 191
Summary 194

10 Embedding Word in an Excel Worksheet 195

Embedding an Entire Word Document
  into an Excel Worksheet 197
Setting Up the Excel Worksheet 198
Embedding the First Document 199
Returning to the Excel Worksheet 200
Embedding the Second Document 202
Editing an Embedded Object 203
Setting Object Properties 204
Preventing an Object from Printing 207
Printing an Embedded Object 207
Deleting an Embedded Object 208

xiii

Embedding Part of a Word Document
into an Excel Worksheet 208
Copying the Existing Data in Word 208
Preparing the Excel Worksheet 209
Embedding the Partial Document into Excel 210
Summary 212

11 Embedding a Harvard Graphics Presentation in Quattro Pro 213

Preparing the Quattro Pro Notebook 215
Embedding the Harvard Graphics Presentation 216
Changing the Label 219
Changing the Icon 220
Completing the Embedding Process 222
Viewing the Embedded Object 223
Deleting the Embedded Object 225
Summary 226

Index 227

Introduction

In this book, you learn how to master the techniques of integrating your Windows applications so that they exchange data with each other automatically. For example, you learn how to copy a Lotus 1-2-3 for Windows spreadsheet into a WordPerfect for Windows document with dynamic ("hot") links so that Windows automatically updates the WordPerfect document if you make changes to the 1-2-3 spreadsheet. You learn how you can embed an Excel chart into a Word for Windows document so that starting Excel and editing the chart is as easy as double-clicking the chart that appears within Word. You will find many more specific examples, as well.

This book also provides a clear, conceptual introduction to every aspect of Windows application integration. If you have tried to understand this subject, you probably have had difficulty finding clear definitions or explanations of terms such as *object linking and embedding (OLE)* or *dynamic data exchange (DDE)*, both of which are fundamental to integrating Windows applications. This book presents a clear, readable introduction to these concepts. No matter which Windows applications you're using, this conceptual introduction will assist you as you integrate the applications you're using. When you finish reading this book, you will know how to apply the full power of Microsoft Windows' integration capabilities to your everyday work with your personal computer.

Why Integrate Windows Applications?

If you're like most Windows users, you're probably content to use your applications without integrating them. Why in the world would you want to link a 1-2-3 worksheet to a WordPerfect document?

The best way to understand the benefits of application integration is to ponder an example. Suppose that you're working on an analysis of a firm that your company wants to buy. In your Quattro Pro for Windows document, you type in all the figures, add the formulas, and Bingo! You get the results. Using the Clipboard's Copy and Paste commands, you copy this figure to your Ami Pro document, which you've prepared for the managing board.

You then discover a mistake in one of your formulas—a mistake that throws your results off by a wide margin. You correct the mistake and save your worksheet. Just then, someone comes into your office for a lengthy discussion, and you forget to recopy the altered result to the Ami Pro document. You then print up your Ami Pro report for the board, complete with the wrong result.

As you discuss your results at the board meeting, someone points out that your figure is incorrect. You remember, suddenly, that you forgot to update that figure in the Ami Pro report! In unison, the board members' heads swivel around to ponder you in the moment of your disarray.

Although this example may seem extreme, such situations have indeed happened. But the technology's already in place to make sure that this needn't happen again. Today, users work with several applications at a time—that's one of the reasons users have switched to Microsoft Windows. You don't need to continue updating data manually because Windows provides the technology to do so automatically.

Incorporated into Microsoft Windows are two sets of standards that permit application integration. The first (and earliest), *dynamic data exchange (DDE)*, establishes the basis for *linking*, in which the changes you make to a source document are updated automatically in copies you have made of this document and inserted in other documents—even those of other applications. Windows has included DDE capabilities from Version 2.0.

The second standard that permits application integration, *object linking and embedding (OLE)*, provides easy-to-use menu commands for linking, and it also makes possible a new kind of application integration called *embedding*. With embedding, you can create a *compound document* in which the various parts were created by different applications. Such a document could contain text created by Ami Pro, a beautiful title created by Microsoft WordArt, a presentation-quality graphic created by Microsoft Excel, and a spreadsheet table created by Quattro Pro for Windows. To edit such a document, you just place the cursor in the portion you want to edit, and Windows starts the application that created the object. Windows Version 3.1 was the first version to fully support OLE.

You have more to learn about DDE and OLE. For now, however, two points are worth stressing:

- **Although DDE and OLE sound complicated, any Windows user can learn to link and embed**. This is especially true with Windows applications that fully support OLE, the most recent of the two application integration standards. To create links or compound documents, you just choose commands from menus.

- **Learning how to use DDE and OLE will increase your Windows competence and productivity by a huge margin**. These subjects aren't just weird, esoteric topics that would be explored only by a computer nut. They are very useful techniques that you can use in your everyday work.

Why a Book on Linking?

Of all the features of Microsoft Windows and Windows applications, DDE and OLE are among the least documented. In many cases, you will search your manuals in vain to find clear explanations of what these features are for, how they work, and what happens if they don't work.

Industry observers have continually been surprised to find that ordinary personal computer users aren't content to use their systems on an elementary level. Personal computer users have learned how to write macros. They have gone to extremes to exchange data between incompatible systems or applications. And a surprising percentage of them, as *PC Magazine* discovered in a recent survey, have even tried some assembly language programming. You can safely conclude that Windows users will explore DDE and OLE. This book provides the conceptual background and tutorials that most people will need, if they want to master DDE and OLE techniques.

Who Should Read This Book?

This book is written for every Windows user, from beginning to advanced, who wants to learn how to use DDE and OLE to integrate Windows applications. If you're a beginner, you will find plenty of easy-to-use techniques that you can implement just by choosing commands from menus. You can safely skip the more advanced material, if you want, or put if off until later. If you're a more advanced user, familiar with macros and eager to learn more about them, you will discover that this book progresses deeply into the mysteries of DDE, including DDE macro commands.

How Is This Book Organized?

In line with the best corporate computer training programs, this book emphasizes both concepts and skills.

> **NOTE** Application integration is currently in transition, thanks to the amazing new capabilities of Windows 3.1. Not all Windows applications currently support the OLE standard, which makes linking much easier and embedding possible. Applications that do not support OLE may nevertheless support DDE, the older standard, although some applications support neither. If your applications support DDE but not OLE, you can use the older DDE techniques, which are somewhat more difficult to use, to create dynamic links with these applications. Because OLE is so much easier to use, this book begins by discussing the OLE procedures for linking and embedding. If your applications do not support OLE, don't despair. You will find plenty of information about linking these applications in subsequent chapters.

The following provides a quick overview of the material covered in this book:

Part I, "Understanding Linking and Embedding Basics," provides a conceptual overview of linking and embedding.

Chapter 1, "Understanding Linking and Embedding," provides a conceptual integration to linking and embedding, the two fundamental processes discussed in this book. You learn the terms you need to know to understand OLE and DDE concepts and processes.

Chapter 2, "Creating and Managing Links," teaches you how to use OLE to create "hot links" (dynamic links) between one application's source document (the document that contains the source data, such as a chart or spreadsheet) and a destination document. When you change the source document, Windows automatically updates the destination document.

Chapter 3, "Embedding Objects," fully surveys the topic of creating compound documents with OLE-capable applications.

Chapter 4, "Packaging Objects," discusses Windows 3.1's useful new accessory, Object Packager, which enables you to minimize linked or embedded material and to insert it into documents as an icon. When you double-click the icon, Windows starts the application that created the material, allowing you to view or edit it. This chapter fully discusses the use of Object Packager, including the creation of interactive documents.

Chapter 5, "Understanding Dynamic Data Exchange (DDE)," delves into the older Windows integration standard, DDE. Even though OLE makes linking and embedding much easier to achieve, in practice, there are good reasons for exploring DDE. Some applications don't yet support OLE, so you need to understand DDE if you want to create links. With DDE, you can take advantage of linking capabilities that OLE doesn't implement, including using DDE commands in application macros.

Part II, "Exploring Linking and Embedding Techniques," presents keystroke-by-keystroke tutorials, which guide you through the process of linking specific Windows applications.

Chapter 6, "Linking between 1-2-3 and Ami Pro," presents the techniques you can use to create dynamic links between these two widely used applications. You learn how to link Ami Pro text to a 1-2-3 worksheet, and you learn how to link a 1-2-3 worksheet to an Ami Pro document.

Chapter 7, "Linking a Named Range in 1-2-3 to WordPerfect," presents tutorials that guide you through the process of linking these two applications, neither of which are yet capable of OLE.

Chapter 8, "Linking between Ami Pro and WordPerfect," presents some very interesting ways you can create links between these two word processing applications, including linking an Ami Pro agenda to a WordPerfect document. You also discover how you can use Object Packager to package WordPerfect documents, even though WordPerfect isn't yet capable of OLE.

Chapter 9, "Linking an Embedded Excel Chart to a Word Memo," presents a tutorial that explores this tricky process, which isn't as easy as most OLE-based operations.

Chapter 10, "Embedding Word in an Excel Worksheet," reverses the data flow discussed in Chapter 9 by embedding Word objects in Excel worksheets.

Chapter 11, "Embedding a Harvard Graphics Presentation in Quattro Pro," guides you through the extension of Quattro Pro's capabilities so that, in effect, they encompass all those of Harvard Graphics. You learn why embedding may be the most powerful and useful of all the techniques discussed in this book.

Linking Windows 3.1 explores OLE and DDE thoroughly—and frankly, if you like Windows, you're in for a treat. After you try linking and embedding, chances are that you will be amazed at the computer power sitting on your desktop. Personal computing has come a long way in just ten years. Computers today are as powerful (or more powerful) than the corporate mainframes of fifteen years ago.

What's more, Windows shows what computing will look like in the future, when computers will enable you to focus entirely on the document you're creating, rather than on the particulars of the application you happen to be using at the time. In these systems, applications will be no more than sets of tools, which you can bring to bear on your documents as you please. By understanding linking and embedding, you are taking giant steps into the future of personal computing.

PART ONE

Understanding Linking and Embedding Basics

Understanding Linking and Embedding

Creating and Managing Links

Embedding Objects

Packaging Objects

Understanding Dynamic Data Exchange (DDE)

CHAPTER ONE

Understanding Linking and Embedding

Linking is easy to do, but the underlying concepts are new to most personal computer users. This chapter provides a conceptual overview of application linking. To apply OLE and DDE successfully, you need to learn some basic distinctions and a few terms. In this chapter, you also see some examples of linking in action—to the extent that we can show these dynamic processes in a printed work!

Understanding the Need for Linking and Embedding

As a Windows user, you've already learned that working with Windows helps you break down the boundaries separating applications. Under versions of DOS, you worked with just one program at a time; transferring data from one program to another could be difficult. (Often, you had to write the data to an intermediary file, in some bizarre format, which only one other application could read.) With Windows, you can open two, three, or more applications at a time. You can switch from one application to another just by pressing Alt+Esc (or by choosing Switch To from the Control menu). If you're working on a report, you can switch to Microsoft Excel and run a "what-if" scenario, without having to quit Microsoft Word for Windows. Using the Clipboard, you can paste information from one application to another—for example, a Lotus 1-2-3 for Windows worksheet into a WordPerfect for Windows document.

Pasting via the Clipboard is a useful technique, but as you have no doubt discovered, it does have two serious drawbacks:

- After you paste information into an application using the Paste command (Edit menu), this information contains no link to its source. If you make changes to the source document, these changes are not reflected in the copy. Suppose that you copy an Excel worksheet into a Word document, only to find that you used the wrong variable in your analysis. You go back to Excel and make the change, but your Word document still contains the wrong figure.

- If you find that the pasted information contains an error, you cannot correct the error by using the tools of the application that created the information. Suppose, again, that you've copied an Excel worksheet into a Word document. This time, you find you've forgotten to format a range as currency (with dollar signs, commas, and two decimal places). You could fix this problem with Word by retyping all the figures manually, but what a pain! In Excel, you can do it in seconds, just by selecting the range and choosing Currency from the style list box.

Standard Clipboard copying allows you only one remedy if the copied information needs updating or editing: You must delete the copy, switch back to the application that created the information, make the corrections, and repeat the whole procedure. If you keep finding more mistakes, you have to repeat the procedure more than once!

Linking and embedding are designed to deal with the shortcomings of Clipboard copying, although in different ways. In the next section, you learn a few basic terms that will help you to understand the difference between linking and embedding.

Learning the Basic Terms

You will find the following terms useful for the discussions on linking and embedding:

- *Object Linking and Embedding (OLE)*. A set of standards for application programs to follow so that they can function as OLE clients, servers, or both. These standards also tell programmers how to include linking and embedding commands on pull-down menus and dialog boxes. OLE makes use of DDE. From the user's point of view, OLE's chief benefit is that it makes DDE functions much more accessible than they used to be (DDE has been around since earlier versions of Windows, but OLE has appeared only recently in most of the popular Windows applications).

- *Object*. A whole document or part of a document, such as a part of an Excel spreadsheet or a Paintbrush drawing, that was produced by a particular application. For OLE and DDE purposes, you will encounter references to Excel objects, Ami Pro objects, and so on. Here, objects just means "documents" or "selected portions of documents."

- *Server Application*. A Windows application capable of providing an object to other Windows applications. Not all Windows applications are capable of performing as a server application. Among the Windows 3.1 accessories, for example, only Paintbrush and Sound Recorder are server applications. Write and Cardfile cannot function as servers.

- *Client Application*. A Windows application capable of *receiving* an object created by a server application. Not all Windows applications are capable of performing as client applications. Using Windows 3.1 accessories again as an example, Write and Cardfile can function as client applications, but Paintbrush and Sound Recorder cannot.

- *Source Document*. The document from which you copy the object (part of the document or the whole document). You create the source document with the server application.

- *Destination Document*. The document into which you paste or embed the object. You create the destination document with the client application.

- *OLE-capable Application*. Can function as a server application or a client application, or both.

NOTE The Windows accessories are unusual because two of them are capable of performing server, but not client, roles (Paintbrush and Sound Recorder), while two more are capable of performing client, but not server, roles (Write and Cardfile). This is not the norm. Most OLE-capable applications can function as servers and clients.

Understanding Linking

When you link one document with another, you copy a document or part of a document via the Clipboard. In figure 1.1, for example, you see selected information being copied to the Clipboard from Quattro Pro for Windows. The only difference between ordinary Clipboard copying and linking is what happens when you paste. With linking, the command to paste may vary between applications. You choose a special Edit menu command, such as Link, Paste Link, or Paste Special, that creates the dynamic link between the server and client applications. In figure 1.2, you see Microsoft Word for Windows' Paste Special command (Edit menu), which pops up a dialog box containing the Paste Link option.

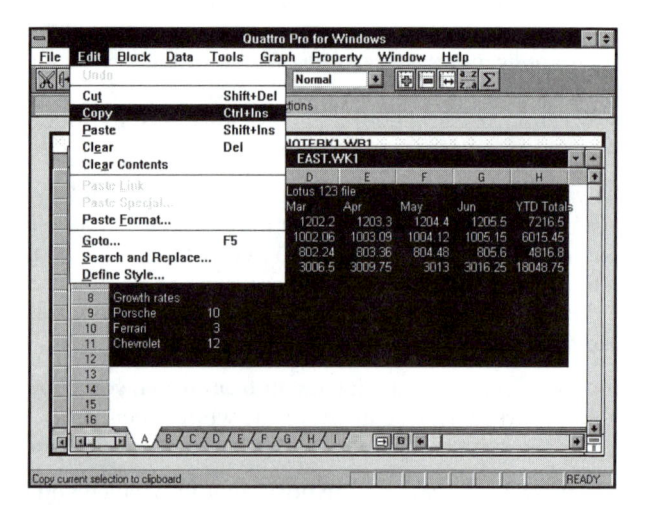

FIG. 1.1 *Copying a selection via the Clipboard (Quattro Pro for Windows).*

When you use a linking command—such as Link, Paste Link, or Paste Special—to paste the object in your document, Windows stores hidden information about the source of the file. Windows uses this information to update the copy of the object that you place in the destination document. If the destination file is open when you change the source document, the update is automatic and instantaneous. If the destination file is closed, you are prompted to update the destination file the next time you open it.

Understanding Linking and Embedding **13**

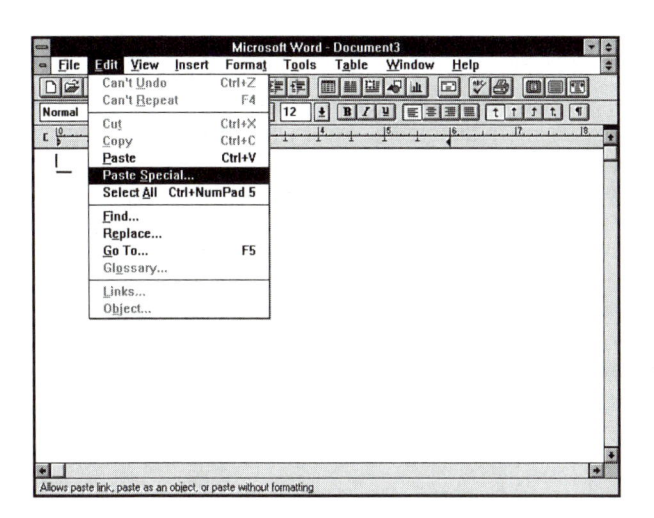

FIG. 1.2 *Linking the copied object using the Paste Special command (Microsoft Word for Windows 2.0).*

After you create a link, you can edit the linked object directly in many cases. But if you would like to use the server application's tools to edit the object, you can easily start the server application and display the source document. In some cases, you simply double-click the object; in others, you must use an Edit menu command, such as Update Link. Windows starts the server application, displays the object within the server application's workspace, and allows you to edit the object. After you make the changes, you choose a special command, usually Update, that appears on the File menu of the server application. This command updates the copied object, closes the server application, and activates the client application.

Because linking creates actively updated links and facilitates editing, it addresses both shortcomings of the Clipboard copying technique (discussed earlier). You also can create more than one copy of an object. Suppose that you create a Quattro Pro worksheet you want to copy to three different WordPerfect documents. You can use linking to place a copy of this object into all three documents. If you make changes to the source document, Windows updates all three copies automatically. This is true even if you edit the source document by double-clicking one of the copies within Word-Perfect. Which copy of the object you edit doesn't matter; all the copies get updated.

> **CAUTION**
>
> After you start linking, don't delete your source documents or move them to different directories! Windows records links with hidden information about the source document's location. If you erase the source document or move it out of its original directory, the client application will not be able to locate the source document, and you will see an error message. You can fix this problem by redirecting the link, as you will learn in Chapter 2, but the best practice is to leave your documents where they are. Because you will not be moving documents after starting with OLE, now's the time to think about a more rational directory structure for your hard disk!

Understanding Embedding

Embedding is different from linking. When you link an object, you establish links between the source document and the linked object (or objects, if you made more than one copy). The linked object is just an on-screen simulation, or copy, of the real file, the source document. The linked object doesn't contain the hidden information needed to alter the source document. For this reason, the copied object isn't really editable. It just seems to be, because when you double-click the object, Windows starts the server application, displays the source document, and enables you to edit the source document. When you choose Update, Windows deletes the old copied object, overwriting it with the new, improved version.

When you embed an object, you actually put into the destination document all of the information the server application needs to enable you to edit the object. The result is a *compound document*—a document that contains supporting information for more than one application. For example, suppose that you embed a Microsoft Graph column chart into a Word for Windows document. (Microsoft Graph is a business graphics package included with Word for Windows 2.0.) The result is a compound document that contains some parts created by Microsoft Graph and other parts usable by Word for Windows (see fig. 1.3).

Now suppose that you want to edit the embedded object. You double-click the object, and Windows starts the server application—Microsoft Graph, in this case. You see the object in the server application's workspace (see fig. 1.4), and all the server application's tools are available for your use. What you *don't* see

Understanding Linking and Embedding **15**

is the source document, because the source document isn't needed. The embedded object contains all the hidden information required by the server application. When you double-click the embedded object to edit it, Windows starts the server application. You actually edit the embedded object, not the source document.

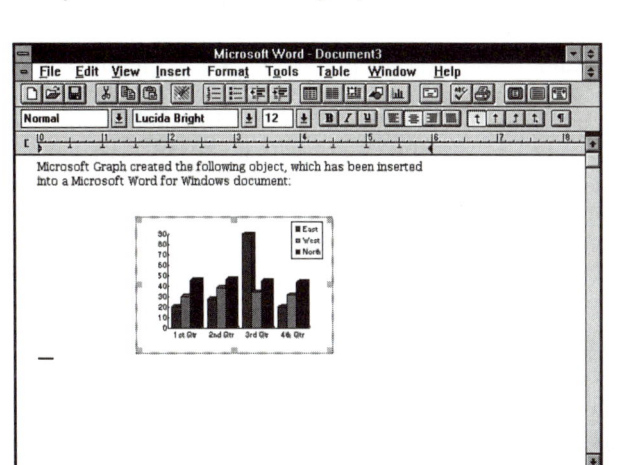

FIG. 1.3 *Microsoft Graph inserted in Microsoft Word for Windows.*

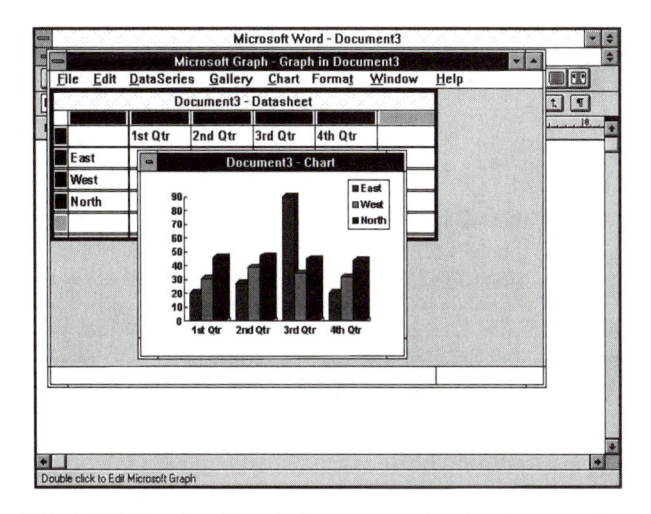

FIG. 1.4 *Editing the object in the server application (Microsoft Graph).*

With embedding, *no link is created between the source document and the destination document.* The embedded object stands on its own. When you make changes to the embedded object, these changes do not affect the source document.

If no link is created between the source document and the destination document, why bother with embedding? Why not just use the regular Clipboard methods? Embedding creates a fully editable copy of the original document. As you modify the embedded object, you have available to you all of the tools and resources of the application that created it. Suppose that you have created a fantastic graphic with Paintbrush, and you want to keep the graphic just the way it is. But you're creating a Write document that calls for a slight modification to the graphic. After embedding the object in the Write document, you can modify the embedded graphic without affecting the original.

> **NOTE** Be aware that compound documents take up a lot more disk space than documents containing linked objects. When you embed rather than link, Windows places into the destination document all the hidden information that the server information needs for you to edit the object. This information takes up much more disk space than a link, which contains only a representation of a file together with a hidden note about the source document's location.

Choosing between Linking and Embedding

Linking and embedding facilitate the editing and updating of copied information placed in a destination document. With either technique, you just double-click the object to have Windows start the server application, display the object, and give you all the tools you need to make the needed change.

Both techniques amount to a massive increase in the amount of application computing power available to you as you work with documents. You can bring all the tools of two, three, or more applications to bear on the work you're doing in a single document. When you need text processing power, you have a word processing program. When you need number-crunching power, you have a spreadsheet. When you need graphics capabilities, you have graphics programs. With linking and embedding, you can use all of these tools, and more, to create a single document. To shape your document just as you like, you have a wide range of tools readily available.

The difference between linking and embedding is simple. With linking, you can create two or more dynamically linked copies of the source object; a change to any one of them is reflected automatically in all the others. With embedding, editing is convenient, but the changes affect only the embedded object.

Linking is useful when you want to maintain one authoritative version of an object, which you may want to copy many times. This object could be an entire document, a portion of a document, or just a tiny little cell that happens to contain the bottom line result of a huge worksheet. Suppose that you keep your firm's price list in an Excel worksheet. You often copy all or part of this price list to Word documents, such as reports or proposals. You always want a change in the Excel worksheet to be reflected automatically in all the copies you have placed in Word documents. After all, you wouldn't want to quote the wrong price! You choose linking.

Embedding is useful when you want to place just one copy of an object in a file, and you don't want the changes you make to this object to be reflected in the original or in any other copies. For example, suppose that you embed your firm's price list in a proposal. For just one client and this client only, however, you want to cut all your prices by 10 percent. You don't want this change to be reflected in the original Excel worksheet, so you choose embedding. After embedding the object, you double-click it; Windows starts Excel and displays the embedded object, not the source object. You can use all of Excel's number-crunching prowess to cut the prices by the requisite 10 percent, but without affecting the original Excel worksheet. Here, embedding is the best choice.

Does the ordinary Clipboard copying technique still have a role to play, now that linking and embedding are available? Windows 3.1 still supports Clipboard copying and pasting, with Cut or Copy and Paste, and for good reasons. Many applications don't support OLE and DDE, the technological foundations of linking and embedding. In addition, at times you know in advance that you will not need to edit or update the copied information. In such cases, ordinary pasting is preferable because it places much less demand on your computer system's microprocessor. Even so, you will want to use linking or embedding often. Doing so is like expanding the capabilities of your application programs by a huge factor.

Understanding Packaging

A Windows 3.1 accessory, called *Object Packager*, adds a new dimension to linking and embedding. With Object Packager, you can insert a linked or embedded object that has been reduced to an icon, just like the icons that represent programs in the Program Manager. Object Packager's icons, however, appear in the destination document. When you double-click the icon, Windows "unpacks" the icon and displays the object.

Packaging is useful if you're inserting or embedding a very lengthy object, or an object so complex that it takes a long time for your PC to scroll through it. While you're editing the document, you can package all the objects, which speeds scrolling considerably. You then can unpack them when you're ready to print.

Another nifty way to use packaged objects is in a document that your correspondent can read on-screen, with the same application that created it. Suppose that your friend Danielle has Word and Excel. You can send her a Word document with an Excel object packaged in it, and the following message (see fig. 1.5):

```
Danielle, just click this icon to see that report
I told you about:
```

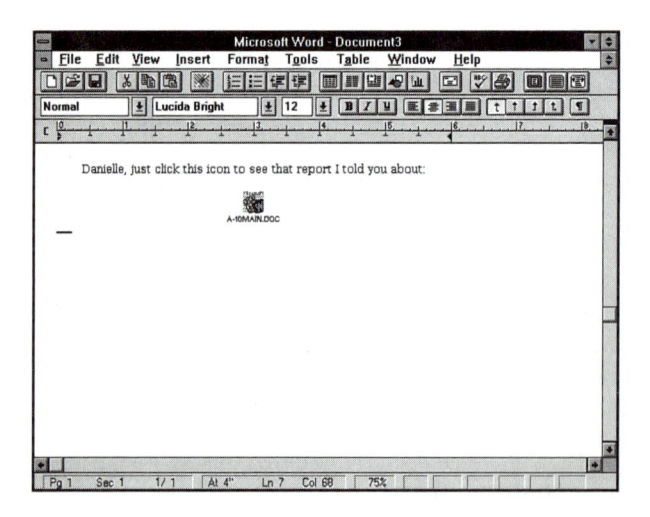

FIG. 1.5 *Packaged object in Word for Windows document.*

Understanding DDE

Dynamic Data Exchange (DDE) is the underlying data exchange architecture for Windows (and, incidentally, OS/2) applications. DDE enables compatible applications to communicate with each other. In all such communications, one application is a client and the other is a server. The client can request data from the server, and it can also tell the server which commands to execute.

When one DDE application communicates with another, the resulting interaction is called a *conversation*. The DDE exchange begins with one application initiating the conversation, and it continues as the other application acknowledges the conversation and receives the data. Finally, one of the applications terminates the conversation. Linking makes use of the communication channels that DDE makes possible. When you insert a linked object into your document, you insert a DDE command. This command says, in effect, "Hello, server application. Would you send me an update if you see a change in such-and-such a location of such-and-such a document?"

The easiest way to use DDE is to use the Paste Link or Paste Special commands that appear on the Edit menus of OLE-capable server applications. With some applications, however, you can write your own DDE commands. In Microsoft Word for Windows 2.0, for example, you can insert a Link field (called a DDE field in earlier versions). In this field, you use the client application to write a DDE command that initiates a conversation with a server application. This command locates the data in the source document and echoes the data at the field's location in the destination document. As with linking, the link is dynamic: if you change the source document, you see a change in the Word field's contents. To illustrate, you can use this command to place in your Word document the value that appears in the bottom line of a worksheet. In Word, as well as other applications, you also can include DDE commands in *macros*—named scripts that automatically carry out a sequence of the application's commands. To use DDE commands in fields or macros, however, you must learn how to write a DDE command by using precisely the right command nomenclature and syntax.

Because linking is easy to accomplish using menu commands, is it worth the trouble to learn how to write DDE commands correctly? Yes, if you want to take advantage of an advanced DDE feature that's not readily available via command menus. DDE commands can instruct the server application to execute one or more of the server application's commands. For example, you can write an Excel macro that instructs Microsoft Q+E, a dBASE-compatible data manager included with Excel 4.0, to perform a query on a database and report the result to Excel—and all without your intervention.

The use of DDE to execute commands remotely is fairly advanced, and learning how to write these commands successfully isn't easy. The basics are the same for all DDE-capable applications, but maddeningly, most implement the command syntax in somewhat different ways. Still, this discussion probably has whet the appetite of those readers who enjoy getting the most out of their systems. Although this book doesn't attempt to document every last reference detail of DDE commands, you will find enough discussion of the subject that you can start writing your own DDE commands. Chapter 5, "Understanding Dynamic Data Exchange (DDE)," discusses DDE in more detail.

> **TIP** In non-Microsoft applications, embedding isn't yet as well-supported as linking. To explore embedding at the technological state-of-the-art, try exploring the Microsoft applications included with Microsoft Word for Windows 2.0, including Microsoft Draw, Microsoft Graph, Equation Editor, and WordArt. All of these applications have been optimized for embedding so that they work as a natural extension of Word. To start one of these applications, choose Object from the Insert menu, and pick an application from the Object Type list box.

Summary

In this chapter, you learned the difference between linking and embedding, and you explored additional concepts: object packaging and dynamic data exchange (DDE). The next chapters examine each of these topics in more detail.

CHAPTER TWO

Creating and Managing Links

Linking is almost as easy as copying with the Clipboard. In the server application, you copy the data to the Clipboard, just as you would in an ordinary Clipboard copy-and-paste operation. In the client application, you choose Paste Link or Paste Special from the Edit menu (in place of the usual Paste command). The client application inserts the data from the Clipboard, just as if you were copying and pasting.

The underlying differences between ordinary Clipboard copying and linking aren't apparent to the user—until you see that the copied data is dynamically updated! When you link, you copy hidden technical information in addition to the copied object you see on-screen. When the client application inserts the linked object, it also inserts hidden information that identifies the server application and the name of the source document. In addition, the client application assigns a unique name to the link and specifies the frequency of updating (automatic by default, in most cases). This hidden information enables Windows to detect whether the source document has changed; if a change has occurred, Windows updates the destination document automatically. If the destination document is open, the update occurs instantly. If the destination document is closed, Windows displays a dialog box, the next time you open a document, asking whether you want to update the link.

I — Understanding Linking and Embedding Basics

Links are easy to create. As in all outstanding technology, the user need not learn the technical details—and, for the most part, isn't even aware of them. With linking, however, you must *manage* the links after you've created them—and that's where some complexity occurs. You need to consider the following information when creating links:

- Links aren't always updated automatically; in some cases, you may have to update the links manually. In Microsoft Word for Windows 2.0, links between Word documents must be updated manually. In Word for Windows, automatic updating is available only for links with external documents (documents created by another OLE-compatible application).

- You may need to choose the appropriate data type, such as Rich Text Format (RTF) or unformatted text, for the paste operation. In some applications, linking is available only when you choose the correct data type. (The term *data type* refers to the format, such as RTF, Picture, or Bitmap, that is used to transfer the data via the Clipboard.)

- Applications vary in the linking features they provide. Some do not implement linking completely. WordPerfect for Windows, for example, enables you to insert linked objects into a document. WordPerfect for Windows provides no tools, however, for you to start the server application from within WordPerfect so that you can edit the source document.

- After creating the link, you must learn special procedures for redirecting the link, repairing broken links, and breaking links.

- You may encounter error messages informing you that Windows couldn't find the server application or the source document. Other errors also may occur.

In short, you have plenty to learn about linking. This chapter illustrates the procedures you use to create links, edit linked documents, open documents that contain links, control existing links, and troubleshoot linking problems.

Despite such variations, the underlying concepts of linking are the same for all OLE-capable Windows applications. Because the general procedures are similar, you can learn all the fundamentals of linking. By reading this chapter, you will gain a good understanding of what's involved in creating links and keeping them operating smoothly.

TIP As you read this chapter, keep in mind that linking procedures still vary among applications. As yet, no hard-and-fast rules exist about how linking commands should be located on menus. This also is true for applications created by the same software publisher. To view a list of the links in a Microsoft Word for Windows destination document, for example, you choose Links from the Edit menu. In Microsoft Excel, however, you find the Links command in the File menu. This chapter gives the general outlines of the fundamental linking procedures, but you need to look up the specifics in the second part of this book, which provides many keystroke-by-keystroke tutorials for linking specific applications.

Linking to Other Applications

The most common use of linking is to link one application's source document with *another* application's destination document. In this section, you learn how to create a dynamic link between two applications—a server application (the one you use to create the source document) and the client application (the one you use to create the destination document).

To create a dynamic link between two applications, follow these steps:

1. Start the server application, and display or create the source document.

    Some client applications require that you open the source document first. If you do not do so, the client application may not be aware that Clipboard data is linkable.

    In figure 2.1, you see an illustration being created in Paintbrush, one of the Windows accessories that is capable of functioning as a server application for linking purposes.

2. Start the client application and display or create the destination document.

    You now have opened both files. Both the source file and the destination file must be open.

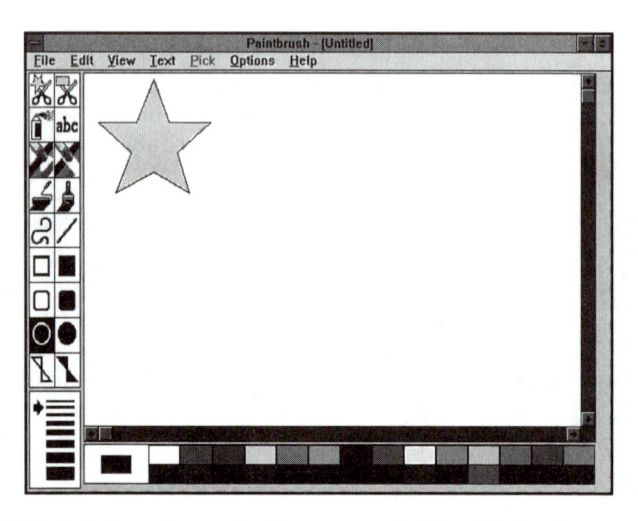

24 *I — Understanding Linking and Embedding Basics*

FIG. 2.1 *Illustration created in server application (Paintbrush).*

3. Choose Switch To from the Control menu, and switch to the server application. Alternatively, press Alt-Esc until you see the server application.

   Important: If you have not yet saved the source document, do so now. You cannot perform linking from a source document that has not been saved.

4. In the source document, select the data you want to copy.

5. Choose Copy from the Edit menu, just as you would if you were copying via the Clipboard.

6. Choose Switch To from the Control Menu, and choose the client application. Alternatively, press Alt-Esc until you see the client application.

7. Position the insertion point where you want the copied data to appear.

8. Choose Paste Link from the Edit menu.

   If the Edit menu has no Paste Link command, choose Links or Paste Special and look for the Paste Link button in the Paste Special dialog box (see fig. 2.2). If the Paste Link button is dimmed, try selecting the Formatted Text data type for text or the Picture data type for graphics.

   The client application inserts the information into your document and creates the link (see fig. 2.3).

Creating and Managing Links **25**

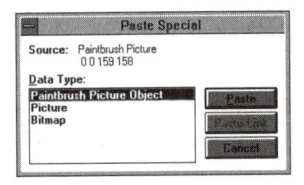

FIG. 2.2 *The Paste Special dialog box (Word for Windows).*

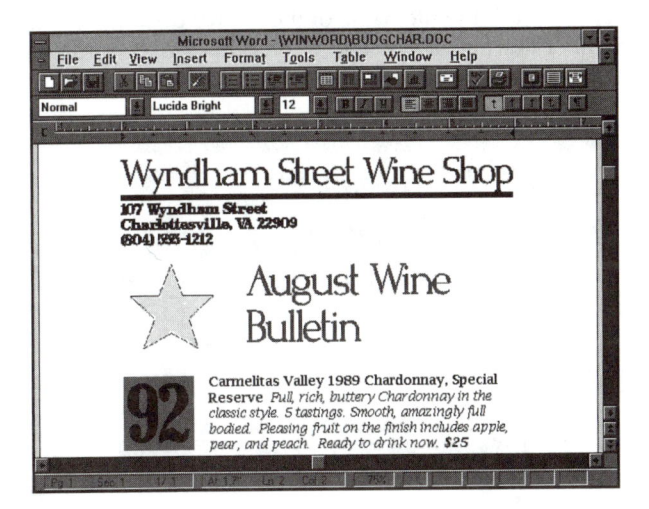

FIG. 2.3 *Linked Paintbrush graphic inserted in a Word for Windows document.*

> **TIP**
>
> With most applications, you can edit, format, size, or scale the linked object within the destination application, but this is usually a bad idea. You can edit a 1-2-3 for Windows worksheet inserted into a WordPerfect document, for example, but the changes you make do not affect the source document. Worse, these changes will be wiped out when the link is updated automatically. Some applications try to save any formatting you've applied to the linked object, but they may not do so consistently. You should edit the object by switching to the source document and then updating the link, as described in the next section.

Understanding How Linking Works

To understand how linking works (and what can go wrong), you will find it helpful to examine the instructions that underlie the Word linkages illustrated in the preceding section. If you choose the Change Links button in the Links dialog box (Edit menu), you see the hidden information that Word stores along with the linked object (see fig. 2.4). This information includes the name of the server application, the file name of the source document, and an item number that specifies the location of the linked information within the source document.

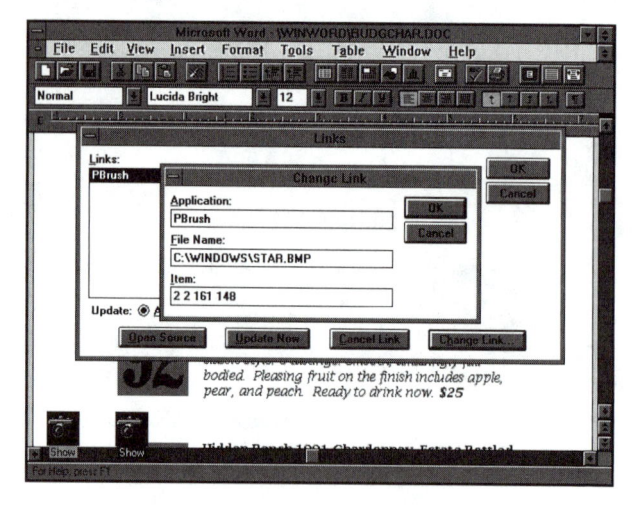

FIG. 2.4 *Information required to create and sustain the link.*

Dynamic linking occurs because the client application stores this information. If you move the source document, the client application will not be able to find the source. In this situation, you see the alert box shown in figure 2.5 when you try to edit or update the linked object.

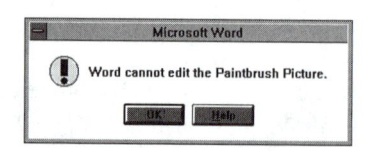

FIG. 2.5 *Alert box informing the user that the source document cannot be located.*

> **TIP** Don't move your source documents. If you're planning to use linking frequently, create a directory called C:\LINKDOCS, in which you store all your source documents. In future hard disk reorganizations, you will remember to leave this directory alone.

Editing Linked Documents

If implemented properly, a client application's linking command should enable you to edit the source document with ease. That's not the case with all client applications, as the preceding WordPerfect for Windows example suggests. Ideally, you should be able to edit the linked object without having to leave the client application. If your application is capable of editing linked objects, you can make corrections in the linked data.

To edit a linked object, follow these steps:

1. In the client application, select the linked object.

    In figure 2.6, the linked object is an Excel chart, which has been inserted within a Word for Windows document. In this chart, a typo has greatly exaggerated the sales of the entry-level Tierra model. To correct the error, you display the source document, make the change, and return to Word for Windows.

2. Double-click the linked object.

    You see the source document in the server application (see fig. 2.7).

> **NOTE** If double-clicking the object doesn't work, try choosing the Edit menu command that enables you to edit or control DDE links, and click the button that opens the source document.

3. In the server application, make the needed change to the source document (see fig. 2.8).

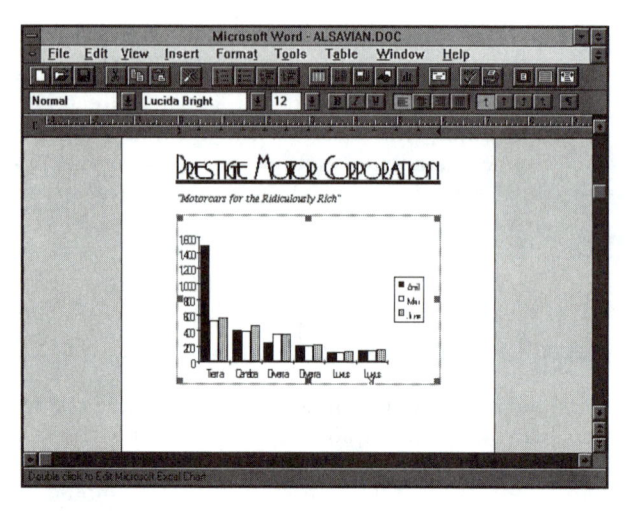

28 *I — Understanding Linking and Embedding Basics*

FIG. 2.6 *Excel chart inserted within a Word for Windows document.*

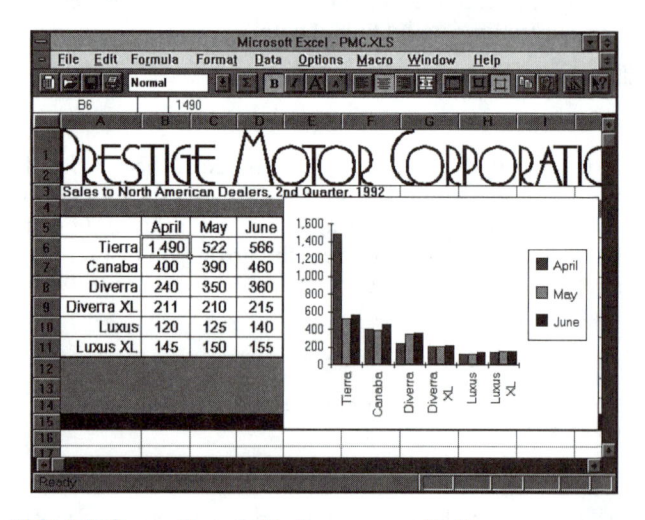

FIG. 2.7 *Source document in the server application.*

4. **Important:** Save the source document.

   If you don't save the document, Windows cannot update the destination document.

5. Close the server application.

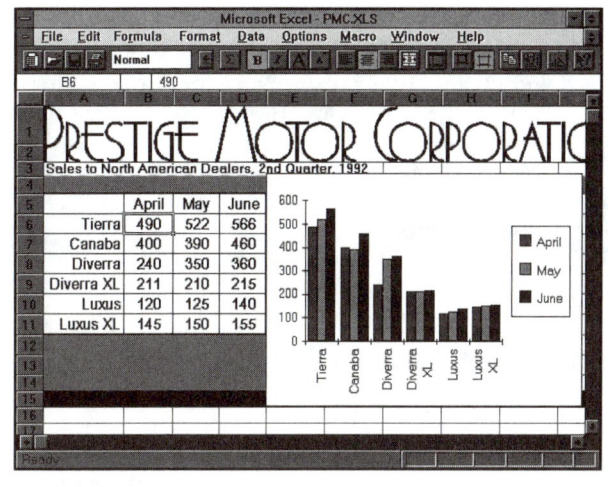

FIG. 2.8 *Making the change to the source document.*

6. If you don't see the destination document, choose Switch To from the Windows control menu and select the client application, or press Alt-Esc until you see the destination document.

   The destination document will reflect the change you've made (see fig. 2.9).

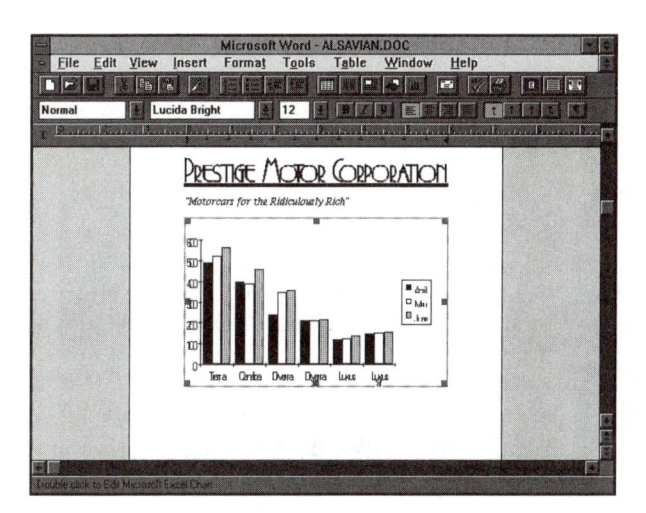

FIG. 2.9 *Change made automatically to the destination document.*

TIP Some applications give you handy shortcuts for this procedure. In Microsoft Word for Windows, for example, the Edit menu displays a command called Microsoft Excel Chart Link when you select a linked object. Choosing this command is the same as choosing Link from the Edit menu and clicking the Open Source button.

Opening Documents That Contain Links

When you open a document that contains automatic links, you see a dialog box such as the one shown in figure 2.10. Windows is asking whether you want the links in your document updated to reflect any changes you may have made to the source documents. Choose Yes to update the links. You may see additional dialog boxes as the application encounters additional links. Choose Yes to reestablish the links. If necessary, Windows will start the server applications so that the links can be activated.

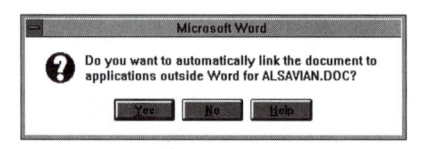

FIG. 2.10 *Opening a document that contains links.*

TIP If no changes have been made to the source document(s), you can save time by choosing No when you see this dialog box (or a variant of it in other applications). If you choose Yes, Windows attempts to start all the server applications, which can consume a few minutes if you've inserted linked objects from two or more applications. Choose Yes only if the links need updating.

Editing Multiple Links

One of the advantages of linking is that you can create *multiple links*. In a multiple link, one source document is linked to two or more destination documents. In figure 2.11, for example, the same Excel spreadsheet data has been linked to two Microsoft Word documents (SALEMEMO.DOC and SALERPT.DOC). In a multiple link, as in an ordinary (single) link, any changes you make to the copied objects do not affect the source (or any other copies). If you want the changes to be made consistently to all copies of the source object, switch to the source document and make the change.

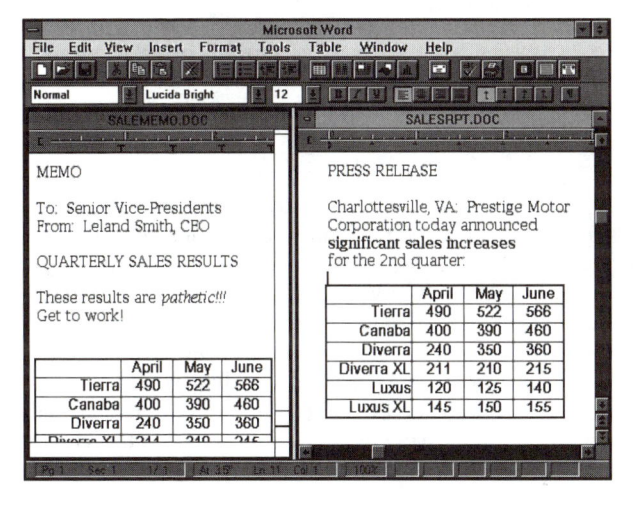

FIG. 2.11 *Excel worksheet linked to two Word documents.*

Controlling Link Settings

When you create a link, your client application inserts the linked object into your document and uses default settings for the *data type* and *update frequency*. With most applications, you can change these defaults.

Data type refers to the format used to copy the information via the Clipboard. Default formats are usually Formatted Text for text objects and Picture for graphic objects. The Formatted Text option uses the Microsoft Rich Text Format (RTF) standard. The Picture option transfers graphics by using object-oriented (vector) graphics techniques. You can choose other data types, but choosing some of them will disable linking.

With most applications, you have two *update frequency* choices: Automatic and Manual. Automatic updating occurs whenever you make a change to the source document. If the destination document is closed at the time you make the change, you will be prompted to update the destination document the next time you open it. If you choose Manual updating, updating occurs only when you choose the Edit menu command that updates the links in the destination document.

In this section, you learn what these settings do, how to change them, and when it's useful to do so.

Choosing the Data Type

In most applications, you can choose between two different commands for performing the paste link operation. The first command (usually called Paste Link on the Edit menu) performs the paste link by using the default link settings. The second command (usually called Paste Special) enables you to choose link settings. Figure 2.12 shows Word for Windows' Paste Special dialog box, from which you can choose data types. In WordPerfect for Windows, you can choose the data type (called *storage type* in WordPerfect's nomenclature) only if you create the link by using the Link Create command (Edit menu). Table 2.1 lists the most common data types.

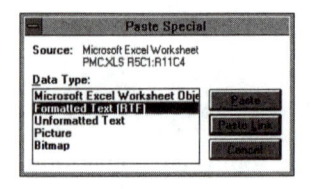

FIG. 2.12 *Paste Special dialog box (Word for Windows).*

Table 2.1. Common Data Types

Type	Description
Object	A representation of the Clipboard contents that includes all the information needed to edit the document. Use this data type for embedding, not for linking (see Chapter 3). In most applications, if you select this option, linking is disabled.
Formatted Text	Text that includes all or most of the formatting applied in the source document by the server application. Formatted text is transferred using the Rich Text Format (RTF) coding scheme. This is the default linking data type for most links involving text.
Unformatted Text	Plain text with no formatting.
Picture	A graphic representation of the Clipboard contents. This is the default linking data type for most links involving graphics. You can size and scale the linked object in the destination document. Because the Picture format is created using object-oriented (vector) graphics, scaling the graphic will not introduce distortions. In some applications, this format is called PICT or METAFILE.
Bit map	A bit-mapped graphic representation of the Clipboard contents. Scaling the bit map may introduce unappealing distortions.
DIB	A bit-mapped graphic representation of the Clipboard contents that conforms to the Device-Independent Bitmap standard.

Even if your application enables you to choose data types, some of the options may be unavailable when you're paste linking graphics. If you're pasting text into the destination document, most applications enable you to choose between pasting the data as formatted or unformatted text. You also can insert the data as a picture. If you're pasting a graphic, your only option is the picture format.

> **TIP** If you're pasting text and you do not want that text modified in the destination document, import the text as a picture.

Controlling Update Frequency

Most applications enable you to choose between automatic updating (the default) and manual updating. If you want to change the update type, you usually must do so after you've created the link. You use an Edit menu command (typically called Edit Link or Link) that displays a list of all the links in your document, together with their current settings. Figure 2.13 shows Word for Windows' link list (produced by choosing Links from the Edit menu). Figure 2.14 shows WordPerfect for Windows' link list (produced by choosing Links Edit from the Edit menu).

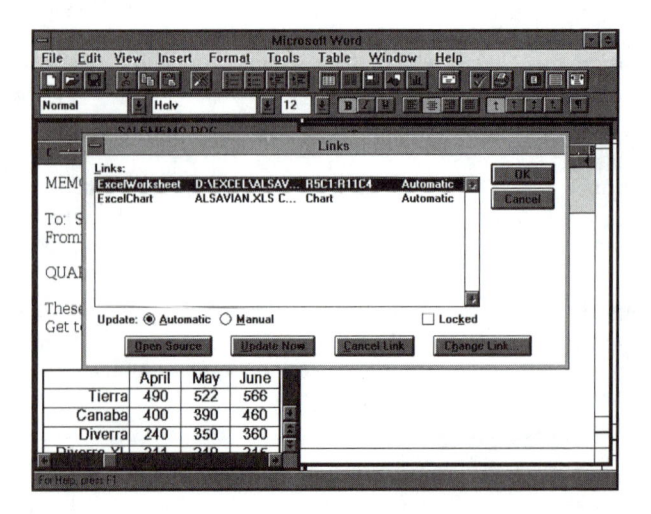

FIG. 2.13 Link list (Word for Windows).

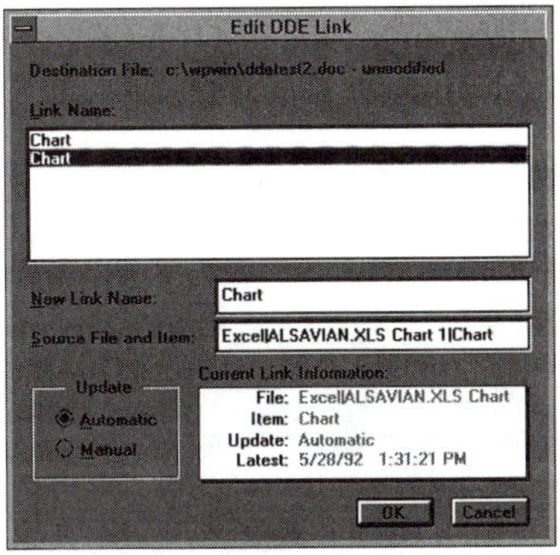

Creating and Managing Links **35**

FIG. 2.14 *Link list (WordPerfect for Windows).*

Why choose manual updating, when the whole point of linking is to create dynamic links between the source and destination documents? After you have edited a document with a lot of links in it, you'll realize the point immediately: Automatic links make very heavy demands on your computer's microprocessor, which is constantly comparing the two documents to see whether they're the same.

> **TIP** If you're editing a destination document that has lots of links, switch them to manual until you're finished editing, and then switch back to automatic.

To choose manual updating, follow these steps:

1. In the destination document, choose the command that enables you to edit the links in the document.

    This command is usually called Links or Edit Links, which you will find in the Edit menu. An exception is Microsoft Excel: You must choose Links from the File menu to produce the link list. After you choose this command, you see the link list (refer to figs. 2.13 and 2.14). The link list dialog box indicates the source of the link and whether the link is set to automatic or manual.

2. Select the link you want to change.

In some applications, you can Shift-click to select more than one link in the list. To Shift-click, hold down the Shift key as you click the links you want to select.

3. Choose Manual.
4. Choose OK.

> **TIP** If you want to change only one of the links in your document, select it before choosing the link editing command. Most applications will display this link highlighted, allowing you to skip step 2.

To switch back to automatic updating, repeat the steps just given, but activate the Automatic option.

Updating Manual Links

If you choose manual updating for any of the links in your destination document, Windows will not update this document automatically when you make changes to the source document. To update the destination document, you must choose an update command. In most Windows applications, the update command is available as an option in the link list.

To update the manual links in a document, follow these steps:

1. Display the Link list dialog box.

    You will find the appropriate command, usually called Links or Link Options on the Edit menu—except in Microsoft Excel, where it's on the File menu.

2. In the link list, highlight the manual link.
3. Choose the Update button.
4. Choose OK.

Breaking the Link

If a dynamic link no longer serves any need, you can break the link. Doing so does not erase the object you pasted into your document; it merely erases the hidden information that specifies the source file's location.

To break a link, follow these steps:

1. In the destination document, choose the command (such as Edit Link, Edit Link Options, or Edit Link Delete) that displays the document's link list so that you can break a link.
2. Highlight the link you want to break.
3. Choose the button that cancels the link.

    This button is called Cancel Link or Delete.
4. Choose OK to confirm the deletion.

    Some applications will display an alert box warning you that you are about to sever a link. If you're certain you have broken the correct link, choose OK. To cancel the break, choose Cancel.

After you break the link, you still see the formerly linked information in your document. Windows will not update this information, however, if you make changes to the source document.

> **TIP** Some applications, such as Microsoft Word for Windows, enable you to lock linked objects. If you lock an object, Windows cannot update the link, even if it is set to automatic linking. You still can modify the linked object within the destination application, however, and the destination retains all the link information. Locking is preferable to breaking the link because, should you change your mind and want to restore dynamic linking, you can do so easily. To restore linking to a broken link, you must redirect the link, as explained in the following section.

Restoring a Broken Link

You can break a link in two ways: deliberately (as just described), or accidentally. Accidental breaks result when you move the source document after creating the link. After moving the source document, Windows cannot find it, so you see an alert dialog box informing you that the source document is missing, or worse, corrupted.

To restore the broken link, follow these steps:

1. Choose the command that displays the link list (such as Edit Link, Edit Link Options, Edit Link Edit, or File Links).

   You see the link list in a dialog box.

2. Choose the option that enables you to change the link. In Microsoft Word for Windows, for example, you click the Change Link button.

   In most applications, another dialog box appears, as in figure 2.15. In other applications, you directly edit a field in the link list.

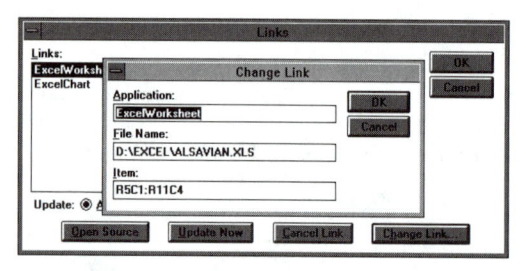

FIG. 2.15 *Redirecting the link.*

3. In the dialog box that appears, carefully change the part of the link command that lists the source document's location.

4. Choose OK.

Troubleshooting Links

Given the complexities of linking, problems sometimes occur. This section reviews linking problems and suggests solution strategies.

The server isn't available.

You have just opened a document, and you choose to update the links in the destination document. Or you have decided to edit the linked object, so you choose the option that opens the source document. You see a message informing you that the server application isn't available.

A server application cannot respond if it's busy displaying a dialog box, printing or downloading, recalculating, saving data, or waiting for user response in a response field. In addition, Windows cannot start the server if its path is not listed in the current PATH command. Try the following suggestions:

- Wait a few moments, and try again. The server application may have completed the task that formerly occupied it.

- Switch to the server application and close all open dialog boxes or text response fields.

- Switch to the server and complete the operation that's consuming its attention, such as printing or recalculating.

- Add a PATH command to your AUTOEXEC.BAT command that lists the server program's directory. To add a PATH command for a directory called EXCEL, for example, you would add the line PATH D:\EXCEL or PATH C:\EXCEL to the AUTOEXEC.BAT file in the root directory of your hard drive. If this file already has a PATH statement, just type a semicolon and add the path name to the list (as in the following example:

    PATH C:\WINDOWS;C:\EXCEL;C:\WPWIN)

The source document isn't available.

You moved the source document to a new subdirectory or disk.

- Move the source document back to the directory it was in when you created the link, or

- Redirect the link.

Your client application cannot access a Microsoft Excel chart you thought you had paste-linked successfully into your document.

To link an Excel chart, you must display the chart in a chart window and choose File Save to save the chart. Next, you must choose File Open to open the named chart. Only then can you copy the chart to the Clipboard and establish a successful link with the client application.

You've copied information to the Clipboard, but the Paste Link command is grayed and unavailable.

You can link only to documents that have been saved.

- Switch to the server application and save the source document.

You double-click a linked object in the destination document, but Windows doesn't start the server application or display the source document.

Some applications, such as WordPerfect for Windows, enable you to insert a linked object into a document, but provide no tools for editing the object. To edit the object, switch to the server application, display the source document, make the needed changes, and save the source document. Windows will update the linked object automatically.

You make changes to the source document, but the changes do not automatically appear in the destination document.

You must save the changes before Windows can update the link. If you save the changes and the destination document still does not reflect the changes you made, display the link list and check the link setting. The link may be set to manual, or the application may not permit automatic updating.

- Save the source document.
- Make sure that the destination document's links are set to automatic linking, if possible.

When you close the source document, you see an alert box warning you that the file contains links to open documents.

Windows is warning you that the linked data in the destination document won't be dynamically updated until the next time you open the source document. That's no problem, as long as you're aware of the fact.

Summary

In this chapter, you fully explored the concepts and methods of linking with OLE-capable applications. You learned how to create, manage, edit, and repair links. You also learned what to do if something goes wrong when linking. In the next chapter, you explore embedding concepts and methods.

CHAPTER THREE

Embedding Objects

In the preceding chapter, you examined dynamic linking, and you saw how this important Windows capability can be used to integrate your Windows applications. In this chapter, you examine embedding, the second of the two integration capabilities made possible by the object linking and embedding (OLE) standard. This chapter surveys the techniques you use to insert embedded objects, edit embedded objects, convert embedded objects to graphics or text, and troubleshoot embedding problems.

This chapter fully explores object embedding. You learn the following:

- Understanding when to use embedding
- Choosing the correct embedding procedure
- Creating an embedded object
- Editing an embedded object
- Deleting embedded objects or transforming them into static pictures
- Canceling embedding without deleting the object

This chapter concludes by surveying the *OLE servers* that Microsoft packages with Word for Windows 2.0 applications such as Microsoft Graph, Microsoft WordArt, and Equation Editor. These OLE servers do not run by themselves; they are used for embedding. Although packaged with Word and Excel, these useful programs are also available to other OLE-capable applications that you have installed on your system.

Understanding When To Use Embedding

Embedding differs from linking in two important ways:

- When you embed an object, you actually put into the destination document all the information that the server application requires for editing the object. The result is a *compound document*, a document that contains data created by more than one application. Therefore, Windows doesn't have to switch back to the source document to locate the embedded object: The destination document "includes" the source document.

- Embedding creates no links, dynamic or otherwise. As you learn in this chapter, you can embed an object by copying data from one document to another. If you then make changes to the original, however, Windows does not update the copy automatically.

What follows from these two differences is simple: you use embedding when ease of object editing is your chief concern, and you don't care about automatic updating. In figure 3.1, you see an example of an embedded object that probably will not need updating but might need editing—the company name that has been incorporated into a Word for Windows letterhead template. Why doesn't this object need updating? Company names don't change very often. (The handsome type was created in Microsoft WordArt, an OLE-capable application that is packaged with Word for Windows.) Embedding the company name as an object enables you to edit the name easily. Just by double-clicking the object, you can try different typefaces, as shown in figure 3.2, or correct a spelling error.

> **TIP**
> Embedding creates fewer editing problems than does linking. As discussed in the preceding chapter, problems may occur when a linked object is edited: when the edit starts from the client application, Windows must locate the source document as well as the server application. With embedding, however, editing is faster, easier, and less subject to error.

Embedding Objects **43**

FIG. 3.1 *WordArt object embedded in a Word for Windows document.*

FIG. 3.2 *Edited WordArt object embedded in a Word for Windows document.*

After you have embedded an object into your document, you have a *compound document*, a document created by more than one application.

When you work with a compound document that contains several embedded objects, such as the one in figure 3.3, you soon think in terms of the document, rather than the specific application with which you are working. In the Quattro Pro for Windows document in figure 3.3, you see a Microsoft WordArt object (the theater company's name in the upper left corner) and a Microsoft Graph bar graph. When you double-click the theater company's name, you see that Windows starts the server application (Microsoft WordArt). The data appears. You can edit the company's name quickly and easily. Then, after you exit the server application, you can see that the destination document shows the editing changes to the company's name.

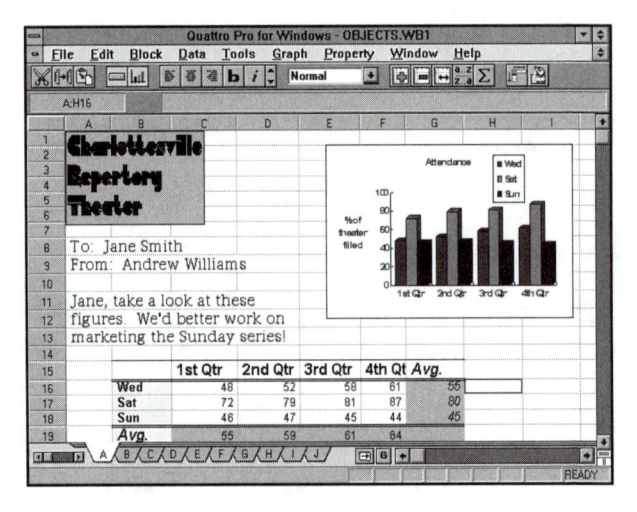

FIG. 3.3 *Microsoft WordArt and Microsoft Graph objects in a Quattro Pro for Windows document.*

> **NOTE** Because compound documents store all the editing data needed by each application used to create an object, they require more disk space than do normal documents. On the other hand, linking requires much less disk space. When Windows links, you see only a picture of your data (the unformatted text) in the destination document. Therefore, if you're short on disk space, you may want to link rather than embed.

When properly implemented, an application with embedding capabilities has a seemingly endless set of alternative command menus, expanding the application's usefulness to an amazing

Embedding Objects **45**

degree. With Microsoft Word for Windows, for example, you can switch almost instantly to applications that create graphs, drawings, artistic typography effects, and mathematical equations.

Embedding undoubtedly points the way to the end-user computing systems of the future. Unfortunately, the future hasn't yet arrived. As of this writing, most of the OLE-capable applications that are discussed in this book are from Microsoft—specifically, Word, Excel, and the Windows 3.1 OLE-capable accessories (Write, Paintbrush, Cardfile, and Sound Recorder). OLE-capable applications from sources other than Microsoft are Ami Pro for Windows 2.0 and Quattro Pro for Windows 1.0. As other software publishers realize that OLE gives applications a competitive advantage, the publishers no doubt will incorporate embedding capabilities into their software.

> **TIP** You can tell at a glance whether your application can serve as a client application for embedding. Just look for a command called Insert Object. (In some applications, this Insert Object command is on the Edit menu. In others, an Object command is on the Insert menu.) Note that some applications can function as either a server or a client but not both. Quattro Pro for Windows, for example, can function as a client for embedding but not as a server.

Choosing the Correct Embedding Procedure

You can embed an object in two ways. The first way is to create the object (such as a chart or drawing) in the server application and then use the Clipboard to copy the object to the destination document. These steps are identical to the first two steps in linking. However, you insert the object by choosing the link list and choosing the Object data type instead of selecting the usual linking datatype options (Formatted Text, Picture, and so on). After you choose the Object data type, the Paste Link button grays, indicating that linking has become unavailable. The client application inserts the object, but no link is created.

The second way to embed an object is to start from the client application. Choose the Insert Object or Insert New Object command. A list of OLE-capable applications appears (see fig. 3.4). You choose an application. Windows starts the application, displaying a blank workspace with a list of all the server application options. You can open an existing document or create a new one. To exit, choose Update from the File menu. The server application quits, and you see the object in the destination document.

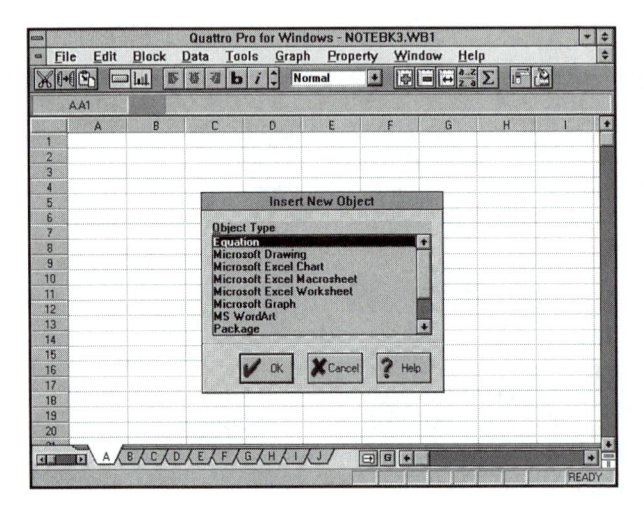

FIG. 3.4 *Insert New Object dialog box (Quattro Pro for Windows).*

> **TIP** Before you can use an OLE-compatible application as a server application for embedding, you must start the program at least once. With that initial start, the program registers on the Windows applications list. Open and quit each OLE-compatible application that you want to use before attempting to embed objects. You need to perform this task only once.

Creating an Embedded Object

As you have just learned, you can use two methods to embed objects in an OLE-capable client application. You can start from the server application, the best technique to use when you want to embed part of a document that you have already created and saved with the server application. You also can start from the client application. Starting from the client application is the best technique to use when you want to create the object from scratch. The two following sections give the steps for using both techniques.

Starting from the Server Application

The technique of starting from the server application closely resembles linking through the Clipboard. This method is best used to embed information from a previously created server application document. For example, you can use this technique to embed into a Word for Windows document a portion of an Excel worksheet you have saved.

To embed an object from the server application, follow these steps:

1. Open the server application.
2. Open the document that contains the information you want to embed.
3. Select the information you want to embed.

> **TIP** If you're selecting a graphic, make sure that you select the entire graphic. Look for the size/move handles on the edges of the graphic.

4. Choose Copy from the Edit menu.
5. Switch to the client application, and place the insertion point where you want the object to appear.
6. Choose the Edit menu command that lets you choose the data type as you paste. Typically, this command is called Paste Special. (If you choose Paste Link, Windows inserts the object as a linked object, not an embedded object.)

The dialog box that appears contains a list of formats from which you can choose the Object type (also called ObjectLink, Embedded OLE, or Native), ensuring that the data will be imported as an embedded object.

Figure 3.5 shows the Paste Special dialog box in Word for Windows. As you can see, you can choose one from among three data types for the paste operation. Only one of the data types, Microsoft Excel Chart Object, will embed the chart in the Word file.

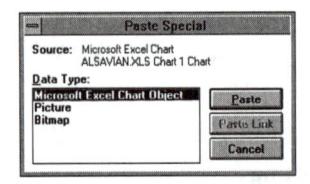

FIG. 3.5 *Paste Special dialog box (Word for Windows).*

7. Choose the Object data type.
8. Choose Paste. Do not choose Paste Link because you're embedding, not linking. (In most applications, the Paste Link option dims when you choose the Object data type.)

   The client application inserts the object at the insertion point location (see fig. 3.6).

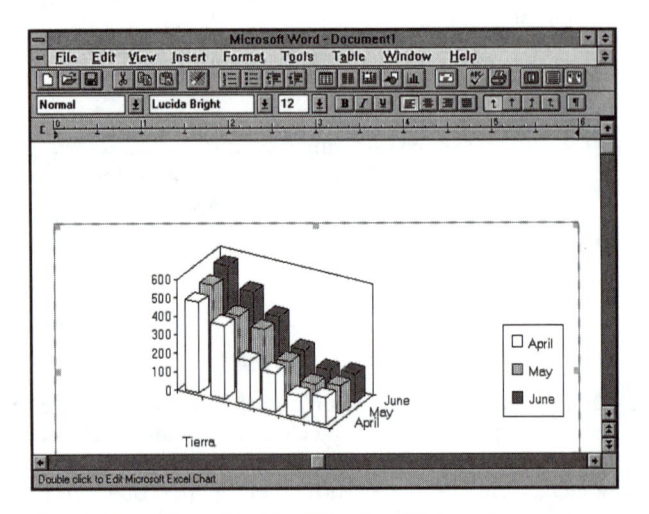

FIG. 3.6 *Excel Chart object in a Word for Windows document.*

9. Save the destination document.
10. Switch back to the server application, and save or discard the source document.

    Yes, you read that correctly! Discarding the source document is indeed an option. When you inserted the object into the client application, you created a compound document. This document contains all the information the server application needs to open the object and enable you to edit the document. When you saved the destination document in step 8, you saved all your work, including the work you did when you created the object.

Starting from the Client Application

When you start embedding from the server application, you use the familiar Clipboard copying method as if you were linking, but you choose the Object data type. This technique differs only slightly from the linking techniques you learned in Chapter 2. When you create an embedded object starting from the client application, however, a new command (called Object or Insert Object) comes into play. In both Word and Excel, you find this command on the Insert menu.

This technique is best used when you need to create the embedded object from scratch. From the client application, you choose Insert Object from the Edit menu. A dialog box appears, showing which applications are capable of functioning as OLE servers for embedding purposes. After you choose an application, Windows switches to the server application. You see a new, blank workspace in which you create the new object. When you choose Update from the server application's File menu, the server application closes and you see the object in the destination document.

> **TIP** If you try to open an existing file while using the server application, you see a message indicating that opening the file will break the link to the destination document. Breaking the link is no catastrophe. Go ahead and open the document. To embed the object, follow the steps in the section "Starting from the Server Application," beginning with step 2.

To embed an object starting from the client application, follow these steps:

1. Choose Object from the Insert menu.

    You see an Object type list, such as the list displayed by Word for Windows, shown in figure 3.7.

I — Understanding Linking and Embedding Basics

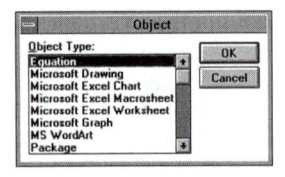

FIG. 3.7 *Object type list (Word for Windows).*

2. Choose the server application you want to use, and click OK. The server application appears.

3. Create the object.

   In figure 3.8, you see an Excel worksheet containing an invoice. The document name, Worksheet in SUZANNE.DOC, is the name of the Word for Windows document from which you began the embedding process.

FIG. 3.8 *Object (worksheet) created in the server application.*

4. Choose Update from the File menu. This command appears only when you access the server application through the Insert Object command.

5. Close the server application. (In some applications, this step isn't necessary; the application closes automatically after you choose Update from the File menu.)

Embedding Objects **51**

> **NOTE** You aren't prompted to save the object you created. When you choose Update from the File menu, you place the object in the destination document. You then save the object when you save the destination document.

After you close the server application, you see the client application and the destination document (see fig. 3.9).

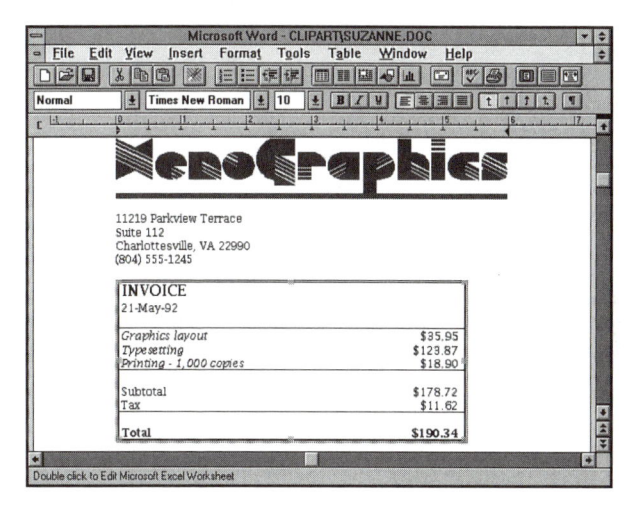

FIG. 3.9 *Excel worksheet inserted as an embedded object into a Word for Windows document.*

6. Save the destination document.

> **TIP** If you decide that you don't want to embed the object after creating it, choose Close in the File menu of the server application. You see a dialog box asking whether you want to update the destination document. Choose No.

Editing Embedded Objects

Editing an embedded object is simplicity itself. You don't need to worry about whether the source document has moved; it is part of the document that contains the object.

To edit an embedded object, follow these steps:

1. Double-click the embedded object, or use the Edit menu to choose the command that includes the word *Object* (such as Microsoft Excel for Windows Object or Microsoft Drawing Object).

> **NOTE** Some embedded objects are designed to perform actions when you double-click them. For example, Sound Recorder objects produce a sound when double-clicked. For these objects, you must choose the Object command from the Edit menu to initiate editing.

   If the server application isn't active, Windows starts the application. Your object appears on-screen in the server application workspace.

2. Edit the object.
3. Choose Update from the File menu.
4. Close the server application. (In some applications, this step isn't necessary; the application closes automatically after you choose Update from the File menu.)

> **TIP** In some applications, you find an Exit & Return command on the File menu. If you have this command, choose it instead of Update. Exit & Return updates the object and closes the application all in one step.

Deleting an Embedded Object

You can easily delete an embedded object. Before you delete, however, remember that this object may be the only copy of the object on disk.

To delete an embedded object, follow these steps:
1. Select the object.
2. Choose Cut or Clear from the Edit menu.

The following procedure shows you how to save an embedded object in a separate file before you delete the object from the source document.

To save an embedded object into a separate file, follow these steps:
1. In the destination document, double-click the embedded object or choose Object from the Edit menu.
2. In the server application workspace, choose Save As or Save Copy As from the File menu and save the object.
3. Choose Exit, and when you're prompted to update the destination document, choose No.

You see the client application and source document again. Now you may delete the embedded object without fear of losing your work.

Canceling Embedding without Deleting the Object

In a compound document, embedded objects take up a great deal of space. If you want to cut down on the amount of space a file requires, you can convert objects into pictures or unformatted text. The object then becomes a static rather than a dynamic object. You cannot edit the object, and double-clicking it does not start the server application. The static object takes up much less room, however, and with most applications, still looks exactly the same.

The procedure for canceling embedding without deleting the object varies widely from application to application. In Microsoft Word for Windows, for example, you highlight the embedded object and then press the Unlink Field key (Ctrl-Shift-F9). In Quattro Pro for Windows, you right-click the object, bringing up the Microsoft Excel Worksheet properties menu. After choosing Object Settings, you see the Object Settings dialog box. In this dialog box, you can choose the Change to Picture button to transform the object into a picture. These methods are just two examples of the different procedures for canceling embedding.

Using Microsoft's OLE Servers

Microsoft Word for Windows and Excel include applications (Equation Editor, Microsoft Draw, Microsoft Graph, and Microsoft WordArt) that illustrate the many advantages of OLE. The applications are designed to function only as servers for embedding; these applications do not run by themselves. They are accessible only through the Insert Object command. You can, however, use Microsoft's OLE servers with any application that is capable of functioning as a client application for OLE purposes. Because these applications are so useful and can be employed with non-Microsoft applications, you should explore their capabilities.

Equation Editor provides useful tools for constructing mathematical equations, such as the one shown in figure 3.10. To build a formula, you type values and operators directly into the application workspace and then choose symbols from the symbol palettes at the top of the window. Many of these symbols include room for additional values. By choosing these symbols, you can quickly build a complex and attractive equation. When you choose Update from the File menu, Equation Editor inserts the formula as an embedded object into your application.

> **NOTE** Equation Editor does not solve equations. Its purpose is to provide a way to type equations quickly without having to fuss with equation typesetting commands, subscripts, or superscripts.

Microsoft Draw is an *object-oriented* (also called *vector*) graphics program. Unlike a paint program (also called a bit-mapped graphics program), Microsoft Draw gives you the tools to create shapes that you can select independently—shapes such as lines, ovals, rectangles, arcs, and polygons. With this drawing program, you can quickly create effective illustrations that (unlike bit-mapped graphics) print at your printer's highest resolution. You also can import bit-mapped graphics and move them around independently until you have created the effect you want (see fig. 3.11).

Microsoft Graph, shown in figure 3.12, is an easy-to-use business graphics program that duplicates the graphics functions of Excel. Creating a graph with Microsoft Graph is much easier and quicker than creating one with Excel, which is first and foremost a spreadsheet program. With Graph, you just type the values into the mini-spreadsheet, and you create a chart in short order.

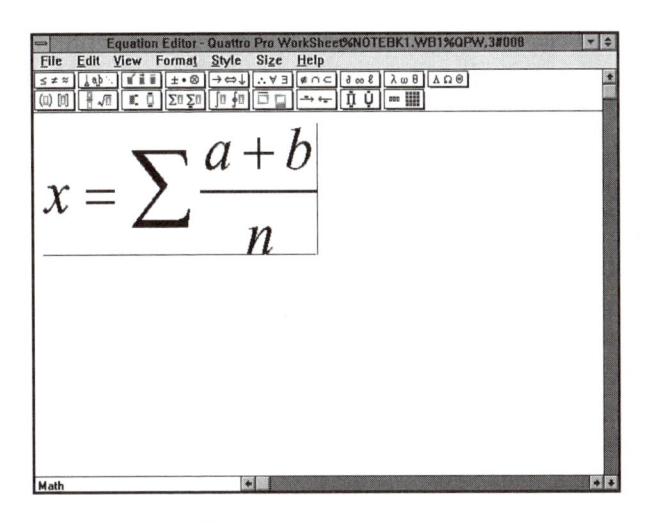

FIG. 3.10 *Equation Editor.*

FIG. 3.11 *Using Microsoft Draw.*

Microsoft WordArt is an especially nifty program that's useful for working with display type (see fig. 3.13). WordArt comes with 19 beautiful display typefaces from which you can choose. The display type effects used in this book's illustrations were created using WordArt.

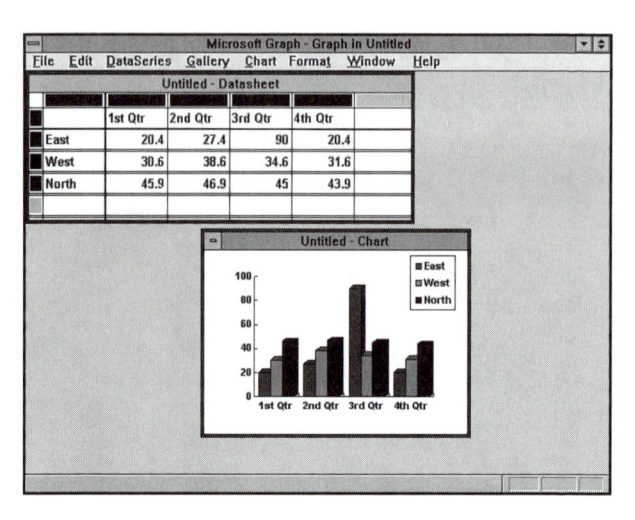

56 *I — Understanding Linking and Embedding Basics*

FIG. 3.12 *A graph created with Microsoft Graph.*

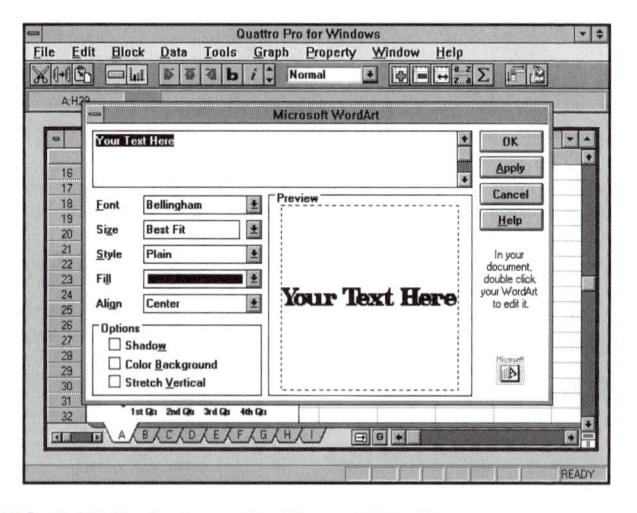

FIG. 3.13 *Display type using Microsoft WordArt.*

Troubleshooting Embedding Problems

This section reviews embedding problems and offers solutions.

You choose Insert Object, but the server application you want to use isn't on the list of server applications.

This problem may have one of several possible causes. First, the application may not be capable of embedding. Many applications that are capable of linking are not capable of embedding. Second, you may have moved the application to a new location. Third, a configuration file may have become corrupted. Finally, you may have deleted the application. To correct the problem, try one or several of the following solutions:

- Check the documentation to make sure that the application is capable of functioning as a server application.

- Reinstall the server application.

- Add to your AUTOEXEC.BAT command a PATH command that lists the server program's directory. To add a PATH command for a directory called EXCEL, for example, you add the line

   PATH D:\EXCEL

   or

   PATH C:\EXCEL

   Add the line to the AUTOEXEC.BAT file in the root directory of your hard drive. If a PATH statement is already in this file, type a semicolon and add the path name to the list, as in the following example:

   PATH C:\WINDOWS;C:\EXCEL;C:\WPWIN)

The server application isn't available.

You have just double-clicked an object so that you can edit it. You see a message informing you that the server application isn't available.

A server application cannot respond when it's displaying a dialog box, printing, downloading to the printer, recalculating, saving data, or waiting for user response in a response field. In addition, Windows cannot start the server if its path is not listed in the current PATH command. Try the following:

- Wait a few moments, and try again. The server application may have completed the task that formerly occupied it.

- Switch to the server application, and close all open dialog boxes or text response fields.

- Switch to the server and complete the operation that is consuming its attention, such as printing or recalculating.

- Add to your AUTOEXEC.BAT command a PATH command that lists the server program's directory. To add a PATH command for a directory called EXCEL, for example, you would add the line

    PATH D:\EXCEL

    or

    PATH C:\EXCEL

    Add the line to the AUTOEXEC.BAT file in the root directory of your hard drive. If a PATH statement is already in this file, type a semicolon and add the path name to the list, as in the following example:

    PATH C:\WINDOWS;C:\EXCEL;C:\WPWIN)

Summary

In this chapter, you learned how to embed objects. With embedding, you place into your document all the information needed by the server application to edit the file. Embedding is useful when you don't need dynamic updating but want to edit the object easily. You can embed in two ways: starting from the server application, or starting from the client application.

CHAPTER FOUR

Packaging Objects

Chapters 2 and 3 discussed linking and embedding, two methods of placing an object into a destination document. After you link or embed an object, you see a representation of the source document on-screen, such as an Excel worksheet range within a Word document. In this chapter, you learn another way to link and embed—by packaging objects. Instead of placing a representation of the object into the destination document, you can insert a package. A *package* is a linked or embedded object minimized to an icon. The package contains the embedded or linked object (all or part of a document). All you see in the destination document is the icon. To see what's in the package, you double-click the icon. Windows starts the server application, and you see the object on-screen in a fully editable form.

You can package an object by using the Object Packager, an accessory you can find in the Accessories group in a standard Windows 3.1 installation (see fig. 4.1). As you will see in this chapter, however, most OLE-capable applications enable you to bypass Object Packager completely: File Manager enables you to package the document by using Clipboard copying or by using drag-and-drop editing with the mouse. Just which method you choose depends on the capabilities of your applications and on your packaging objectives.

Why package an embedded or linked object? Packaging documents gives you a way to create an *interactive document* you can give to a colleague, correspondent, or coworker. In an interactive document created with Object Packager, text is kept to a minimum. If readers want more information on a subject, they just double-click the Object Packager icon. When necessary, Windows then starts the server application. Figure 4.2 shows an interactive letter containing a package.

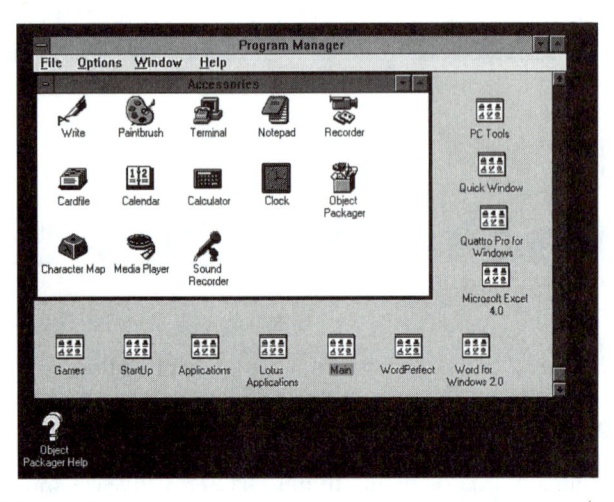

60 I — *Understanding Linking and Embedding Basics*

FIG. 4.1 *Object packager icon in the Accessories group.*

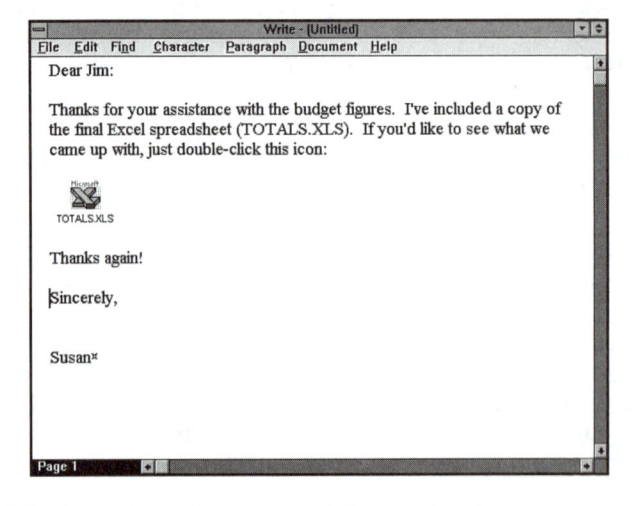

FIG. 4.2 *An interactive letter containing a package icon.*

What happens when you double-click a package depends on what's in it:

- *Text, Spreadsheets, or Graphics*. When you double-click a package containing a text, spreadsheet, or graphic document, Windows displays the object in the server application.

■ *Sounds and Animations*. When you double-click a package containing a sound or animation object, Windows activates the object when you double-click it—in other words, you hear the sound or see the animation.

Packaging is less useful for printing. When you print a document containing a package, your printer prints the document and the object icon; however, you cannot double-click an icon printed on paper.

> **TIP** At this writing, OLE is not well implemented in many applications, and many of the procedures in this chapter may not work with some of your applications—even though they're supposedly OLE-capable. For example, Microsoft Word for Windows 2.0 cannot function as a client for some of the procedures discussed in this chapter. As new software versions emerge, however, they probably will take full advantage of the new Windows 3.1 features, including Object Packager. To see how packaging should work, experiment with the Write and Paintbrush accessories packaged with Windows 3.1. Because Paintbrush is capable of functioning only as a server, and Write, only as a client, you can use Paintbrush files for your source documents and Write for your destination documents.

> **NOTE** You can package an entire document created by any application, even if the application is not OLE-capable. Object Packager does have certain limitations, however. First, you can package part of a document only if the application that created the document is OLE-capable. Second, you can insert a package into a document only if the package was created by an OLE-capable server application.

This chapter fully explores every facet of this useful Windows 3.1 accessory. First, this chapter introduces many options for packaging. You can package an entire document using File Manager techniques, or you can package part of a document with the Object Packager. You can package a linked or an embedded object, and, under certain conditions, you can package without using Object Packager at all. Next, you learn how to activate or edit the packaged object. Finally, you learn how to create your own icons and how to package DOS commands.

> **TIP** A common reason for packaging is to create an interactive document that you can give to a colleague on a floppy disk. If you are sharing a disk, embed the object rather than link it. With an embedded object, the destination document contains all the information your colleague needs to open the document and edit it on his system (assuming this system is equipped with the same applications you used). With a linked object, Windows cannot find the source document on your colleague's system.

Packaging Options

You can package objects in the following three ways:

- *Using File Manager and Clipboard*. Using the File Manager, you copy a document icon to the Clipboard, and then embed or link the icon to the destination document. This feature isn't available, however, in all OLE-capable applications.

- *Using Drag-and-Drop Editing*. You drag a document icon from the File Manager window into the destination document window. This feature isn't available in all OLE-capable applications.

- *Using Object Packager*. You import a file into Object Packager, and then copy the package into the destination document. Any application capable of functioning as an OLE client should be able to accept a package from Object Packager. When you use Object Packager, you can change the icon and label of the package.

Just which packaging technique you choose depends on what you are trying to accomplish.

- *Are you packaging an entire document or just part of a document?* The easiest way to package an entire document is to use the Clipboard or the drag-and-drop technique. If you want to package part of a document, you must use Object Packager.

■ *Do you want to change the icon or label?* By default, the package's icon is the same as the icon of the application that created it. You may want to change the icon or its label to something more descriptive of the file contents. If you want to change the icon or label, use Object Packager.

Packaging an Entire Document

You can package a document created by any application, whether or not it is capable of object linking and embedding (OLE). Although you can package an entire document using Object Packager, the easier techniques are the File Manager techniques using either Clipboard copying or drag-and-drop editing.

> **NOTE** Some applications do not accept packages copied by the Clipboard or edited by drag-and-drop. If these two techniques do not work, try using Object Packager.

Packaging with the Clipboard

Using the File Manager and the Clipboard, you can easily package an entire document. This technique is a good choice if you prefer to work with full-screen windows; the drag-and-drop technique discussed in the next section requires you to display the File Manager and the destination document simultaneously.

To package an object with the File Manager and the Clipboard, follow these steps:

1. Open the File Manager.

2. In the file list window, highlight the name of the document you want to package.

   You can package a document created by any application, even one that isn't OLE-capable.

3. Choose Copy from the File menu, or use the F8 keyboard shortcut.

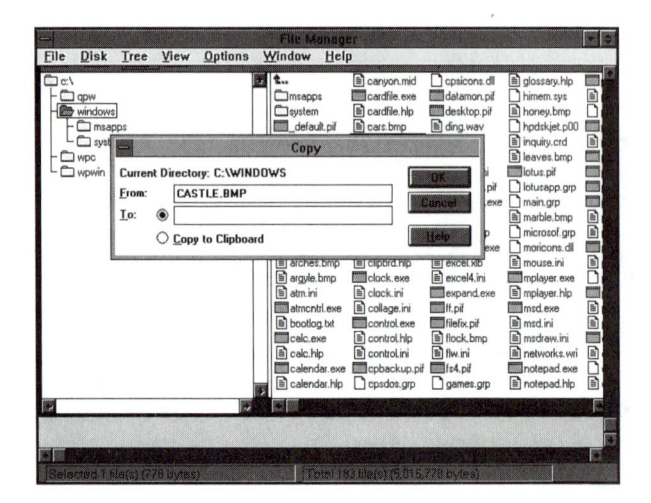

64 *I — Understanding Linking and Embedding Basics*

The Copy dialog box appears (see fig. 4.3).

FIG. 4.3 *The Copy dialog box (File Manager).*

4. Activate the Copy to Clipboard option.
5. Choose OK.

   File Manager copies the document icon to the Clipboard.

6. In the client application, open the destination document.

   The application must be capable of functioning as a client for OLE purposes.

7. Position the insertion point where you want the package to appear.
8. Do one of the following:

   To insert the object as an embedded object, choose Paste.

   To insert the object as a linked object, choose Paste Link.

After you choose Paste or Paste Link, Windows inserts the source document icon into the destination document (see fig. 4.4). By default, the icon is the file name of the client application, and the label is the file name of the document. If you double-click the icon, you see the source document in the client application, even if the client application isn't capable of OLE.

Packaging Objects **65**

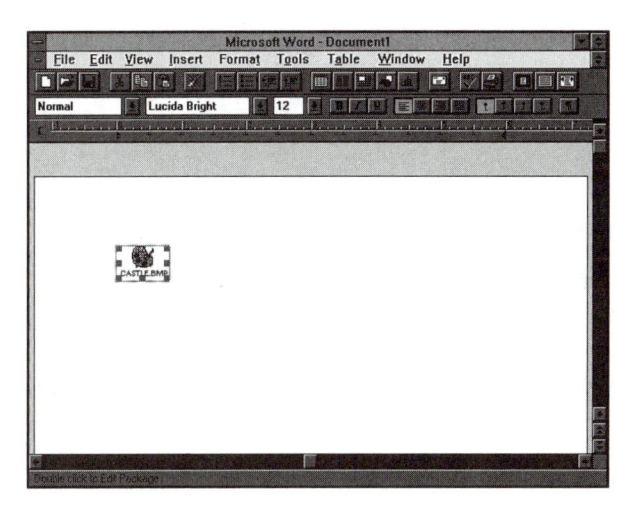

FIG. 4.4 *Source document icon inserted into destination document.*

> **NOTE** If you package an object from an application that isn't OLE-capable, the icon you see isn't that of the client application: Windows uses the icon of the Object Packager.

Packaging with Drag-and-Drop

In this section, you learn an even easier way to package an entire document. However, not all applications, even those fully capable of OLE, support this technique. For example, Microsoft Excel doesn't support drag-and-drop packaging.

To package an entire document with the mouse, follow these steps:

1. Open File Manager, and size the File Manager window so that it occupies the top half of the screen.

2. Open the destination document, and size the client application window so that it occupies the bottom half of the screen (see fig. 4.5).

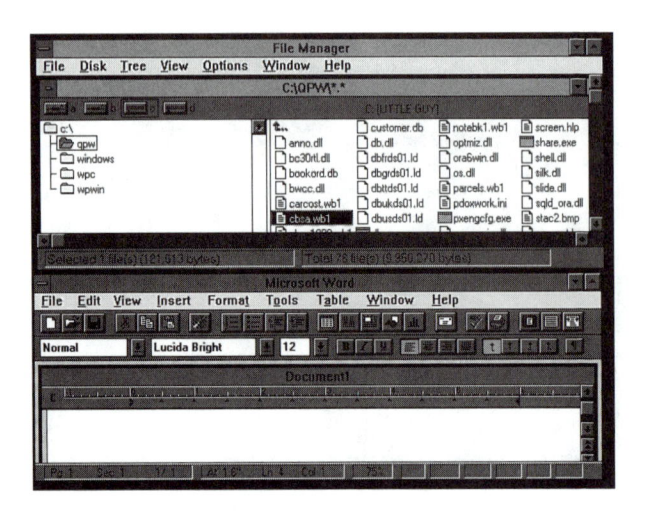

66 I — Understanding Linking and Embedding Basics

FIG. 4.5 *Sizing the File Manager and client application for drag-and-drop packaging.*

3. Do one of the following:

    To embed the object, drag the source document icon from the File Manager to the destination document. Release the mouse button when you have the icon where you want the package to appear.

    To link the object, hold down the Shift and Ctrl keys, and then drag the source document icon from the File Manager to the destination document. Release the mouse button when you have the icon where you want the package to appear.

    Windows inserts the package into your document.

> **NOTE** If your application doesn't accept drag-and-drop packaging, it may open the document or refuse to accept it. If the application refuses to accept the document, the application title bar blinks. Clicking the mouse displays an error message that may not be relevant to packaging. Just click OK. You still may be able to insert the package; try using Object Packager, as described in the next section.

Packaging an Entire Document Using Object Packager

Although Object Packager does not offer the fastest way to insert a package into your destination document, with some applications it provides the only way to do so. For example, Microsoft Excel does not accept packages copied by the Clipboard or dragged from the File Manager. However, Excel does accept a package from Object Packager.

To package an entire document with Object Packager, follow these steps:

1. From the Accessories program group, choose Object Packager.

2. You see the Object Packager - Package window (see fig. 4.6). This window gives you the tools needed to create a package. The Object Packager window is split into two smaller windows. The left window (the Appearance window) will display the package icon. The right window (the Content window) will contain the name of the source document.

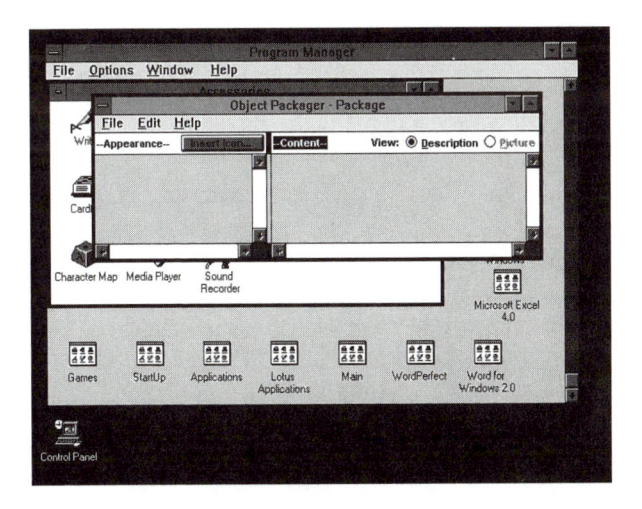

FIG. 4.6 *The Object Packager–Package window.*

3. Activate the Content window by clicking within it or by pressing Tab.

4. From the File menu, choose Import.

You see the Import dialog box (see fig. 4.7). This dialog box provides the tools you need to find the source document.

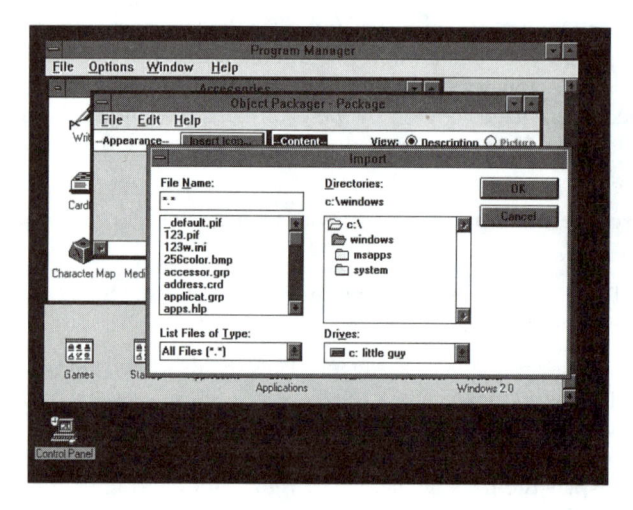

FIG. 4.7 *The Import dialog box.*

5. Type the name of the source document in the File Name text box, or use the Drives and Directories list box to choose the correct directory, and highlight the file name in the File Name list box.

6. Choose OK.

   Object Packager creates the icon and returns you to the Object Packager window. You see the icon in the Appearance window and the file name in the Content window (see fig. 4.8). By default, Object Packager uses the server application icon. If the source document icon isn't capable of OLE, Object Packager uses the Object Packager icon.

7. If you want to change the icon, click the Insert Icon button and choose a new icon from the Insert Icon dialog box. Choose OK to confirm your choice.

8. If you want to change the label Object Packager inserts under the icon after the package is placed in the destination document, choose Label from the Edit menu. Type a new label in the Label text box, and choose OK.

   By default, Object Packager uses the document file name as the label.

Packaging Objects **69**

> **TIP** By default, Object Packager opens the icons in PROGMAN.EXE (Program Manager). To see more icons, type MORICONS.DLL in the File Name list box of the Insert Icons dialog box, and choose OK. To find the icon of the source document application, choose Browse, and use the Browse dialog box to find the application EXE file. (Choose *.EXE in the List Files of Type box to restrict the file display to EXE files.)

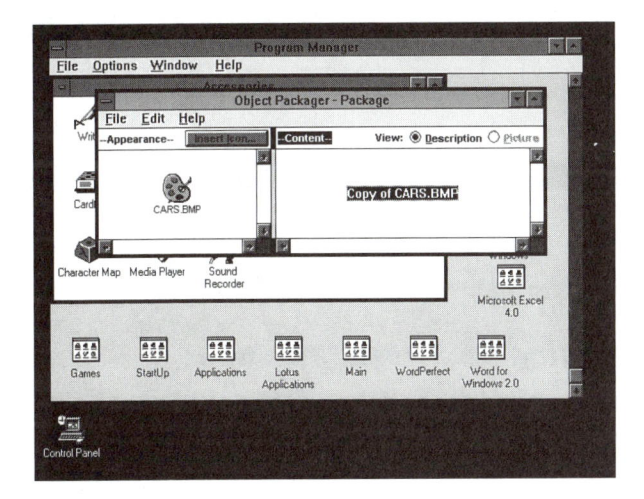

FIG. 4.8 *The icon and file name in the Object Packager window.*

9. From the Edit menu, choose Copy Package.

10. Switch to the application into which you want to insert the package. The application must be capable of functioning as a client application for OLE purposes.

11. Open the document into which you want to insert the package.

12. Position the insertion point where you want the package to appear.

13. Do one of the following:

    To insert the package as an embedded object, choose Paste.

    To insert the package as a linked object, choose Paste Link.

Windows places the icon in the document (see fig. 4.9).

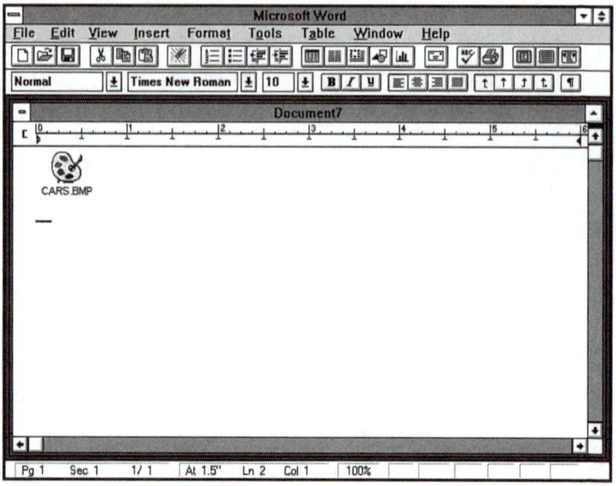

FIG. 4.9 *The icon inserted into a document.*

Packaging Part of a Document

To package part of a document, you must use Object Packager. You cannot package part of a document using the File Manager techniques discussed in the preceding section. In addition, the source document must have been created by an application capable of functioning as a server for OLE purposes.

You begin by selecting the portion of the document you want to package and by copying this portion to the Clipboard. In Object Packager, you paste the Clipboard contents into a package, and then you copy the package to the destination document. You can create an embedded or linked package this way.

> **NOTE** Not all applications, even those capable of functioning as OLE clients, will accept objects containing portions of a document. If you see an error message after trying the following procedure, your application cannot function as an OLE client for this purpose.

To package part of a document, follow these steps:

1. Open the document containing the information you want to package.

   NOTE If you want to link the package to this document, you must name and save the document at this time, if you have not already done so.

2. Select the information.
3. From the Edit menu, choose Copy.
4. Switch to Object Packager.
5. Activate the Contents window.
6. Do one of the following:

   Choose Paste from the Edit menu to create an embedded object package.

   Choose Paste Link from the Edit menu to create a linked object package.

   TIP If you pasted the Clipboard contents into the Appearance window by mistake, just choose Delete from the Edit menu, or press the Del key. Select the Content window, and try again.

7. If you want to change the icon, click the Insert Icon button and choose a new icon from the Insert Icon dialog box. Choose OK to confirm your choice.

8. If you want to change the label Object Packager will insert under the icon after the package is placed in the destination document, choose Label from the Edit menu. Type a new label in the Label text box, and choose OK.

9. From the Edit menu, choose Copy Package.
10. Open the document into which you want to insert the package.
11. Position the cursor where you want the package to appear.

12. From the Edit menu, choose Paste. You don't need to choose Paste Link or Paste Special.

    Windows inserts the package into your document.

Activating the Packaged Object

After you have inserted a package into your destination document, you can easily activate or edit the package. With an inserted sound or animation sequence, activating the package plays the sound or initiates the animation. With an inserted spreadsheet, text document, or graphic, activating the package enables you to edit the source document.

Just what you do to activate the package varies from application to application. In many applications, you can just double-click the package to activate it. Windows plays the sound, initiates the animation, or displays the source document. In other applications, you must use a menu command, such as Edit Object. In still others, you choose Package Object from the Edit menu and then choose Activate Contents from the cascading menu.

Editing the Package with Object Packager

If the Edit menu on your client application has a Package Object command, you can edit the packaged object in three ways: you can change the icon, change the label, and edit the source document.

To edit an object with Object Packager, follow these steps:

1. In the destination application, select the package.
2. Choose Package Object from the Edit menu.

> **TIP** If you don't find a Package Object command, your application may offer another way to edit the package. In Quattro Pro for Windows, for example, you right-click the package, and then choose Object Settings from the pop-up menu. In the Object Settings property menu, you choose Edit Package to display the Object Packager.

Object Packager starts and displays the package in its application workspace (see fig. 4.10).

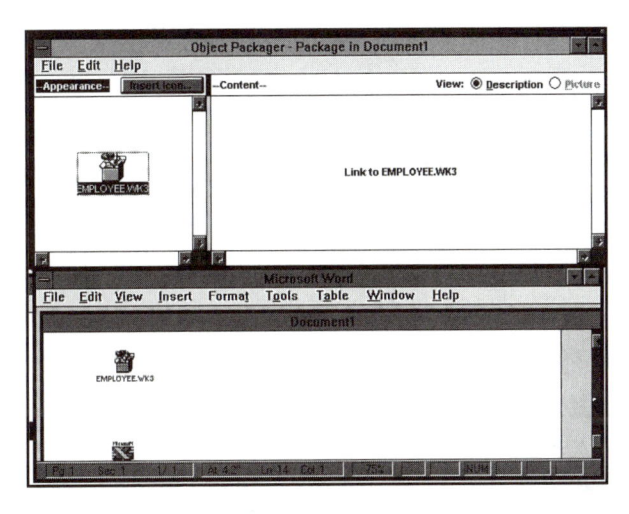

FIG. 4.10 *Editing the packaged object.*

3. To change the label, choose Label from the Edit menu. You see the Label dialog box (see fig. 4.11). Type a new label, and click OK.

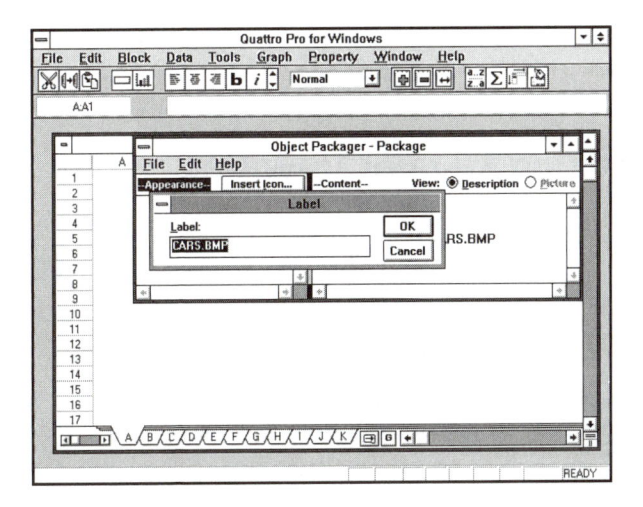

FIG. 4.11 *The Label dialog box.*

4. To change the icon, click the Insert Icon button in the Appearance area. You see the Insert Icon dialog box. Type a new icon file name, or use Browse to find an icon file. Highlight the icon you want, and choose OK.

5. To change the source document, highlight the icon in the Appearance window and press Del; then highlight the text in the Content window and press Del. Choose Import from the File menu, and when the Import dialog box appears, find and select the new source file. Choose OK to confirm your choice.

6. To display a picture of the package contents in the Content window, choose the Picture option

> **NOTE** You can display a picture only when the object was created by using an OLE server application, and when the Clipboard was used to copy the object into Object Packager.

7. To view and edit the source document, double-click the text in the Content area. Save your changes and exit the server application; you will see Object Packager again.

8. Choose Update from the File menu to update the package object.

9. Choose Exit from the File menu to return to the destination document.

Choosing Manual Updating

If you decide to insert a package linked to the source document instead of embedding the package, you can choose manual updating when you create the link. However, you must use Object Packager.

To create a package with manual linking, follow these steps:

1. In the File Manager, highlight the document you want to package and choose Copy from the Edit menu.

2. Switch to Object Packager.

3. With the Content window highlighted, choose Paste Link from the Edit menu.

Object Packager creates the package using linking. In the Content window, the text indicates that the package contains a link (see fig. 4.12).

4. Choose Links from the Edit menu.

   You see the Links dialog box (see fig. 4.13).

5. Choose Manual.
6. Choose OK.
7. From the Edit menu, choose Copy Package.
8. Switch to the destination document.
9. Choose Paste from the Edit menu to insert the linked package in your document.

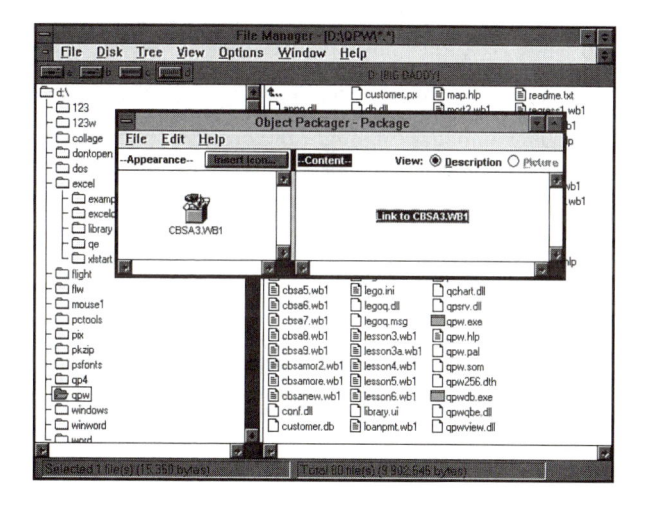

FIG. 4.12 *Linking with Object Packager.*

To update a manually linked package, follow these steps:

1. In the destination document, highlight the linked object and choose Package Object from the Edit menu.
2. In the cascading menu, choose Edit Object.

   Windows displays Object Packager.

3. Choose Links from the Edit menu.

   You see the Links dialog box.

4. Choose Update Now.

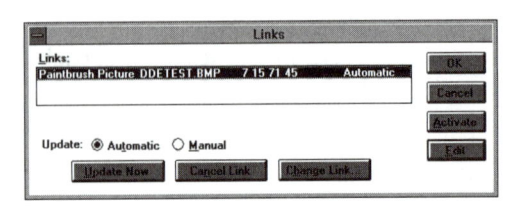

FIG. 4.13 *The Links dialog box.*

Creating Your Own Icons

The default Windows icons in PROGMAN.EXE and the icons in MORICONS.DLL are not really intended for packaging, but for use in group windows. You may want to create your own icon for the packages you insert. The following steps show how to create your own icon while creating a package with Object Packager.

To create a package with a custom icon, follow these steps:

1. In the File Manager, highlight the entire document you want to package, and choose Copy from the File menu.

    or

    For a partial document, open the source document, select the information you want to package, and choose Copy from the File menu.

2. Switch to Object Packager.

3. Activate the Content window by clicking it or pressing Tab.

4. Do one of the following:

    Choose Paste from the Edit menu to create an embedded object.

    or

    Choose Paste Link from the Edit menu to create a linked object.

    Object Packager creates the package using the default icon.

5. Select the Appearance window.

6. Choose Copy from the Edit menu.

7. Switch to Paintbrush.

    Paintbrush is one of the Windows accessories.

8. Choose Paste from the Edit menu.

   You see the icon in the Paintbrush window.

9. Modify the icon, or delete it and create a new one.

10. Select the icon you have modified or created.

11. Choose Copy from the Edit menu.

    If you want to save the icon, choose Save from the File menu, type a file name, and choose OK.

12. Switch to Object Packager.

13. Choose Paste from the Edit menu.

    Object Packager inserts your icon in the Appearance window (see fig. 4.14).

14. Choose Copy Package from the Edit menu.

15. Open the destination document.

16. Position the cursor where you want the package to appear.

17. Choose Paste from the Edit menu.

    Your application inserts the package into your document (see fig. 4.15).

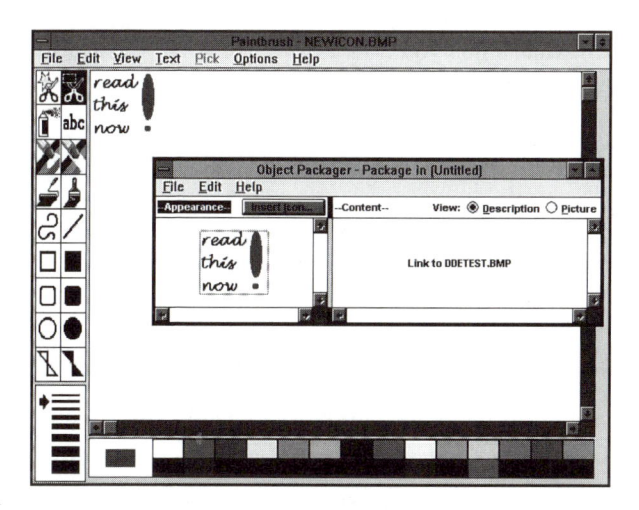

FIG. 4.14 *Inserting the custom icon into the Appearance window.*

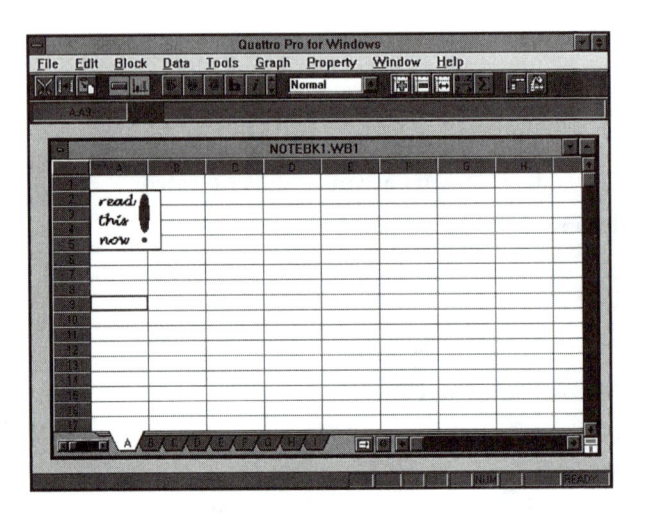

FIG. 4.15 *Custom package icon in the destination document (Quattro Pro for Windows).*

Packaging a DOS Command

An unusual feature of Object Packager is its capability to package a DOS command line. You can use this feature to create interesting interactive documents. For example, you can include a DOS command line that, when you double-click the icon, starts another application or launches a batch file.

> **CAUTION**
>
> Don't package commands that perform destructive acts, such as formatting disks or erasing files.

To package a DOS command, follow these steps:

1. Start Object Packager and activate the Content window.
2. From the Edit menu, choose Command Line.

   You see the Command Line dialog box (see fig. 4.16).

3. In the Command text box, type the DOS command you want to package.

   If you're typing the name of a program or file, be sure to include the full path name, such as C:\WP51\WP.

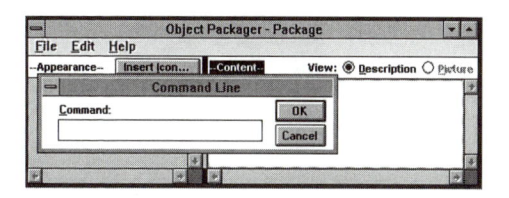

FIG. 4.16 *The Command Line dialog box.*

4. Choose OK.

    Object Packager shows the command in the Content window (see fig. 4.17).

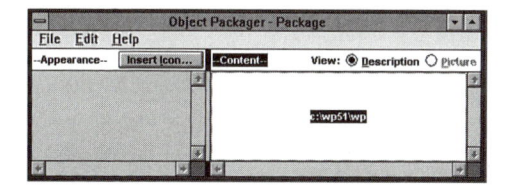

FIG. 4.17 *A DOS command in the Content window.*

5. Choose the Insert Icon button.

    You see the Insert Icon dialog box (see fig. 4.18). In the Current Icon box, you see many icons.

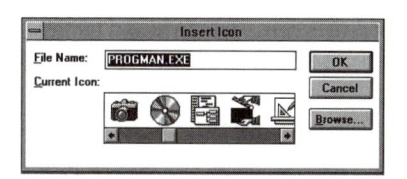

FIG. 4.18 *The Insert Icon dialog box.*

6. Click the right scroll arrow to display additional icons. When you see the icon you want, click the icon to highlight it.

7. Choose OK.

    Object Packager shows the selected icon in the Appearance window (see fig. 4.19).

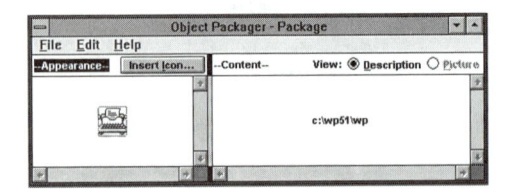

FIG. 4.19 *The selected icon in the Appearance window.*

8. From the Edit menu, choose Copy Package.
9. Open the destination document.
10. From the Edit menu, choose Paste. You also can press the Ctrl-V keyboard shortcut.

You see the package's icon in the destination document (see fig. 4.20).

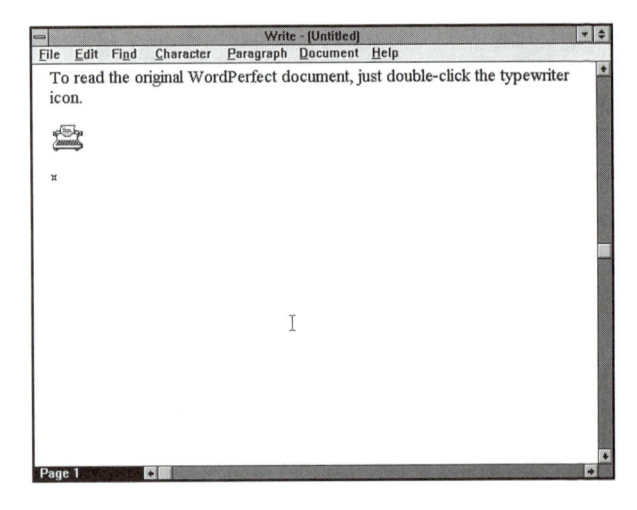

FIG. 4.20 *The package icon in a document.*

Putting It All Together: Creating Interactive Documents

An interactive document invites the user to click packages to see animations, hear sounds, and view documents. In figure 4.21, you see these three capabilities combined in a useful way. This Write document contains an embedded sound (created with Sound Recorder) and four embedded objects stored in packages: a Write document, an Excel spreadsheet, an Excel chart, and a Paintbrush graphic. Just by double-clicking the icons, new team members get a quick introduction to the project—complete with an inspiring, audible message from the Project Director.

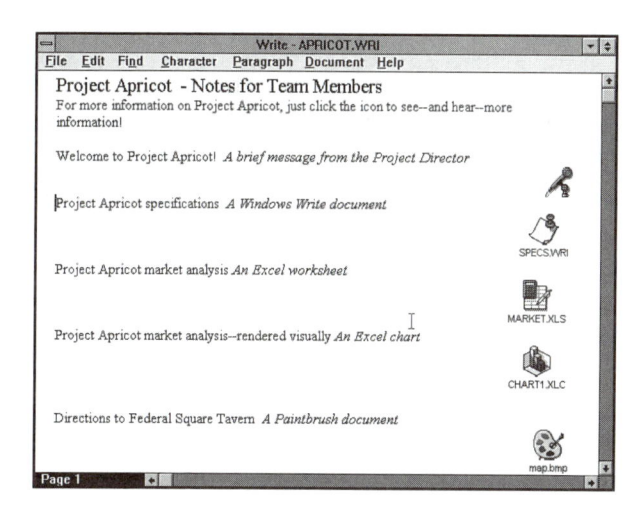

FIG. 4.21 *An interactive document combining several capabilities.*

Using Other Object Packager Commands

Object Packager offers many commands not discussed in the previous sections on packaging procedures. You may find some of these commands useful.

- To delete an icon in the Appearance window or text in the Content window, highlight the icon or text and choose Delete from the Edit menu. Alternatively, press the Del key.

- To undo your last Object Packager action, choose Undo from the Edit menu or use the Ctrl+Z shortcut.

- To edit the source document before completing the packaging operation, highlight the document name in the Content window and choose Edit Object from the Edit menu.

- To view a picture of the source document, choose Picture in the View area of the Content window.

For more information on using Windows 3.1 Object Packager, you can refer to Que's *Using Windows 3.1,* Special Edition.

Summary

In this chapter, you learned how to use File Manager and Object Packager to package linked or embedded objects—in other words, insert an object into a document so that the object is minimized to an icon. When you double-click the object, Windows displays the document. You can use Object Packager to create interactive documents full of packages.

CHAPTER FIVE

Understanding Dynamic Data Exchange (DDE)

In previous chapters, you learned how to integrate Windows applications by linking, embedding, and packaging objects. These techniques make use of Microsoft's object linking and embedding (OLE) standards, which enable you to perform linking and embedding operations by choosing commands from menus. In this chapter, you peer beneath OLE to the underlying communication capabilities that make OLE possible. These capabilities are made possible by Microsoft's dynamic data exchange (DDE) standards, which specify how Windows applications can be written to exchange data with other active applications.

One way to understand the relationship between DDE and OLE is to think of DOS and Windows' File Manager. DOS integrates your system's components so that they can work together harmoniously, handling tasks such as storing and retrieving files. Typing DOS commands directly, however, is tedious. The File Manager makes DOS easy to use by providing menu commands for common DOS operations. DDE underlies OLE in much the same way, but few people like to use it. With most applications, using DDE requires that you master a complicated command syntax, requiring that you type the command using exactly the correct sequence of instructions, punctuation marks, and command keynames. Just as the File Manager makes DOS accessible for the average user, OLE makes DDE more accessible by providing menu commands for dynamic linking operations. OLE also makes two non-DDE operations, embedding and packaging, possible for the first time. (For more information on using the File Manager, refer to Que's *Using Windows 3.1,* Special Edition.)

If OLE is a user-friendly version of dynamic data exchange, why learn about DDE and its hard-to-write commands? The purpose of OLE, after all, is to make linking and embedding easier for the average user. If your need to link Windows applications does not extend beyond the linking, embedding, and packaging techniques already discussed, you don't need to understand DDE, and you can cheerfully skip this chapter. Linking, embedding, and packaging provide all the application integration prowess that most users need. But you may want to explore DDE more fully for three reasons:

- *Many Windows applications do not yet support OLE, so you need to understand DDE if you want to create dynamic links.* In Chapter 7, "Linking a Named Range in 1-2-3 to WordPerfect," you learn how to create DDE links with two applications that do not currently support OLE. Although these applications provide dialog boxes to make dynamic linking easier to achieve, you will find it helpful to understand the underlying concepts of DDE as you attempt to link these applications.

- *Some useful DDE functions are not implemented in the Edit menu techniques of linking and embedding.* If you learn to write DDE commands yourself (instead of using Edit menu linking and embedding techniques), you can send data to the server application, execute the server application's commands remotely, run server application macros, and import data from specialized storage locations, such as glossaries and bookmarks. Each of these topics is discussed at greater length in this chapter. The point to keep in mind for now is that DDE enables you to exchange data in ways that OLE techniques do not fully implement.

- *If you understand DDE, you can use the DDE capabilities included in many applications' macro capabilities.* A macro is a stored set of keystrokes and commands that, when played back, perform a series of actions, such as selecting a block of cells and choosing a font. Many Windows applications—including Microsoft Word, Microsoft Excel, Quattro Pro for Windows, and Ami Pro—include DDE macro commands. If you understand DDE, you can write macros that perform DDE functions such as exchanging data with other applications.

This chapter explores the world of DDE that lies beneath your applications' object linking and embedding (OLE) capabilities. You learn how DDE works so that you can identify the DDE functions not implemented in OLE-style linking. You also find an introduction to the use of DDE techniques in macros. Although this chapter does not attempt to cover the specifics of DDE syntax in all the applications this book mentions, it provides the perspective that enables you to learn and apply these specifics in short order.

Understanding the Purpose of DDE

With DOS, people typically ran just one application at a time—so far as most system designers were concerned, one was enough. After all, the purpose of personal computing is to provide users with a stand-alone, single-user workstation. Because most people have difficulty doing two things at once, or so the reasoning went, a personal computer need not provide *multitasking* capabilities—the capability to run more than one program at a time.

Personal computer users soon proved wrong the assumption that they wanted to run only one program at a time. Many users want to perform functions off-screen (printing a lengthy file, indexing a huge database, or downloading data from an on-line information service, for example) as they continue to work with a document on-screen. Moreover, they want to move data from one application to another, preferably without having to quit the first in order to access the second. With DOS, however, running more than one program at a time isn't possible without resorting to risky tricks, such as using terminate-and-stay resident (TSR) programs that are notoriously prone to cause system crashes.

One of the reasons for Microsoft Windows' widespread adoption is that it effectively addresses user's multitasking needs. With Windows running in the Standard or 386 Enhanced mode, you can open two or more applications and set them to work simultaneously; while Excel prints your workbook, complete with spreadsheets and charts, you can work on your report with Ami Pro. Moreover, Windows simplifies transferring data from one application to another; you don't have to quit the first application to start the second.

Because Windows can run more than one program at a time, an advanced computing capability called *interprocess communication* is made available to personal computer users. In interprocess communication, applications running simultaneously can send messages to each other. In essence, dynamic data exchange (DDE) is a *protocol* (a set of documented standards) for interprocess communication in the Windows computing environment. With DDE, a Windows application can instruct another application to perform tasks such as sending data, carrying out a command, or executing a macro.

Interprocess communication is made possible by the underlying message-based design of Microsoft Windows. Windows is an *event-driven* program; in other words, it doesn't do anything until something happens—the mouse is clicked or a key pressed, for example. So long as nothing is happening, the program goes through a *ready loop* over and over, with infinite patience. As soon as an event occurs, however, the event—such as a key press— transmits a message that propagates through the system until an application receives it and acts on it. DDE messages fit into the message loop along with other messages that stem from events, enabling one application to send a message to another. Excel can send a message to a program that is actively monitoring stock prices from an on-line information service, for example. As the stock prices change, Excel receives the changing data and recalculates a stock analysis spreadsheet accordingly.

Dynamic data exchange (DDE) originated in early versions of Microsoft Excel. Excel's development team created DDE to demonstrate how applications could use Windows' internal communication structure to send messages to each other and incorporated this into Version 2.0 of Microsoft Windows. Microsoft made a DDE development kit available to other application publishers, and many took advantage of it. Not until Version 3.1 of Windows with its full OLE support, however, did users begin making more than occasional use of dynamic linking and dynamic data exchange.

> **TIP** Because DDE predates OLE, many applications that provide little or no support for menu-based OLE functions are fully capable of supporting DDE. If you have hunted in vain in your applications for commands such as Paste Link or Insert Object, take heart: your application may still support DDE, and you may be able to try some of the DDE techniques discussed in this chapter. Many of the tutorials in the remaining chapters of this book detail ways to link applications that don't support OLE.

This discussion may seem to imply that DDE is obsolete, replaced by the more friendly OLE menu commands. As you learn more about DDE, however, you see that it offers some unique capabilities not available with OLE. To understand these capabilities more fully, you will find it helpful to understand the structure of DDE messages.

Understanding the Structure of DDE Messages

The following analogy may help you understand DDE messages. Imagine that you're a manager and you're calling an employee. When you pick up the telephone to call, you *initiate* the conversation. If your employee is at the other end, you succeed in your attempt to connect a *channel* of communication, and you receive an *acknowledgment* that signals the beginning of your *conversation*. You then transmit messages to your employee. When you're finished, you *terminate* the conversation. DDE messages are just as simple, and the terms used here are, in fact, the ones used to describe a dynamic data exchange.

In DDE, a conversation is initiated by the *client application*; on the other end of the "phone" is the *server application*. The term *client* is somewhat misleading because the client—the boss, in telephone terms—is very much in control of the conversation. The "client-as-boss" can tell the server to send data, to choose and carry out the server's own commands, and even to run the server's own macros. The client application could even include a DDE command to have the server carry out a command that would wipe out its own data.

> **TIP**
>
> If you don't want your applications to be manipulated by DDE clients, most applications give you a way of ignoring external DDE orders. In Microsoft Excel, for example, you can choose Workspace from the Options menu and activate the Ignore Remote Requests check box to protect Excel from external DDE orders. By default, this option is not activated (see fig. 5.1). After activating this option, applications trying to access Excel get the electronic equivalent of "I'm sorry, she's not at her desk right now."

I — Understanding Linking and Embedding Basics

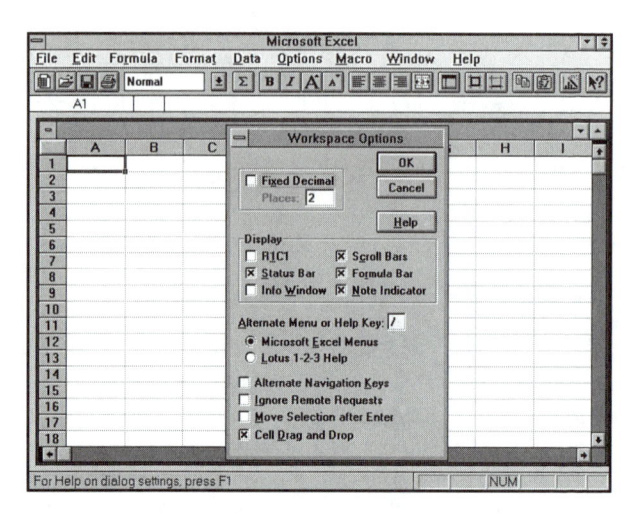

FIG. 5.1 *Excel workspace options.*

A DDE conversation has a *topic* and an *item*, the subject of which is determined by the client application. In general, the *topic* is the name of a file, and the *item* refers to the specific location of the data, such as a range in a spreadsheet. All DDE commands therefore have a three-part structure, consisting of the name of the application being addressed, the topic, and the item (data location).

You know enough about DDE now to see an actual DDE command—and you can create one yourself using a neat trick. When you paste-link data using the OLE techniques discussed in Chapter 2, many applications actually create a DDE command, unbeknownst to you, that usually is hidden from view. In Microsoft Word for Windows, for example, paste-linking the contents of a Quattro Pro for Windows cell results in the automatic creation of a DDEAUTO field, which doesn't appear in your document unless you choose a command. Figure 5.2 shows a typical figure ($1,400.00) in a typical Microsoft Word letter that has been paste-linked into Word. When you choose Word's Field Codes command (View menu), you toggle on the display of codes and commands that underlie text generated by fields, such as the DDEAUTO field. Figure 5.3 shows the DDEAUTO command Word automatically created when the contents of the Quattro Pro cell were paste-linked into the Word document.

Understanding Dynamic Data Exchange (DDE)

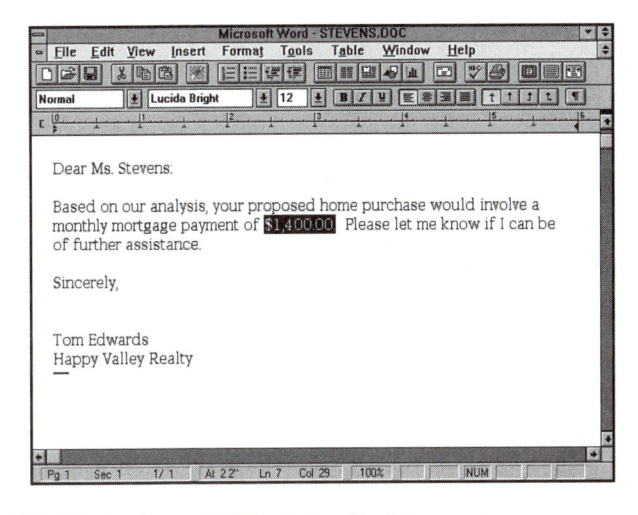

FIG. 5.2 *A value paste-linked into a Word document.*

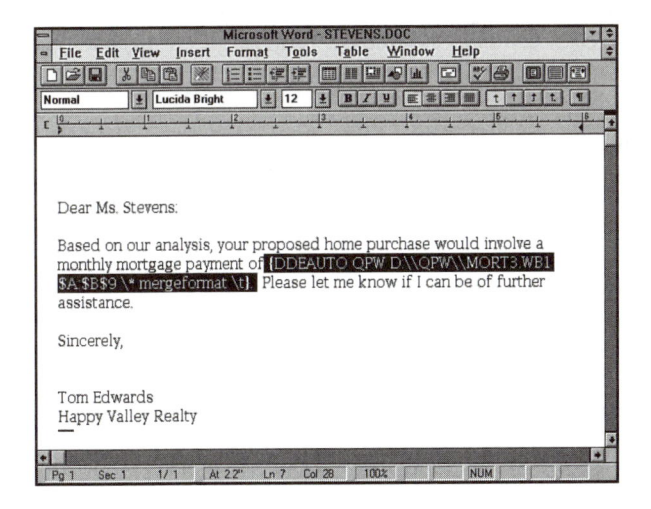

FIG. 5.3 *DDEAUTO command underlying the value in the Word document.*

I — Understanding Linking and Embedding Basics

> **TIP** Never type a lengthy DDE command if you can use your application to build one automatically. In the example just given, Word constructed the entire command when the Quattro Pro for Windows data was paste-linked into Word. You need not learn the complicated syntax of DDE commands if your application can build the command for you automatically.

A closer look at this command may help you understand it. First, you see the command keyname DDEAUTO. This command sets up a DDE link that is automatically updated; that is, if you change the Quattro Pro for Windows cell that this command references, the change is reflected in the Word document. Next, you see the application name, QPW (Quattro Pro for Windows). Following the application name is the topic—the file D:\QPW\MORT3.WB1—and the item—data location: cell B9 on notebook page A. The dollar signs indicate an *absolute cell reference*, the default reference method for linking purposes. An absolute cell reference ensures that this command refers to cell B9 and only cell B9. The rest of the information specifies the data format Word will use as it imports the data.

To summarize what you have learned in this section, every DDE exchange begins when a client application initiates a *conversation* with a server. The conversation is about a *topic* (usually a file) and an *item* (usually a data location). When you link documents using the Edit menu techniques of paste-linking, many applications automatically create and store a DDE command like the Word command seen here. These commands can tell you a great deal about the structure of DDE messages and how your application requires you to type DDE commands. But don't type a DDE command if your application can create it automatically when you paste-link data using Edit menu commands. In the next section, you learn about some DDE capabilities that go beyond OLE-style linking. To take advantage of these capabilities, you must type the DDE command yourself—and you may find the results well worth learning how to do so.

> **TIP** If you are linking to a spreadsheet program, place the cell pointer in the cell that contains the linked data. The status line shows the DDE formula the program created automatically when you paste-linked the data into your spreadsheet. In figure 5.4,

for example, you see the DDELINK formula that Quattro Pro inserts in a cell when you paste-link an Excel cell into a Quattro Pro worksheet. The formula contains all the necessary elements of a DDE command: the application name (EXCEL), the topic (SHEET1), and the item (cell R9C2).

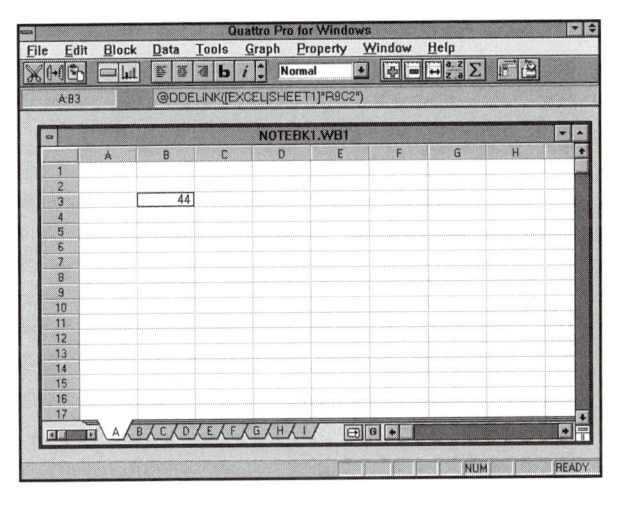

FIG. 5.4 *DDELINK formula automatically created by paste-linking data.*

Understanding Windows' DDE Message Set

DDE is made possible by the interprocess communication capabilities built into Microsoft Windows. In this section, you look more closely at Windows' DDE capabilities in order to understand just what you can accomplish with DDE.

To enable DDE, Windows provides *protocols* (standard procedures) for applications to use in communicating with each other. The protocols are implemented in the DDE *message set*, a set of nine commands that Windows recognizes and processes.

- **WM_DDE_EXECUTE.** Sends a *command string* (a series of characters) to another application. Using this command, the client application can start the server application, tell the server application to execute one of its own commands, or run one of the server application's macros.

- **WM_DDE_INITIATE.** Opens a channel for the DDE conversation. Each channel is given a unique number, such as Channel 1 or Channel 2. More than one channel can be open at a time.

- **WM_DDE_INITIATEACK.** Acknowledges that a DDE conversation has begun. With this command, the server application is able to say "Hello."

- **WM_DDE_REQUEST.** Requests data from another application. This command creates a dynamic link through which source document data is imported into the destination document.

- **WM_DDE_ADVISE.** Requests another application to update the requested data whenever it changes. This command establishes a "hot" or dynamic link that causes changes in the source document to be automatically reflected in the destination document.

- **WM_DDE_UNADVISE.** Tells another application to stop updating data. This command freezes a "hot" or automatic link so that it is no longer automatically updated.

- **WM_DDE_ACK.** Acknowledges a request. This command enables the server application to say "OK" when the client makes a request.

- **WM_DDE_POKE.** Sends data to another application. This command enables the *client* application to force data into one of the *server* application's documents, reversing the normal flow of data in linking operations.

- **WM_DDE_TERMINATE.** Ends the DDE conversation and closes the channel.

This list of Windows DDE commands shows you what DDE can accomplish. As you may have already inferred, DDE can do more than create dynamic links. In the next section, you learn ways you can use DDE to go far beyond OLE-style linking. You may even find some good reasons to learn how to write DDE commands yourself.

Using Advanced DDE Capabilities

So far in this chapter, DDE has been described as if it were a manual, type-it-yourself, more or less obsolete way of creating dynamic links that you can create much more easily using the OLE menu commands. This perception is true in part. OLE is much easier to use, and when you're using DDE, you must deal with more complex concepts.

DDE has some unique features not implemented in OLE, however. With DDE, you can do much more than create links to selected data in the server application, as you can with OLE. Specifically, you can link to data units not accessible through the OLE menu techniques, such as bookmarks in a word processing program, named ranges in a spreadsheet program, and the results of database queries in a database management program. The sections to follow illustrate these uses of DDE commands. In subsequent chapters, you find tutorials that show you how to take advantage of these DDE capabilities for specific applications not capable of OLE, such as WordPerfect for Windows and Lotus 1-2-3 for Windows.

Accessing Bookmarks in Word Processing Documents

DDE commands include an application name, a topic, and an item. The term *item* usually refers to the data location—selected text in a document. Some applications, however, permit you to access items other than the selection. In this section, you learn how a DDE command can access data stored as a *bookmark* in Microsoft Word for Windows.

In Word, a *bookmark* is a fixed unit of text (such as one or two paragraphs or pages) to which you have assigned a bookmark name. Doing so has several advantages. Because bookmarks are named, you can jump to a bookmark quickly just by choosing its name from a menu—a real advantage in a lengthy, complex document. For DDE purposes, however, the virtue of bookmarks stems from your capability to address them as items in a DDE command.

From the DDE perspective, a Microsoft Word bookmark is one of several items that can be remotely referenced in a DDE command. In figure 5.5, you see a Microsoft Word document that contains a passage of *boilerplate text*—text stored in a fixed form to be used repeatedly, without variation—that has been defined as a bookmark. In many firms, for reasons of legal liability and customer service, the same text must be used every time a letter or analysis is prepared. In figure 5.6, you see a Quattro Pro for Windows spreadsheet in which this bookmark, called "Disclaimer," is referenced by a DDELINK command. (Look for the command in the formula bar.) As you can see, this command differs from previous DDE commands you have seen in this chapter in only one way: the item is a bookmark.

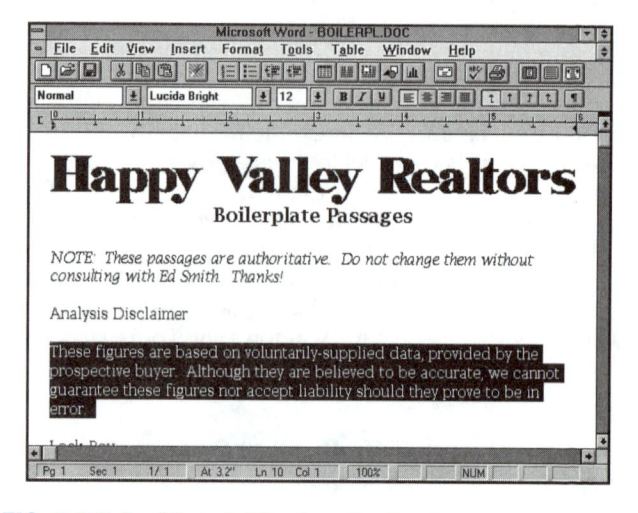

FIG. 5.5 *Boilerplate text defined as a bookmark.*

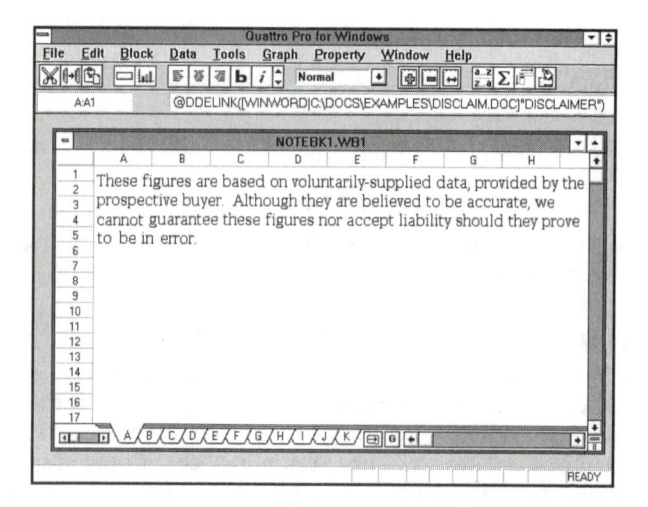

FIG. 5.6 *DDELINK formula in Quattro Pro referencing bookmark in Word document.*

> **TIP** If you want to create an external reference to a bookmark, the following is an easier alternative to learning how to type the DDE command. Just select the original bookmark text in the server application, choose Copy from the Edit menu, and paste-link the bookmark text into the destination spreadsheet. Then place the pointer in the cell containing the external reference formula that your spreadsheet program constructed automatically when the paste-link occurred. Carefully delete the item name from the existing formula and type in the name of the bookmark. Do not disturb any punctuation, such as quotation marks. After you press Enter, the formula should successfully reference the bookmark—without you having to learn how to type the command using the correct syntax.

Ami Pro for Windows also supports bookmarks. Chapter 6, "Linking between 1-2-3 and Ami Pro," contains tutorials that extensively illustrate the process of linking to an Ami Pro bookmark.

Accessing Spreadsheet Ranges

In spreadsheet programs, you can write DDE commands that access data stored in named *ranges*. By naming ranges of cells, you often can avoid having to type cell references. Instead of typing the range B9..B43, for example, you can just type the name of the range, SALES. When you name a range, you can access the range as an item in a DDE command. In Quattro Pro for Windows, the following command links to the range MAY_SALES in the Excel spreadsheet FIRSTQTR.XLS:

@DDELINK([EXCEL|D:\EXCEL\FIRSTQTR.XLS]"MAY_SALES")

As you learn in Chapter 7, "Linking a Named Range in 1-2-3 to WordPerfect," WordPerfect for Windows provides menus that establish links to spreadsheet ranges. This feature is desirable because you don't have to learn how to type complicated DDE commands such as the Quattro Pro for Windows command just given.

Accessing Databases

In the preceding two sections, you learned about writing DDE commands that access named units of data in word processing

I — *Understanding Linking and Embedding Basics*

programs (bookmarks) and spreadsheet programs (named ranges). In this section, you learn that you can access data stored in DDE-capable database management programs, such as Microsoft Q&E (a database management program packaged with Microsoft Excel), in a wide variety of ways. The capabilities illustrated here are those of Microsoft Q&E, but other DDE-capable database management programs may have similar capabilities.

The following Quattro Pro for Windows function typifies the DDE commands this chapter has discussed. You see the application name (QE, short for Microsoft Q&E), the topic (in this case, the window titled Query1), and the item (the data location R3C1:R3C7, a row of data in the Q&E database). This command was constructed by paste-linking a row of Q&E data (see fig. 5.7) into a Quattro Pro spreadsheet (see fig. 5.8).

@DDELINK([QE|D:\EXCEL\QE\EMPLIST.QEF]"R3C1:R3C7")

	FIRST_NAME	LAST_NAME	EMP_ID	HIRE_DATE	SALARY	DEPT	EXEMPT	INTERESTS
1	Tyler	Bennett	E10297	6/1/77	32000.00	D101	Y	
2	John	Rappl	E21437	7/15/87	47000.00	D050	Y	Sports:II
3	George	Woltman	E00127	8/7/82	53500.00	D101	Y	Sports:II
4	Adam	Smith	E63535	1/15/88	18000.00	D202	N	
5	David	McClellan	E04242	7/27/82	41500.00	D101	Y	Sports:II
6	Rich	Holcomb	E01234	6/1/83	49500.00	D202	Y	
7	Nathan	Adams	E41298	2/15/88	21900.00	D050	N	
8	Richard	Potter	E43128	4/12/86	15900.00	D101	N	
9	David	Motsinger	E27002	5/5/85	19250.00	D202	N	
10	Tim	Sampair	E03033	12/2/87	27000.00	D101	Y	
11	Kim	Arlich	E10001	7/30/85	57000.00	D190	Y	
12	Timothy	Grove	E16398	1/21/85	29900.00	D190	Y	

FIG. 5.7 *Copying a row of data from a Q&E database.*

This command is much easier to create using the copy-and-paste-link techniques made possible by OLE than by typing it manually. As figure 5.8 shows (note the formula bar), Quattro Pro constructs the formula automatically. You can do much more, however, if you are willing to edit a function such as this one. Just by substituting items, you can make DDE go to work for you in an impressive way.

If you edit the @DDELINK function as follows,

@DDELINK([QE|D:\EXCEL\QE\EMPLIST.QEF]"ALL")

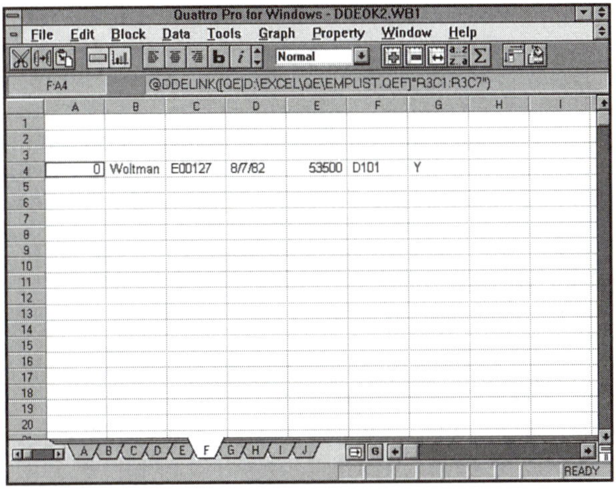

Understanding Dynamic Data Exchange (DDE) **97**

FIG. 5.8 *Data copied into Quattro Pro for Windows spreadsheet.*

Quattro Pro imports all the data in the database. The following command imports all the data and includes the header names (field names) and row numbers:

@DDELINK([QE|D:\EXCEL\QE\EMPLIST.QEF]
"ALL/HEADERS/ROWNUM")

As these examples illustrate, investigating just which items your application enables DDE to access can be well worth your time.

> **TIP** Because relatively few users make use of DDE commands, you probably will not find much information on DDE in your applications' manuals. You may have difficulty determining which items your application supports. If the manual contains no chapter or appendix on DDE, check the index under "Dynamic data exchange" or "DDE."

Using DDE Commands in Macros

A *macro* is a series of recorded actions that, when played back, carry out these actions automatically, just as if you have performed them yourself. Many applications include macro capabilities. You can use macros to carry out actions that you otherwise accomplish manually by choosing a series of commands, such as centering and bolding a return address. With some applications, you can turn on a macro recorder that captures your actions and records them so you can play them back later. Other applications permit you to write and record macros. With these applications, you can draw from a treasure trove of macro commands that enable you to create much more complex and impressive macros than those you can create by recording.

DDE-capable applications that enable you to write your own macros typically include DDE macro commands. You can use these commands to gain full control of Windows' DDE capabilities. In the preceding section, you learned how to modify DDE commands created by paste-linking operations in order to access items such as bookmarks, ranges, and databases. In this section, you learn how DDE macro commands give you access to the full range of DDE capabilities, including forcing the DDE server to list available information, sending data to the server application, and executing the server application's commands.

> **NOTE** If you're new to macros, by all means try reading this section. Keep in mind, however, that the scope of this book does not include detailing all the procedures and knowledge you need to write Excel or Quattro Pro macros effectively.

Understanding DDE Macro Commands

DDE macro commands differ from the DDE commands covered thus far in this chapter, the ones that applications automatically insert in your document when you paste-link data (such as Word's DDEAUTO and Quattro Pro's @DDELINK). Commands such as DDEAUTO are very much like a spreadsheet program's built-in commands in that they perform several actions. @AVG, for example, sums a range, counts the number of cells, and divides the sum by the number of cells. In the same way, a DDE command such as @DDELINK or DDEAUTO sets several of the basic Windows DDE messages in action. @DDELINK, for example, sets in motion these Windows DDE messages: WM_DDE_INITIATE, WM_DDE_REQUEST, WM_DDE_ADVISE, and WM_DDE_TERMINATE. WM_DDE_EXECUTE may be needed as well if the server application isn't running.

Understanding Dynamic Data Exchange (DDE) **99**

DDE macro commands, in contrast to commands such as @DDELINK or DDEAUTO, accomplish just one action, such as initiating the DDE conversation or requesting data from the server. They closely parallel the Windows commands discussed earlier in "Understanding Windows' DDE Message Set." Using DDE macro commands, you can gain full control over all the capabilities that DDE offers.

A glance at the DDE macros available in Quattro Pro for Windows (see table 5.1) shows how closely DDE macro commands parallel the Windows DDE message set. (For simplicity, table 5.1 lists only the command macro keynames.) As you can see, these macros enable you to carry out DDE tasks that cannot be accomplished with the Edit menus of OLE-capable applications, such as sending data to the server application or executing the server application's commands remotely. Each DDE-capable application has its own names for these commands, but they usually are similar and are often identical to Quattro Pro commands. For the sake of simplicity, the remainder of this section uses Quattro Pro's macro commands to illustrate advanced DDE applications.

Table 5.1. DDE Macro Commands (Quattro Pro for Windows)

Command	Function
{EXEC}	Starts an application
{INITIATE}	Opens a channel for a DDE conversation
{REQUEST}	Requests data to be dynamically paste-linked
{POKE}	Sends data to the server application
{EXECUTE}	Tells the server application to carry out a command
{TERMINATE}	Ends a DDE conversation

Looking at a DDE Macro

When you write a DDE macro, you must include all the actions needed to establish and terminate a DDE conversation. The following macro, written in the Quattro Pro for Windows' macro language, retrieves the bookmark text stored under Disclaimer in the Word document (refer to fig. 5.6):

{INITIATE "Winword","BOILERPL.DOC",dde_channel}
{REQUEST dde_channel,"Disclaimer",A9}
{TERMINATE dde-channel}

An English translation of this macro may read, "Start a DDE conversation with the application Winword (Word for Windows) and use the topic BOILERPL.DOC (a file name). When the application responds by stating the number of the DDE channel that has been opened, store this number in the variable *dde_channel*. From the server application, use this channel to request the data stored under the bookmark name Disclaimer and paste-link this data into cell A9. Then hang up the phone."

This example illustrates that DDE macros must always include the INITIATE and TERMINATE commands. All the following examples include these commands.

Using the SYSTEM Topic

Every DDE conversation involves an application, a topic, and an item, which may be optional in some cases. Usually the topic is a file name, as in the preceding example, in which the file BOILERPL.DOC was accessed. However, you can obtain some very useful information that may not be found in your application's documentation by using the SYSTEM topic. With the SYSTEM topic, you can instruct the server application to transmit a list of the topics and formats it can make available through DDE channels. Some applications make additional information available when you use the SYSTEM topic.

To use the system topic, write a macro such as the following Quattro Pro for Windows macro:

{INITIATE "QE","SYSTEM", dde_channel}
{REQUEST dde_channel,"SysItems",A9}
{TERMINATE dde_channel}

In English, this macro reads, "Initiate a DDE conversation with the application named QE (Microsoft Q&E, the database manager packaged with Excel). When the application responds with the number of the DDE channel that has been created, store this number under the variable *dde_channel*. Ask the server to send a list of SysItems, the items that can be accessed through the SYSTEM topic. When the server responds, place the list in cell A9 and hang up." Figure 5.9 shows the results of the SYSITEMS macro.

Understanding Dynamic Data Exchange (DDE) **101**

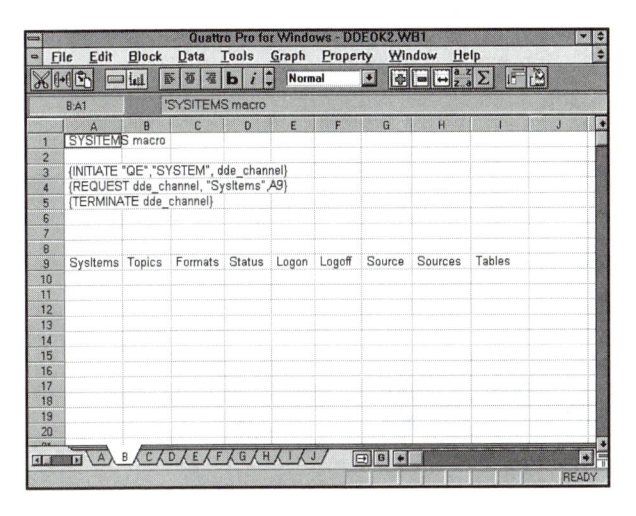

FIG. 5.9 *List of SYSTEM topics generated by SysItems macro.*

The SysItems list is a table of contents of information that the SYSTEM topic can transmit via DDE. Figure 5.10 shows the results of a macro that asks Q&E to transmit the available topics; figure 5.11 shows the results of a macro that asks Q&E to transmit the formats it can use to transmit data via the DDE channel. (The two formats available are BIFF, an Excel format, and unformatted TEXT.) Figure 5.12 shows the results of the same macro, with the application name changed to Winword (Word for Windows' moniker for DDE purposes).

Just which items are available under the SYSTEM topic varies from application to application, but you usually will find the items listed in table 5.2. Not all applications support all these items, and some support additional items.

Table 5.2. Items Typically Found under the SYSTEM Topic

Item	Description
SysItems	Lists all the items available under the SYSTEM topic.
Topics	Lists all the server application files currently open.
Status	States the application's current mode, such as READY or BUSY.

continues

Table 5.2. Continued

Item	Description
Formats	Lists the data formats in which the server application can transmit information via DDE links.
Selection	Describes the location of the current selection in the server application.

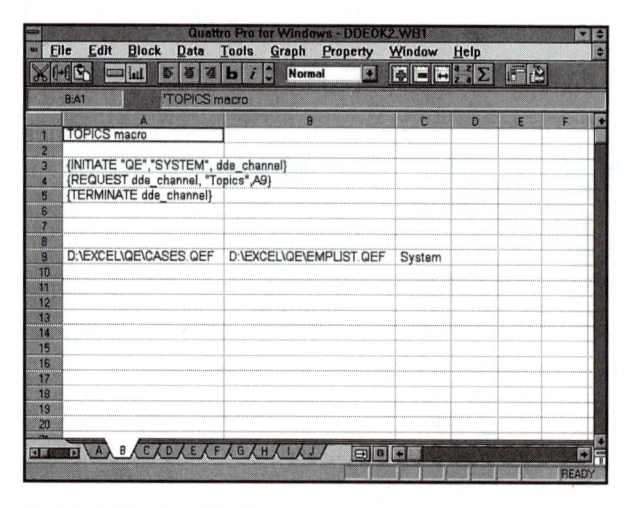

FIG. 5.10 *Results of the SysItems macro.*

Sending Data to the Server Application

Throughout this book, you have seen that the server application obediently provides data to the client. But Windows' DDE message set includes a command, WM_DDE_POKE, that enables the client to send data to the server application—literally, to force the data into the server application. (The command's name, POKE, is indeed accurate—although SHOVE may be more to the point.)

Understanding Dynamic Data Exchange (DDE)

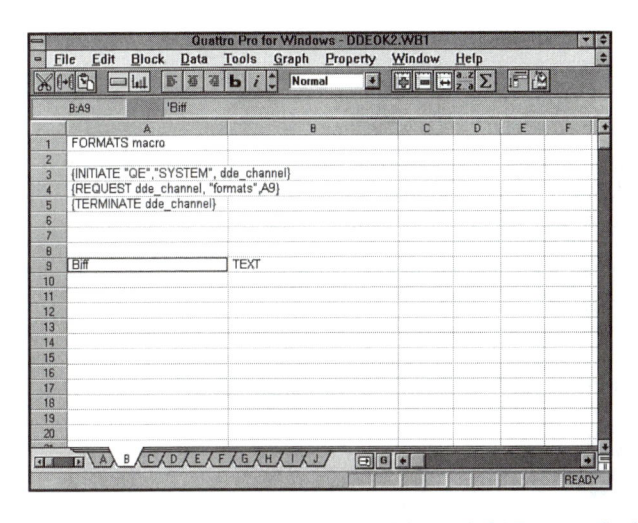

FIG. 5.11 *Results of the Formats macro (Microsoft Q&E responding).*

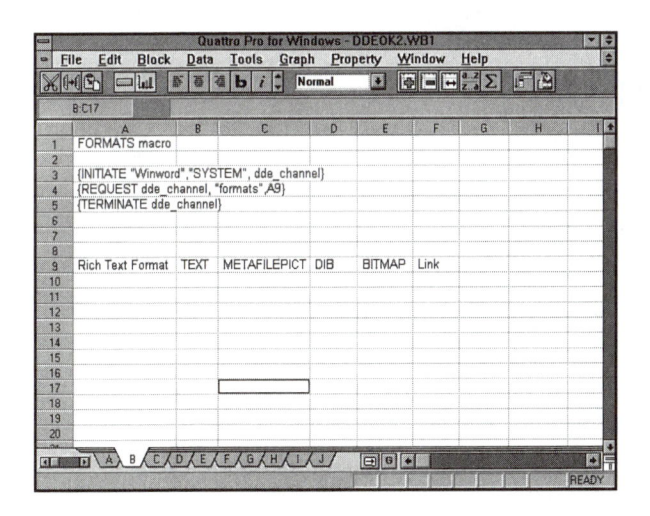

FIG. 5.12 *Results of the Formats macro (Word for Windows responding).*

The following Quattro Pro for Windows macro illustrates a use of the POKE command:

{INITIATE "Excel","first_qtr.xls",dde_channel}
{REQUEST dde_channel,"March",A9}
{POKE dde_channel,"R18C4",A1}
{TERMINATE dde_channel}

This macro works just like the one given earlier that extracts a named range from an Excel worksheet, but with one major difference: it inserts data on the *source worksheet*. The third line of the macro, the one with the POKE statement, performs this trick. It says, in English, "Through the DDE channel that has been established, send the contents of cell A1 and place them in the cell R18C4 in the server application."

The following example shows the usefulness of this command. Suppose that you want to know just when data has been extracted from a source worksheet. If you place today's date in cell A1 of the destination worksheet, this macro inserts this date in the source document. You then know when the data was last extracted.

> **TIP** Reversing the norm, your application's Help screens may actually contain more information about DDE commands than the manuals do. In Help, select the macro topic and look for DDE commands in the alphabetical list of macro commands. You will find helpful information about how to type these commands correctly.

Executing Commands

As just illustrated, you can send data to the server application, reversing the normal flow of data in linking operations. In this section, you learn an even more dramatic trick: through DDE channels, you can send the server application commands that it must execute.

The following Quattro Pro for Windows macro illustrates a macro that can open a file in another application—Excel, in this case.

    {INITIATE "Excel","SYSTEM",dde_channel}
    {EXECUTE dde_channel,"[OPEN(""d:\excel\report.xls"")]",exec_result}
    {TERMINATE dde_channel}

This macro sends Excel an instruction written just as you would type it in Excel's own macro language:

    [OPEN("d:\excel\report.xls")]

The doubled quotation marks are needed in the Quattro Pro macro because the quotes occur within another pair of quotation marks. The EXECUTE command sends the command through the

DDE channel, and when the server application responds, the command stores the response in the variable *exec_result*. From Quattro Pro, you will not see anything happen as a result of the macro. If you switch to Excel, however, you find that Excel has opened the file REPORT.XLS.

Putting It All Together: An Automated DDE Application

In this section, you see a DDE application that fully exploits the hidden power of DDE macro commands. Note that you need a great deal of experience in Microsoft Word for Windows' macro programming language, WordBasic, to understand every statement in the macro program discussed here; these details are beyond the scope of this book. Still, this example demonstrates what can be done with these little-utilized commands. You also can see the true benefit of DDE commands that, when properly implemented, can reduce the server application to an invisible, obedient servant that does not even appear on-screen.

To begin, consider the following scenario. Mary works in a real estate office, and she is constantly asked how much the monthly payment will be on a house with a given price. She can determine the payment using a calculator and write it down, but her office prizes professionalism in all respects, including graphics communications, so Mary and her colleagues prefer to give their clients a written estimate in a formal business letter (see fig. 5.13).

Mary has already developed a Quattro Pro worksheet that calculates the monthly payment (see fig. 5.14). Using Quattro Pro as the server application, Mary used OLE-linking techniques to link the cost of the home (cell B1), down payment (B2), term in years (B3), interest rate (B4), and monthly payment (B9) to the corresponding areas of the Microsoft Word letter. To produce the letter, Mary just opens both documents, types the needed data into the Quattro Pro worksheet, and prints the Microsoft Word letter.

At this point, Mary has gotten the maximum benefit from OLE-linking techniques, but she doesn't like to fuss with two applications, particularly when she has a client sitting across from her. Mary decides to write a WordBasic macro to further automate this application. Her goal is to transform the Quattro Pro server into an invisible, obedient servant—one that she doesn't have to see to produce the letter. You can look more closely at the macro in a moment. For now, you see how it works.

I — Understanding Linking and Embedding Basics

The Country House Company

107 Main St. ♦ Charlottesville, VA 22908 ♦ (804) 555-1234

September 21, 1992

Mr. Tom Smith
567 Birdwhistle Court
Charlottesville, VA 22997

Dear Mr. Smith:

Thank you for your interest in a country home! Based on the home's selling price of $185,000.00, a down payment of $37,000.00, a term of 30 years, and an interest rate of 8.25%, we estimate your monthly payments to be **$1,111.87**.

Sincerely,

Mary Jensen

FIG. 5.13 *Written estimate of monthly payment (Microsoft Word for Windows).*

When Mary needs to produce a new letter for a client, she opens the Word document template that contains the text of the letter, the OLE links, and the WordBasic macro. The macro is set up to run automatically when she opens the document; its first action is to present the dialog box shown in figure 5.15, which is produced by the WordBasic macro.

Mary types the needed data, shown in figure 5.16, and chooses OK. The DDE macro commands then automatically take the values Mary has typed, poke them into the Quattro Pro for Windows spreadsheet fields, and save the Quattro Pro spreadsheet, resulting in the updating of the linked fields in the Word document. Next a letter pops out of the printer, complete with the correct figures, which Mary can give to her client. Quattro Pro never shows its face.

Understanding Dynamic Data Exchange (DDE) **107**

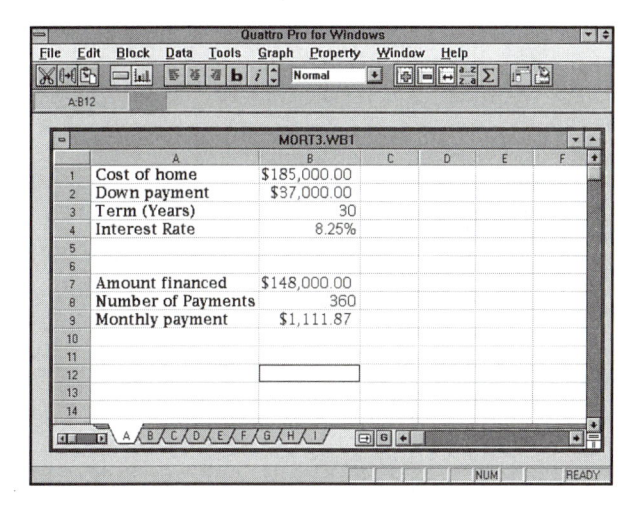

FIG. 5.14 *Quattro Pro spreadsheet for calculating monthly payments.*

FIG. 5.15 *Dialog box produced by WordBasic macro.*

FIG. 5.16 *Dialog box with user-supplied values.*

Figure 5.17 shows the WordBasic macro that governs this application. For now, ignore the code that generates the dialog box; all you need to know about this code is that it creates four variables (Price, Down, Term, and Rate) that receive the values the user types in the dialog box. The DDE commands are as follows:

I — Understanding Linking and Embedding Basics

```
NewChan=DDEInitiate("QPW","MORT3.WB1")
DDEPoke NewChan, "B1",Dlg.Price
DDEPoke NewChan, "B2",Dlg.Down
DDEPoke NewChan, "B3",Dlg.Term
DDEPoke NewChan, "B4",Dlg.Rate
DDEExecute NewChan, "{FileSave}"
DDETerminate NewChan
```

```
Sub MAIN
Begin Dialog UserDialog 450, 150
         OKButton 350, 5, 95, 21
         CancelButton 350, 30, 95, 21
         Text 5, 8, 130, 21, "Selling &Price"
         TextBox 135, 8, 130, 21, .Price
         Text 5, 35, 130, 21, "&Down Payment"
         TextBox 135, 35, 130, 21, .Down
         Text 5, 62, 130, 21, "Term (&Years)"
         TextBox 135, 62, 130, 21, .TERM
         Text 5, 117, 130, 21, "&Interest Rate"
         TextBox 135, 117, 130, 21, .Rate
End Dialog

Dim Dlg As UserDialog
GetCurValues Dlg
On Error Goto Bye
Dialog Dlg
On Error Goto 0

NewChan = DDEInitiate("QPW", "MORT3.WB1")
DDEPoke NewChan, "B1", Dlg.Price
DDEPoke NewChan, "B2", Dlg.Down
DDEPoke NewChan, "B3", Dlg.Term
DDEPoke NewChan, "B4", Dlg.Rate
DDEExecute NewChan, "{FileSave}"
DDETerminate NewChan

FilePrint
Bye:

End Sub
```

FIG. 5.17 *WordBasic macro.*

You're already familiar with most of these commands from the preceding discussion of DDE macro commands. As you recall, every DDE conversation sets up a unique, numbered channel, the value of which (an integer such as 1 or 2) is stored in the variable NewChan. Moreover, the conversation must begin with an INITIATE command and close with a TERMINATE command. Finally, every DDE conversation must involve an application (here, QPW) and a topic (here, MORT3.WB1). The DDEPoke commands take the values stored in the dialog box variables (Dlg.Price, Dlg.Down, and so on), and force them into the appropriate Quattro Pro cells. The DDEExecute command tells Quattro Pro to save the altered worksheet. This step is needed so that the values can link successfully to the Word document.

As you can see, only a few DDE macro commands are needed to set up an impressive application. Such an application, if properly implemented, can hide the complexity of your system by keeping other applications off the screen. You can focus on what's most important for your work, with the other applications supporting you as needed in off-stage roles.

Troubleshooting DDE Commands

This section reviews some of the problems you may encounter when writing macros using DDE commands and suggests strategies for their solution.

You receive a message that a DDE command contains a syntax error.

Syntax errors are common when you are typing macro commands. If you do not type the command perfectly, even the tiniest error can cause a syntax error message: an extraneous space, a comma instead of a period, or a curly brace instead of a parenthesis. Check your command against the documentation until you find the mistake.

You receive a message that your application cannot initiate the link.

The macro failed to establish a link with the server application. Possible reasons include the following:

- The server application is not running. Start the application and display the correct document.

- The server application is busy printing a file. Wait until the file is finished printing.

- The server application is displaying a dialog box that requires user input. Supply the input and close the dialog box.

- The topic you specified does not exist.

- Too many active links are open. Close other documents that contain links.

- The server application does not support DDE. If so, you cannot use DDE macro commands to access this application.

You receive a message that the server application failed to execute the requested process.

This problem has several possible explanations:

- You may have typed the command incorrectly. When you send a command to the server application, you must type it according to the server application's rules for such commands. With Quattro Pro for Windows, for example, external DDE commands must be typed in the same way you type Quattro Pro macro commands. Check the server application's documentation to find out how to type commands that can be remotely executed by DDE.

- A needed document may not be available in the server application. Make sure that the document is available and try the macro again.

Summary

OLE is a user-friendly version of DDE, but learning how to write your own DDE commands is still worthwhile. This chapter illustrated the use of DDE commands to access bookmarks in word processing programs, spreadsheet ranges, and databases. You also learned how you can use DDE commands in macros to perform actions such as opening files and executing another application's commands.

PART TWO

Exploring Linking and Embedding Techniques

Linking between 1-2-3 and Ami Pro

Linking a Named Range in 1-2-3 to WordPerfect

Linking between Ami Pro and WordPerfect

Linking an Embedded Excel Chart to a Word Memo

Embedding Word in an Excel Worksheet

Embedding a Harvard Graphics Presentation in Quattro Pro

CHAPTER SIX

Linking between 1-2-3 and Ami Pro

Lotus 1-2-3 for Windows is a top-rated spreadsheet application and Ami Pro 2.0 is a top-rated word processor. If you have ever tried using 1-2-3's word processing features or Ami Pro's table features, you will understand the value of linking Ami Pro text to 1-2-3 and 1-2-3 spreadsheets to Ami Pro. The beauty of linking is that you can use Ami Pro's powerful word processing features and 1-2-3's sophisticated spreadsheet functions to create one document, bypassing 1-2-3's rather impotent text commands and Ami Pro's limited table capabilities. You can create the spreadsheet in 1-2-3 and the document in Ami Pro and then combine them into one file—either by inserting Ami Pro text into the 1-2-3 spreadsheet file or by inserting the spreadsheet into the Ami Pro document.

When you normally think of linking between Ami Pro and 1-2-3, you imagine linking a 1-2-3 spreadsheet to an Ami Pro document. In some situations, however, linking an Ami Pro document, or a portion of a document, to 1-2-3 can work better. For instance, perhaps you want to take portions of several Ami Pro documents that serve as boilerplates to use in one 1-2-3 report. Using Ami Pro bookmarks, you can insert sections of the various boilerplate documents in the appropriate places in the 1-2-3 spreadsheet file, and at once the new report is complete—you bypass having to create a brand new Ami Pro document.

An Ami Pro bookmark, like other word processor bookmarks, is simply a piece of text that has been assigned a name. Any time you copy a section of an Ami Pro document to the Clipboard and later paste link that selection into 1-2-3, or any application for that matter, Ami Pro creates a bookmark for the selected text. The bookmark name it assigns is DDE_BOOKMARK1. You can create bookmarks yourself whenever you want, however, and later link those bookmarks to 1-2-3 without having to recopy the text. If you plan to link frequently from Ami Pro to 1-2-3, you should get into the habit of using Ami Pro bookmarks. As you're about to discover, using bookmarks makes the linking process from Ami Pro to 1-2-3 smooth and expedient. (For more information on using Ami Pro bookmarks, refer to Que's *Using Ami Pro*.)

The goals of this lesson are as follows:

- Link portions of an Ami Pro document to a 1-2-3 spreadsheet file.
- Link a 1-2-3 spreadsheet to an Ami Pro document.

To accomplish these goals, you will perform the following tasks:

- Save selected text as a bookmark called Networks.
- Prepare the 1-2-3 spreadsheet.
- Link the Networks bookmark to AMILINK.WK3.
- Create a new bookmark in Ami Pro, and then edit the LINK1 link.
- Copy the AMILINK.WK3 spreadsheet.
- Paste-link the 1-2-3 spreadsheet into README.SAM.
- Decrease the amount of rows in the linked spreadsheet.
- Display all the columns of the linked spreadsheet.

Linking Portions of an Ami Pro Document to a 1-2-3 Spreadsheet File

Imagine that you have set up a document in Ami Pro that serves as a boilerplate for proposals you create in 1-2-3 for a civil engineering firm. The boilerplate document is separated into several sections; you use different sections for different types of proposals. Because the boilerplate information changes from time to time, you must link rather than copy sections from the boilerplate to each new proposal. This system has worked relatively well so far, but you are getting tired of having to open the boilerplate document each time you want to create a proposal, copy the first section, switch to 1-2-3 and paste-link the section, return to Ami Pro and copy the second section, return to 1-2-3 and paste-link the second section, return to Ami Pro...and so on.

Fortunately, you can bypass these monotonous steps. If you assign bookmark names to each section in the boilerplate document, you then can use these bookmark names to set up links to 1-2-3, meaning that you don't have to return to the Ami Pro boilerplate at all while creating the links. When you use 1-2-3's Edit Link Options Create command, you must enter an item name for each link you want to establish. An item name simply refers to the portion of text to be linked. Ami Pro bookmarks serve as link item names.

Consider this more specific illustration: One section in the boilerplate document has been assigned the bookmark name *Fees*. You want to include this section immediately after a 1-2-3 spreadsheet that projects estimated man-hours needed for surveying, drafting, blueprinting, and so on. Rather than open the Ami Pro boilerplate, copy the Fees section, return to 1-2-3 and then paste-link the selected text, you can simply create the link from 1-2-3 (without ever having to copy from the boilerplate) and specify Fees as the item to be linked. Imagine how much time and effort this method saves.

Preparing the Ami Pro Document

Before you can link to 1-2-3 using items, you must create bookmarks in the Ami Pro document. So that you will not have to spend time entering a proficient amount of text for this exercise, you will use text from Ami Pro's README.SAM file to establish the link.

NOTE The README.SAM file used in this exercise is from Ami Pro 2.0. If you're using a later version, select any paragraph you want from the README.SAM file to create the bookmark.

Usually you will already have assigned bookmark names to sections of text before you create a link. Keep in mind, then, that the total time spent establishing links normally will be shorter than the time spent during this exercise.

One of the nice things about using bookmarks to link to 1-2-3 is that you can name the bookmarks however you want. Make sure to assign bookmark names that you will remember easily when you are ready to create the links in 1-2-3. For example, don't use names like Bookmark1, Section1, and so on, which do not describe the nature of the bookmark. Instead, use a title like Terms for a section of text that discusses the terms of a contact, and Disclaimer for text that includes disclaimer statements. This way, when you create the link in 1-2-3 later, you can enter the item name without any difficulty.

In the event that you do forget the name or exact spelling of a bookmark, just switch to the Ami Pro document, choose Edit Bookmarks, and scroll though the Bookmark list until you see the name of the bookmark you want to link. If a document serves as a boilerplate or if you intend to link from any one document frequently, consider keeping a list of all bookmark names that you can refer to later when creating links from the document to 1-2-3.

TASK: Save selected text as a bookmark called Networks.

1. Start Ami Pro if it isn't already running.
2. From the File menu, choose Open.
3. Select README.SAM (located in the DOCS directory), and then choose OK.

   The README.SAM document opens (see fig. 6.1).

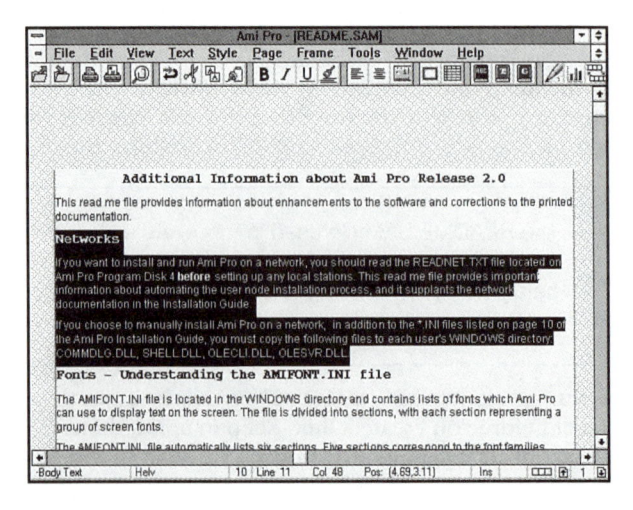

FIG. 6.1 *The README.SAM file with selected text.*

4. Following the example in figure 6.1, highlight the paragraph labeled Networks.

5. From the Edit menu, choose Bookmarks.

    The Bookmarks dialog box appears (see fig. 6.2).

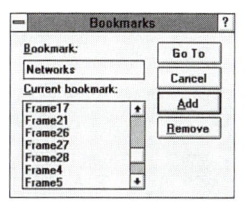

FIG. 6.2 *The Bookmarks dialog box.*

6. In the Bookmark box, type *Networks*.
7. Choose Add.

    The bookmark is created and you are returned to the README.SAM document. The text no longer is selected.

Make sure that you leave README.SAM open while you create the link in 1-2-3. To switch to 1-2-3 while leaving Ami Pro running, you can do one of two things. If 1-2-3 is not already running, click the Ami Pro Minimize button (upper right corner) so that Ami Pro runs in the background. Then start 1-2-3 as you normally would. If 1-2-3 is already running, click the Control box (upper left corner) to display the Control menu, choose Switch To, select 1-2-3, and then choose Switch To again. Alternatively, double-click on 1-2-3.

If an Ami Pro file you are linking from is not open, you can still set up a link in 1-2-3, but the text will not be inserted into the 1-2-3 spreadsheet at that time. The link status will read Inactive in the Edit Link Options dialog box. You can update the link later so that the text is inserted. Making sure that the Ami Pro document you are linking from is open while you set up the link in 1-2-3 is much easier.

Preparing the 1-2-3 Spreadsheet

Again, you're spared some typing. Rather than create a brand new spreadsheet, you will use one of 1-2-3's sample files to receive the Ami Pro bookmark link.

TASK: Prepare the 1-2-3 spreadsheet.

1. Start 1-2-3 if it isn't already running.

2. From the File menu, choose Open.

3. Switch to the SAMPLE directory, select EMPLOYEE.WK3, and then choose OK.

   The EMPLOYEE.WK3 file opens (see fig. 6.3).

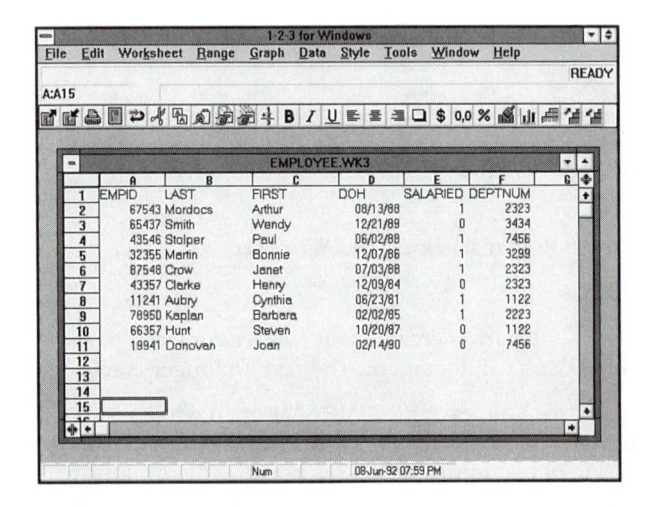

FIG. 6.3 *The EMPLOYEE.WK3 spreadsheet file.*

4. Select the following cell range: A14..G23.

   You don't have to take this step here, but defining the cell range before you start creating the link is faster.

   Make sure that you allow enough room for all of the Ami Pro text to fit. Although the text won't be inserted within the entire cell range (as you will see later), you are better off providing excessive rather than inefficient space for the linked text.

5. From the File menu, choose Save As.

6. In the File Save As dialog box, type *amilink.wk3* as the file name.

Creating the Link

You have already created the bookmark in Ami Pro and now you want to link the bookmark to 1-2-3. Use the 1-2-3 Edit Link Options Create menu command to set up the link.

Linking between 1-2-3 and Ami Pro **119**

Remember, README.SAM should be open while you complete the following steps.

> **NOTE** If you have any problems accessing the Edit Link Options Create dialog box, you probably are running short on memory. Try increasing your virtual memory swap file by following these steps: Double-click the Windows Control Panel icon. Double-click the 386 Enhanced icon. Choose Virtual Memory, and then choose Change. If possible, increase the amount of virtual memory and then choose OK. You have to restart Windows if you do change the amount of memory.

TASK: Link the Networks bookmark to AMILINK.WK3.

1. From the 1-2-3 Edit menu, choose Link Options.

   The Edit Link Options dialog box appears.

2. Choose Create.

   The Edit Link Options Create dialog box, which is similar to figure 6.4, appears. Conveniently, most of the information you need to enter for the link is already input for you.

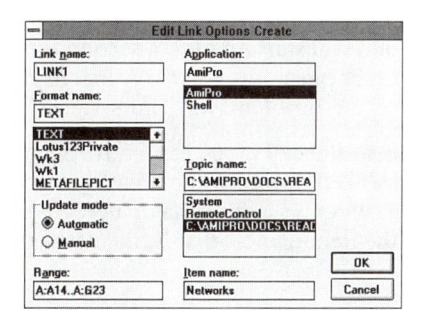

FIG. 6.4 *The Edit Link Options Create dialog box.*

In the Link Name box, the name LINK1 is assigned automatically to the link. If you plan to link several items to a 1-2-3 spreadsheet, you should change the link name so that it is more meaningful; otherwise, you may have a difficult time remembering what text is represented by each link name. You probably should use the item name as the link name. For example, you could enter *Networks* here as the link name—however, leave the link name as it is.

In the Application box, Ami Pro already is displayed but not highlighted. Likewise, the Format Name box already shows TEXT, which is the type of format needed for the link. Because README.SAM was open when you chose the Edit Link Options Create command, the README.SAM file, including its path, is already listed in the Topic Name box. The Topic Name box should almost always include the complete path name of the file you're linking from. If the README.SAM file hadn't been open when you used the link command, you would have had to enter the full path name, C:\AMIPRO\DOCS\README.SAM, in the Topic Name box.

The Update mode is set to Automatic by default. If you want to update a link manually, select the Manual option in the Update Mode box. When the update mode is set to Automatic, any changes made to the Ami Pro document will be reflected immediately in the 1-2-3 spreadsheet. On the other hand, if manual updating is in effect, you must choose Edit Link Options Update to make the linked information current.

When you do update manually, the Ami Pro document doesn't need to be open; 1-2-3 starts Ami Pro and opens the source document for you when you choose Edit Link Options Update. This means that if Ami Pro is running, you should close it before updating linked information; 1-2-3 will not acknowledge that Ami Pro is already running and will start Ami Pro a second time. You want to avoid this situation because running two versions of the same program can create severe problems for your system.

Because you defined the cell range earlier, the Range box already contains the correct cell range for the linked text to be inserted. Alternatively, you can enter a range name here. Note that all you need to enter is the item name—that is, the name of the Ami Pro bookmark.

3. In the Item Name box, type *Networks*.
4. Choose OK.

   The Edit Link Options Create dialog box closes and you are returned to the Edit Link Options box. This is handy if you are going to link several items in a row. For now, though, you want to return to the spreadsheet.

5. In the Edit Link Options dialog box, choose Cancel.

The Edit Link Options dialog box closes and you are returned to AMILINK.WK3. The Networks text appears in rows 14 through 16 (see fig. 6.5). Linked text is never inserted as justified text. You must justify the text after it has been inserted.

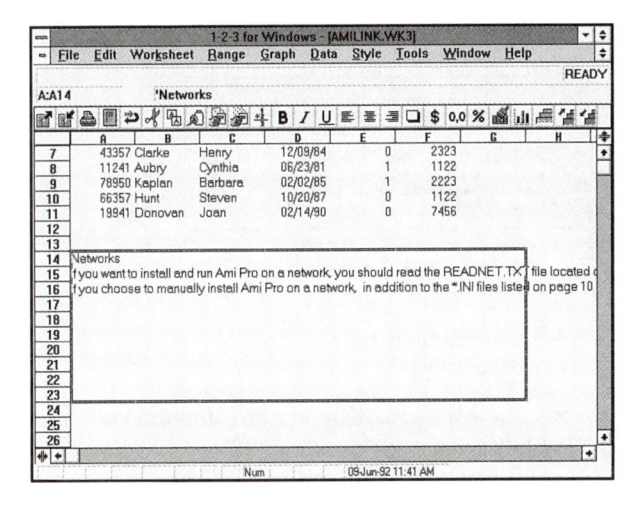

FIG. 6.5 *The linked text appears in AMILINK.WK3.*

6. Select the following cell range: A15..F24.
7. From the Range menu, choose Justify.

   The linked text now occupies the entire cell range, as shown in figure 6.6. The link process is complete.

Changing the Linked Bookmark

A benefit of linking with bookmarks is that if you ever want to replace an existing link with a new one, you can do so easily. Suppose that several other bookmarks exist in the README.SAM file. If you want to use a bookmark other than Networks in the same location in the 1-2-3 spreadsheet, all you have to do is change the item name and instantly the old linked text is replaced with the new text.

To see how easily this works, you're going to create a new bookmark in Ami Pro and then change the link so that the text from the new bookmark is linked to AMILINK.WK3 in place of the Networks text.

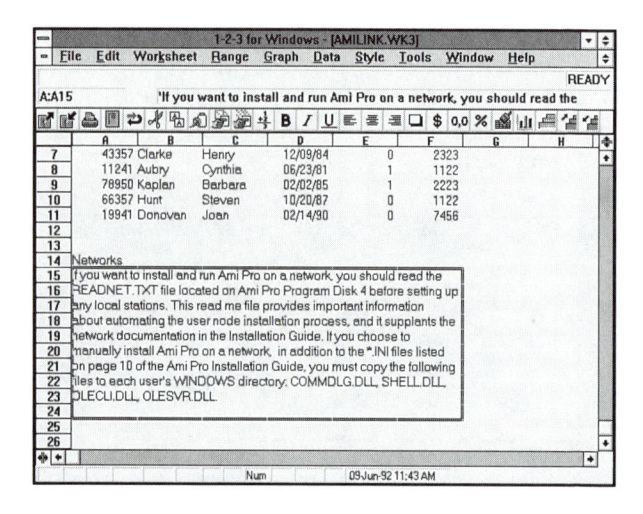

122 *II — Exploring Linking and Embedding Techniques*

FIG. 6.6 *The justified linked text.*

TASK: Create a new bookmark in Ami Pro, and then edit the LINK1 link.

1. Switch to Ami Pro.

2. In the README.SAM file, select the first two paragraphs in the section on Fonts located directly below the Networks discussion (see fig. 6.7).

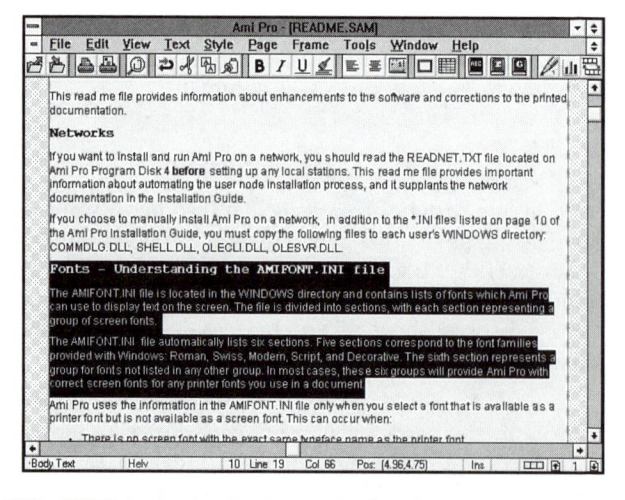

FIG. 6.7 *Selecting text for the new bookmark.*

3. From the Edit menu, choose Bookmarks.
4. In the Bookmark box, type Fonts.
5. Choose Add.
6. Switch to AMILINK.WK3 in 1-2-3 (leave Ami Pro running in the background).
7. From the Edit menu, choose Link Options.

   The Edit Link Options dialog box appears (see fig. 6.8).

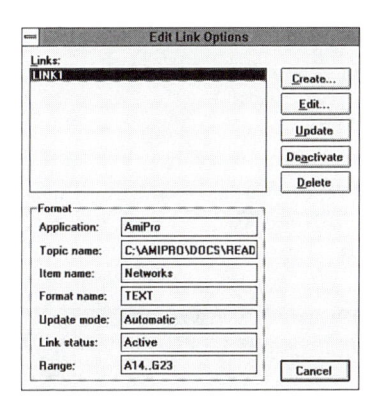

FIG. 6.8 *The Edit Link Options dialog box.*

8. Select LINK1.

   Notice that each box in the Format section of the dialog box now shows information about the link you created earlier. Also, all of the command buttons (Edit, Update, Delete, and so on) become active (no longer dimmed).

9. Choose Edit.

   The Edit Link Options Edit dialog box appears (see fig. 6.9). This looks just like the Edit Link Options Create dialog box, except that an item name already appears in the Item Name box.

10. In the Item Name box, change Networks to Fonts (refer to fig. 6.9).

11. Choose OK.

    The Edit Link Options Edit dialog box closes and you are returned to the Edit Link Options dialog box.

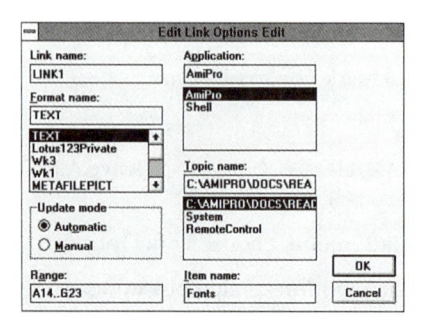

II — Exploring Linking and Embedding Techniques

FIG. 6.9 *The Edit Link Options Edit dialog box.*

12. Choose Cancel.

    As figure 6.10 shows, the Networks text is replaced by the new linked text on Fonts. Notice that the new linked text is not inserted justified, even though the text it replaced had been justified.

FIG. 6.10 *The new linked text replaces the old text.*

Deactivating versus Deleting Text

The Edit Link Options dialog box has a Delete and Deactivate option button. The difference between the two options is significant. You can deactivate a link temporarily so that any changes made to the Ami Pro source document are not reflected in the 1-2-3 spreadsheet. In other words, the linked information in 1-2-3 remains the same regardless if the information in Ami Pro changes. If later you want to update the link so that the most recent information is reflected in the spreadsheet, you can choose the Update option button in the Edit Link Options dialog box. This reactivates the link.

The difference between deactivating and deleting a link is that a deleted link can never be updated again. You have to start from scratch if you want to insert a current version again. When you deactivate a link, the linked information remains in the spreadsheet, but it is disconnected temporarily from the source document. When you delete a link, the linked information also remains in the spreadsheet, but it is disconnected permanently from the source document.

If you want to delete a link and remove the linked information as well, simply select all of the linked information and press the Del key.

Linking a 1-2-3 Spreadsheet to an Ami Pro Document

Imagine that you're creating a weekly report in Ami Pro, which includes a 1-2-3 spreadsheet. The information in the spreadsheet, however, changes from day to day. If you weren't able to link the spreadsheet to the report, you would have to copy and paste the spreadsheet into the report every week in order to have current data. Thanks to linking, you don't have to endlessly copy and paste. You copy and paste-link once, and the task is done.

Copying the Spreadsheet To Be Linked

For the sake of convenience, you will use the same two documents you just used in the last exercise to create the link for this exercise. This time, you will copy the spreadsheet in AMILINK.WK3 and then paste link it into README.SAM.

TASK: Copy the AMILINK.WK3 spreadsheet.

1. Open (or switch to) AMILINK.WK3 in 1-2-3.

2. Select cells A1 to F11.

3. From the Edit menu, choose Copy.

The spreadsheet is now copied to the Clipboard and ready to be linked to the Ami Pro document.

Creating the Link

TASK: Paste link the 1-2-3 spreadsheet into README.SAM.

1. Open (or switch to) README.SAM in Ami Pro.

2. Following the example in figure 6.11, place the insertion point two lines below the last paragraph in the Networks section (which ends in OLESVR.DLL).

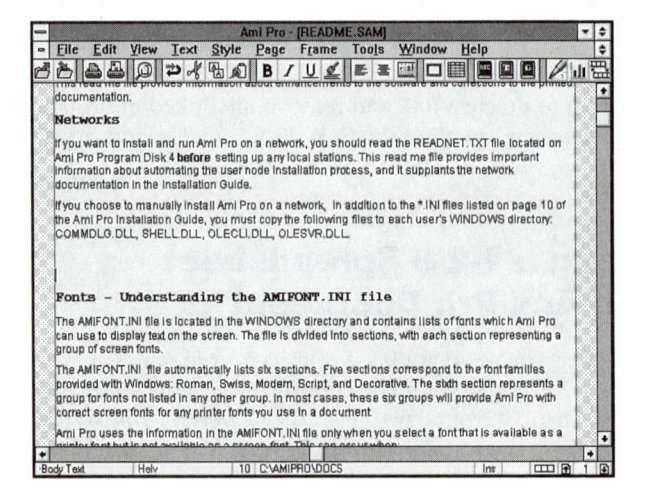

FIG. 6.11 *Preparing README.SAM to receive the link.*

3. From the Edit menu, choose Paste Link.

   Immediately, the 1-2-3 spreadsheet is inserted just after the insertion point (see fig. 6.12). Note that a blue marker appears in the upper left and bottom left corners of the spreadsheet; these markers remind you that the spreadsheet is actively linked to 1-2-3 rather than merely copied from 1-2-3.

Editing the Link

After you link a spreadsheet to Ami Pro, you can change the rows or columns contained in the spreadsheet very easily.

Linking between 1-2-3 and Ami Pro **127**

TASK: Decrease the amount of rows in the linked spreadsheet.

1. From the Ami Pro Edit menu, choose Link Options.

   The Link Options dialog box appears (see fig. 6.13). Each link in the current document is identified in the Links box. The Links box specifies the format of the link (in this case Text), the link status (active or inactive), the source file (including its path), and the item (in this case, a spreadsheet range).

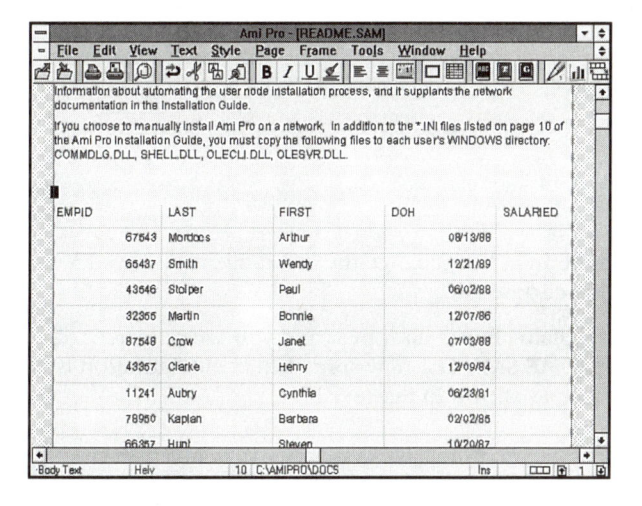

FIG. 6.12 *The linked spreadsheet.*

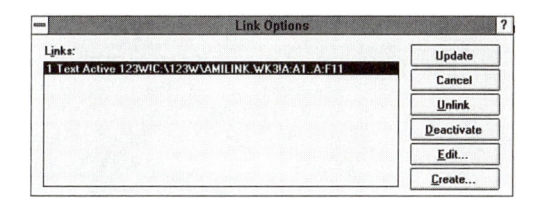

FIG. 6.13 *The Link Options dialog box.*

2. In the Links box, select (highlight) the 1-2-3 link.

   After you select a link, all of the option buttons become active (no longer dimmed).

3. Choose Edit.

128 II — Exploring Linking and Embedding Techniques

The Link dialog box appears (see fig. 6.14). This dialog box displays the name of the server application (in this case 1-2-3), the topic (which is usually the full path name of the source file), and the item (in this case, the cell range A1..F11). You can change any of these items, although you probably will never change the application name—unless you want to link from an entirely different program.

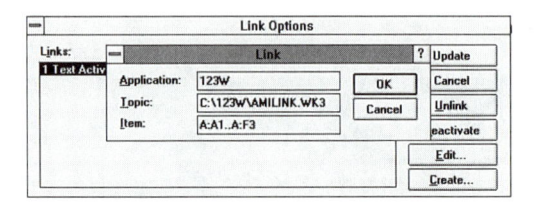

FIG. 6.14 *The Link dialog box.*

4. In the Item box, change the cell range to A:A1..A:F3, and then choose OK.

The dialog boxes disappear and you are returned to README.SAM. The new spreadsheet configuration is now in effect, as shown in figure 6.15.

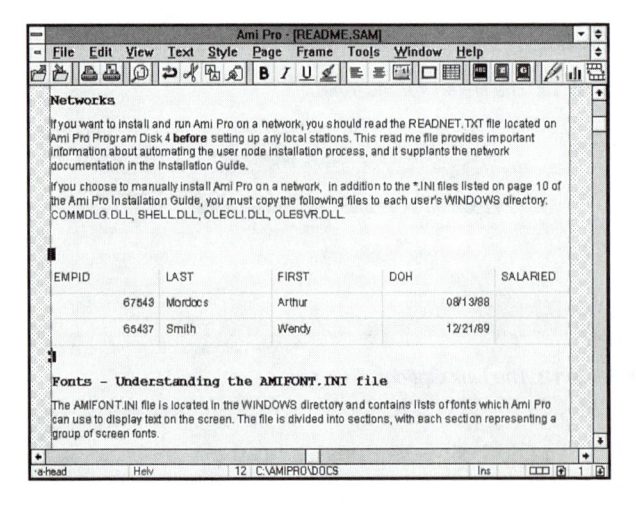

FIG. 6.15 *The new spreadsheet configuration.*

Making Format Changes

You may have noticed that when you linked the 1-2-3 spreadsheet to Ami Pro, some of it was cut—columns E and F do not show up on-screen. You can modify the spreadsheet in Ami Pro so that these columns are visible, but the next time the spreadsheet information is updated, all formatting changes you made to the spreadsheet will be lost. So keep this in mind before you spend a lot of time sprucing up a linked spreadsheet!

One way to avoid this situation is to switch to 1-2-3 and decrease the column width of the columns in the original (source) spreadsheet. Then all of the columns should show up in the Ami Pro document.

Suppose that you are going to print README.SAM, and you need those hidden columns to show just for the printout. If you don't want to switch to 1-2-3, you can quickly modify the linked spreadsheet so that it shows all of its columns before you print the document. Just remember that the next time the spreadsheet is updated, the columns will be hidden again.

TASK: Display all the columns of the linked spreadsheet.

1. Select the entire table.
2. From the Tables menu, choose Column/Row Size.
3. In the Columns Width box, enter *.88*.

   The entire table now shows in the Ami Pro document (see fig. 6.16). Remember, the next time the spreadsheet is updated, the columns will return to their original size.

Deactivating the Link

Ami Pro works similarly to 1-2-3 in regards to deactivating and deleting links. If you choose Deactivate in the Ami Pro Link Options dialog box, the link is temporarily disconnected. If you choose Unlink in the same dialog box (it's Delete in 1-2-3), however, the link is disconnected permanently (the spreadsheet remains in the Ami Pro document, however). After you deactivate a link, you can choose Update in the Link Options dialog box to reactivate the link and insert all current figures in the spreadsheet. You cannot update a link that has been severed using the Unlink option button.

If you want to delete a link and remove the spreadsheet entirely from the Ami Pro document, choose Table, Delete Entire Table.

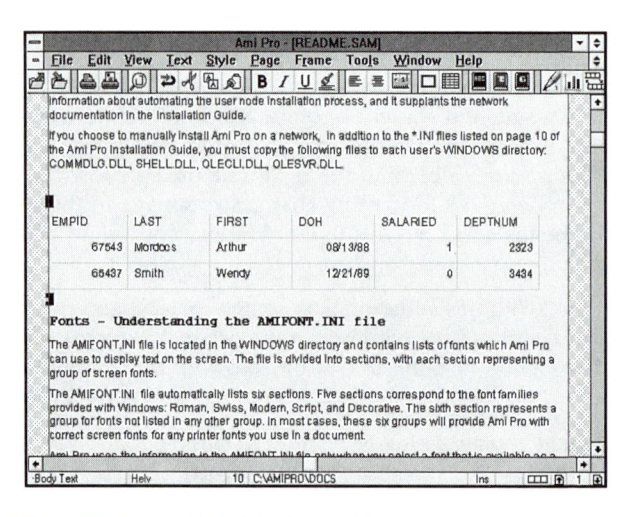

FIG. 6.16 *The modified linked spreadsheet.*

Summary

Linking between 1-2-3 and Ami Pro may seem intimidating at first. The good news is that the process really isn't difficult; linking gets easier each time. Refer to the steps presented in this chapter each time you create a new link until you feel comfortable setting up links on your own.

For more information on using the programs 1-2-3 for Windows and Ami Pro, refer to Que's books *Using 1-2-3 for Windows*, Special Edition, and *Using Ami Pro*.

CHAPTER SEVEN

Linking a Named Range in 1-2-3 to WordPerfect

Currently, neither 1-2-3 nor WordPerfect supports object linking and embedding, although future versions of both programs are expected to support OLE. This means that for now you cannot embed objects in either application; all links between the two applications will be established via DDE.

You can link a spreadsheet to WordPerfect in two ways. WordPerfect has a special Spreadsheet Link menu command that enables you to link an entire spreadsheet, a range of cells, or a named range (a range name being a group of cells that have been assigned a name) to a WordPerfect document. The second way is to use the regular Edit Link Create menu command that you use to link any type of document—memo, report, graphic, spreadsheet. When using the Edit Link Create menu command, however, you must use a range name to establish the link because you must enter an Item name—which, for a spreadsheet, is a range name.

Although both methods accomplish links, the two linking methods are dissimilar in a few significant ways. The circumstances under which you create the link and various effects you want to achieve will determine which method you use. Use table 7.1 to help you decide which method is best for your current situation.

Table 7.1. Spreadsheet Link versus Edit Link Create

	Tools Spreadsheet Create Link	*Edit Link Create*
Prerequisites	You must know the name of the spreadsheet file *and* its path.	You must know the name of the spreadsheet file. The range you want to link must already be named and you must know its name.
Advantages	You can decide whether the spreadsheet data is inserted into the WordPerfect document as text alone or within a table. 1-2-3 does not have to be running nor the spreadsheet file open when you create the link—the spreadsheet datawill be inserted regardless.	Linked data is updated instantly when both files are open. You don't need to know the path of the spreadsheet file. You can assign a name to the link.
Disadvantages	Data is not updated automatically—even if both files are open. You must save the spreadsheet file after you make changes to it before those changes can be reflected in the WordPerfect document. You have to know the path of the spreadsheet file (however, you can use the Select File scroll boxes to find the file).	Only named ranges can be linked this way. Spreadsheet data is always inserted into the WordPerfect document as text alone (for example, not in a table). The worksheet must be open when you create the link for the information to be inserted immediately.

Linking a Named Range in 1-2-3 to WordPerfect **133**

	Tools Spreadsheet Create Link	Edit Link Create
Use if...	You want to link cells that are not named (no range name is designated for those cells).	You want to link cells that are part of a named range (and you know the range name already).
	You want to link a named range, but you cannot remember its name.	You want data inserted as text (not in a table).
Don't use if...	You want changes in the 1-2-3 spreadsheet immediately reflected in the WordPerfect spreadsheet.	You want data inserted in a WordPerfect table.

During this tutorial, you will practice both ways of linking. First you will link a named range to a WordPerfect document using the Edit Link Create command, and then you will link the same 1-2-3 range to the same WordPerfect document using the Spreadsheet Link command.

The goals of this lesson are as follows:

- To link a 1-2-3 named range to a WordPerfect document using the Edit Link Create command

- To link a 1-2-3 named range to a WordPerfect document using the Tools Spreadsheet Create Link command

To achieve these goals, you will perform the following tasks:

- Set up the 1-2-3 spreadsheet, and then name a range of cells.

- Prepare the WordPerfect document to receive the spreadsheet link.

- Link the named range WPWINLINK to the LINK.ME document.

- Modify the format of the linked spreadsheet in WordPerfect, and then update the source spreadsheet in 1-2-3 and see what happens to the WordPerfect spreadsheet.

- Change the name of the WPWINLINK link and set it to manual updating.

- Remove link codes and configure the link to be updated automatically each time you open LINK.ME.

- Remove the table from the linked spreadsheet so that only text remains.

- Update the WPWINLINK link.

- Delete the WPWINLINK link, leaving the spreadsheet intact in WordPerfect.

Using the Edit Link Create Command

As mentioned earlier, you can use the Edit Link Create command to create links between objects other than spreadsheets and WordPerfect. For example, you can use this menu command to link portions of letters, reports, or memos.

The most important thing to remember about using this command is that you must know the *item* that will be linked. An item is simply a named portion of a document, such as a spreadsheet range, a bookmark (as in Ami Pro), or a table. Remember, however, that if you don't know the name of the item you want to link, or if the item is not named, this does not necessarily mean you cannot create a link. If the application you are linking from supports DDE, you can copy the data you want to link to the Clipboard first, open the WordPerfect file you're linking the data to, and then use WordPerfect's Edit Link Paste Link command.

Why not just use this method all of the time? Sometimes the Paste Link command is dimmed, meaning that the command is not available. Also, if you already know the name of the item you're linking, just typing the item's name in the Create DDE Link dialog box is faster than exiting WordPerfect, opening the source application and document, copying the text to the Clipboard, going back into WordPerfect, and then paste linking the data.

Another benefit of using the Create DDE Link dialog box is that you can set up the link in WordPerfect before the item or even the file to be linked from is created. For example, if you are drafting a WordPerfect report and know that you are going to include a few spreadsheet ranges from 1-2-3, but you haven't yet created the spreadsheet, you can set up the link in WordPerfect anyway, as if the spreadsheet file and range names already existed. The links will have the status (no data received) in the Create DDE Link dialog box until the 1-2-3 file and range names are created. After the files and range names are created, the next time you open the WordPerfect document, the linked information will be present in the document.

Setting Up the 1-2-3 Spreadsheet and Named Range

Remember, when using the Edit Link Create command to link a spreadsheet to a WordPerfect document, you must use a named range from the 1-2-3 spreadsheet in order for the link to work. You cannot enter a range of cells (such as A5..E25) as an item.

TASK: Set up the 1-2-3 spreadsheet, and then name a range of cells.

1. Start 1-2-3 if it isn't already running.

2. In an Untitled spreadsheet, click the cell in which you want to enter data.

3. Enter the figures shown for cells A4 to E12, as shown in figure 7.1. If the data is in $, you need to click the $ icon on the toolbar.

   If you want to use the formulas, the salaries increase by six percent each year.

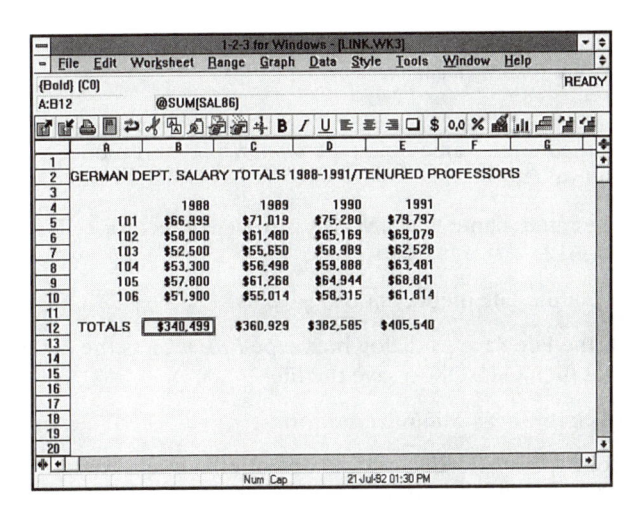

FIG. 7.1 *The 1-2-3 spreadsheet to be linked.*

II — *Exploring Linking and Embedding Techniques*

If you know how to create range names, create a range name called WPWINLINK for cells A4..E12, and then skip to the next task.

4. Highlight cells A4..E12 (refer to fig. 7.2).

5. From the Range menu, choose Name, and then choose Create.

   The Range Name Create dialog box appears (see fig. 7.2). Notice that the range you selected is already specified in the Range box.

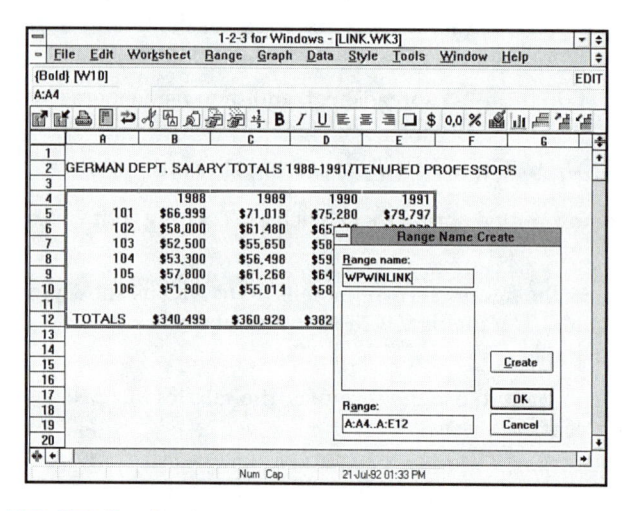

FIG. 7.2 *Creating the range name.*

6. In the Range Name box, type *wpwinlink*, and then choose OK.

   The range name WPWINLINK is now in effect for cells A4..E12.

7. From the File menu, choose Save As.

8. In the File Save As dialog box, type *link.wk3* as the file name, and then click OK to save the file.

9. Click the 1-2-3 Minimize button.

   Your spreadsheet is now set up with the range name WPWINLINK.

Linking a Named Range in 1-2-3 to WordPerfect **137**

Setting Up the WordPerfect Document

Now that the range has been defined in the 1-2-3 spreadsheet file, you are ready to start WordPerfect and prepare the document to receive the link.

TASK: Prepare the WordPerfect document to receive the spreadsheet link.

1. Start WordPerfect if it isn't already running.
2. From the File menu, choose Save.
3. In the Save As dialog box, type *link.me* as the file name and press Enter.
4. Move the insertion point down a couple of lines.
5. Type the following phrase:

    Here is the named range, WPWINLINK, linked from the Lotus spreadsheet to this WordPerfect document:

6. Press the Enter key twice.

You are now ready to create the link.

Creating the DDE Link

Remember, before you can create a link, the document which will be receiving the link must already be saved. Because you saved the WordPerfect document in the preceding steps, you now are ready to establish the link.

TASK: Link the named range WPWINLINK to the LINK.ME document.

1. From the WordPerfect Edit menu, choose Link and then choose Create.

    The Create DDE dialog box appears (see fig. 7.3). Notice that the name of the current file, LINK.ME, is identified in the top line as the destination file.

2. In the Source File and Item box, type the following:

    123W|LINK.WK3|WPWINLINK

    Whenever you establish a link using the Create DDE Link dialog box, you have to identify the source file and item by using the following syntax exactly. Make sure that you enter vertical bars and not backslashes.

Application|file name|item

FIG. 7.3 *The Create DDE Link dialog box.*

The application name is almost always the same name used for the directory containing the application's files. For example, unless you specified otherwise, your 1-2-3 files are stored in a directory called 123W, Ami Pro files are stored in AMIPRO, WordPerfect files are stored in WPWIN. Accordingly, the application names for DDE purposes for these three applications are 123W, AMIPRO, and WPWIN, respectively.

Contrary to what you may be accustomed to, do not include the path for the file name. Notice that the complete path name for the file currently open in 1-2-3 is listed in the Source File and Item box. Nonetheless, all you need to enter is the file name alone.

3. Click inside the Link Name box.

The name you specified as the item in the Source File and Item box is inserted instantly into the Link Name box. You can change this name if you want. For this exercise, however, leave WPWINLINK as the link name.

4. Choose OK.

A pause ensues as WordPerfect loads the spreadsheet range into LINK.ME. After the range is inserted, your screen should look similar to figure 7.4.

Changing the Format of the Linked Data

You may not like the font or font size WordPerfect assigns to a linked spreadsheet. You can do nothing about it, however, if you want to keep the link alive. Well, that's partially true. You can change the formatting temporarily, but the next time the data changes in 1-2-3 and is updated in WordPerfect, all the formatting changes you made to the WordPerfect version are erased forever. You could switch to manual updating, but in doing so you would risk not having the most current spreadsheet figures when you print the WordPerfect document.

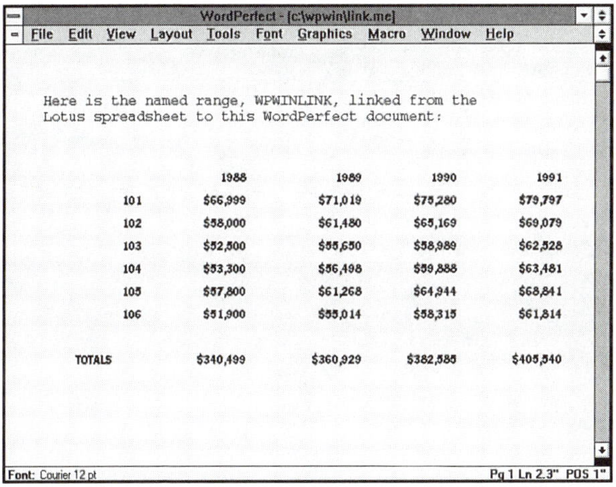

FIG. 7.4 *The linked spreadsheet range.*

The best way to remember that formatting changes made to linked data do not stick is to learn firsthand—which you're about to do.

TASK: Modify the format of the linked spreadsheet in WordPerfect. Then update the source spreadsheet in 1-2-3 and see what happens to the WordPerfect spreadsheet.

1. In WordPerfect, select the entire spreadsheet.
2. Change to a new font and switch to a 14-point font size.

   Your document should look something like figure 7.5.
3. Switch to 1-2-3 LINK.WK3.
4. In cell B5, change the dollar amount to 76,999.

If you used formulas to insert the spreadsheet figures, other cells in row 5 will change accordingly.

5. Switch back to WordPerfect LINK.ME.

   Your document should now resemble figure 7.6. Notice that all formatting changes were lost. Also, LINK.ME was updated immediately to show the new figures you just entered in the 1-2-3 spreadsheet.

The moral of this task is...don't spend a lot of time making format changes that will be lost the next time the source spreadsheet changes!

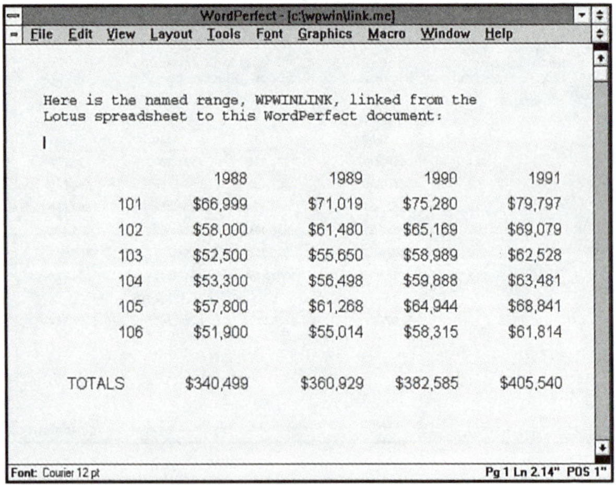

```
WordPerfect - [c:\wpwin\link.me]
File  Edit  View  Layout  Tools  Font  Graphics  Macro  Window  Help

Here is the named range, WPWINLINK, linked from the
Lotus spreadsheet to this WordPerfect document:

                1988        1989        1990        1991
        101   $66,999    $71,019    $75,280    $79,797
        102   $58,000    $61,480    $65,169    $69,079
        103   $52,500    $55,650    $58,989    $62,528
        104   $53,300    $56,498    $59,888    $63,481
        105   $57,800    $61,268    $64,944    $68,841
        106   $51,900    $55,014    $58,315    $61,814

      TOTALS  $340,499   $360,929   $382,585   $405,540

Font: Courier 12 pt                          Pg 1 Ln 2.14" POS 1"
```

FIG. 7.5 *The formatted spreadsheet.*

Editing the DDE Link

In WordPerfect, when you choose Edit Link Edit, the Edit DDE Link dialog box appears (see fig. 7.7). This box has a twofold purpose: it tells facts about each DDE link present in the current document, and it also enables you to edit any of these links.

TASK: Change the name of the WPWINLINK link and set it to manual updating.

1. From the WordPerfect Edit menu, choose Link and then choose Edit.

   The Edit DDE Link dialog box appears (see fig. 7.7). If more than one link is present in the current document, you have

Linking a Named Range in 1-2-3 to WordPerfect **141**

to click on the link name of the link you are interested in getting information on or editing. Because WPWINLINK is the only link in LINK.ME, however, it is highlighted by default.

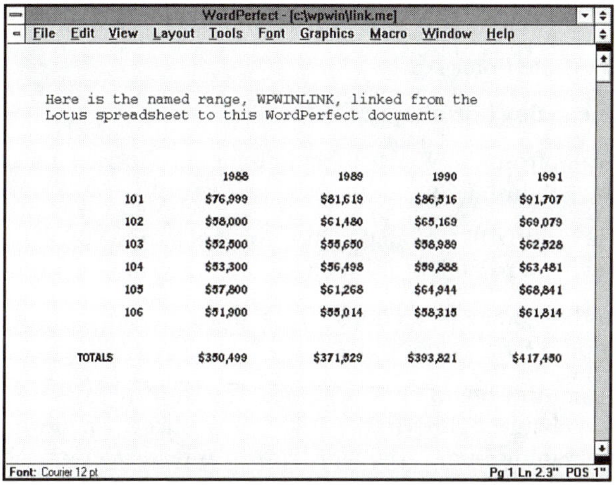

```
┌─────────────────────────────────────────────────────────┐
│                WordPerfect - [c:\wpwin\link.me]         │
│  File  Edit  View  Layout  Tools  Font  Graphics  Macro  Window  Help │
│                                                         │
│  Here is the named range, WPWINLINK, linked from the   │
│  Lotus spreadsheet to this WordPerfect document:       │
│                                                         │
│                  1988      1989      1990      1991    │
│           101   $76,999   $81,619   $86,516   $91,707  │
│           102   $58,000   $61,480   $65,169   $69,079  │
│           103   $52,500   $55,650   $58,989   $62,528  │
│           104   $53,300   $56,498   $59,888   $63,481  │
│           105   $57,800   $61,268   $64,944   $68,841  │
│           106   $51,900   $55,014   $58,315   $61,814  │
│                                                         │
│  TOTALS         $350,499  $371,529  $393,821  $417,450 │
│                                                         │
│ Font: Courier 12 pt                      Pg 1 Ln 2.3" POS 1" │
└─────────────────────────────────────────────────────────┘
```

FIG. 7.6 *The updated WordPerfect spreadsheet.*

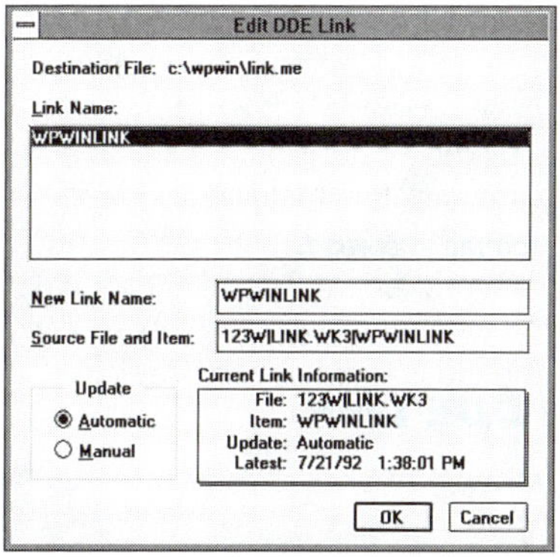

```
┌───────────────────── Edit DDE Link ─────────────────────┐
│ Destination File: c:\wpwin\link.me                      │
│ Link Name:                                              │
│ ┌─────────────────────────────────────────────────────┐│
│ │ WPWINLINK                                           ││
│ └─────────────────────────────────────────────────────┘│
│                                                         │
│ New Link Name:       WPWINLINK                          │
│ Source File and Item: 123W[LINK.WK3[WPWINLINK           │
│                                                         │
│     Update          Current Link Information:           │
│   ● Automatic          File:   123W[LINK.WK3            │
│   ○ Manual             Item:   WPWINLINK                │
│                        Update: Automatic                │
│                        Latest: 7/21/92  1:38:01 PM      │
│                                                         │
│                              [  OK  ]  [ Cancel ]       │
└─────────────────────────────────────────────────────────┘
```

FIG. 7.7 *The Edit DDE Link dialog box.*

The Current Link Information box tells you the name of the file WPWINLINK is linked to, as well as the item that is linked (in this case, the item and link name are the same). The Update field tells you whether automatic or manual updating is in effect. The Latest field displays the date and time of the most recent update.

2. In the New Link Name box, type *German 88-91*.

   If you click somewhere else in the dialog box, the new name you just typed is erased, and the old name shows again. Frustrating? Unlike normal dialog box entries, you must press the Enter key immediately after typing the new name for it to take effect. Clicking OK doesn't work.

3. Press the Enter key.

   The dialog box disappears.

4. Again, from the WordPerfect Edit menu, choose Link and then choose Edit.

   The Edit DDE Link dialog box appears again. Notice that the new link name has taken effect.

5. In the Update box, choose the Manual option, and then choose OK.

   From now on, the link no longer instantly updates each time you change figures in the 1-2-3 spreadsheet. Whenever you do want to update the WordPerfect spreadsheet, simply use the Edit Link Update command each time you want the most recent figures reflected in the WordPerfect document.

> **NOTE** You can change the item being linked if more than one named range is in a 1-2-3 spreadsheet. For example, if you've already established a link to a range name but later want to delete that link and replace it with a new one, you don't have to start from scratch. Simply go into the WordPerfect Edit DDE Link dialog box and type the new range name in the Source File and Item box. The old link data will be replaced instantly with the new link data.

Using the Spreadsheet Link Command

After learning how to use the Edit Link Create command, you may find using the Spreadsheet Link command comparatively easy. Do remember, however, that the two methods do not cancel each other out. In other words, under certain circumstances you will use the Edit Link Create command to establish a link—even though the method is a bit more complicated—to accomplish what the Spreadsheet Link command will not. Generally speaking, you will use the different methods for different reasons, though in some situations, you can use either to accomplish the same result. The important thing to remember about the Edit Link Create command is that you can link items other than spreadsheets. The Spreadsheet Link command can be used to link only spreadsheets (as its name makes clear!).

To refresh your memory, the Spreadsheet Link command does the following:

- Lists all existing range names in the spreadsheet file you want to link from so that you can simply choose the correct named range

- Enables you to choose whether to insert the spreadsheet data in a table or as text alone

- Enables you to create a link without having the server application running or the source file open

- Does not update linked data instantly

Although WordPerfect makes a distinction between DDE linking (the method you just learned) and Spreadsheet linking (the method you're about to learn), both links are established via DDE. That's why in this book, we label the two methods as Edit Link Create and Spreadsheet Link commands. WordPerfect simply labels the second method Spreadsheet to distinguish it from the other link method and to reinforce that only spreadsheets can be linked using this method—not to imply that a utility other than DDE is being used to create the links.

As with the Edit Link Create command, formatting changes made to data linked via the Spreadsheet Link command will not be retained permanently. The next time the WordPerfect linked spreadsheet is updated, all formatting changes will be lost. Keep in mind, however, that if the data in the 1-2-3 spreadsheet does not change frequently, new formatting could remain in WordPerfect a substantial amount of time—perhaps enough time for you to print the WordPerfect document with both current spreadsheet figures *and* special formatting.

Creating the Spreadsheet Link

For the sake of convenience and also for comparison purposes, we'll use the same 1-2-3 spreadsheet (LINK.WK3) and the same WordPerfect document (LINK.ME) to establish the link.

TASK: Link WPWINLINK to LINK.ME using the Spreadsheet Link command.

1. If 1-2-3 is running, close it. Remember, unlike Edit Link Create, you can create spreadsheet links without having the 1-2-3 spreadsheet file open.

2. In WordPerfect, open LINK.ME.

3. Place the insertion point a couple lines below the spreadsheet you linked earlier in this chapter.

4. From the Tools menu, choose Spreadsheet and then choose Create Link.

   The Create Spreadsheet Link dialog box appears (see fig. 7.8). Notice the Type box, from which you can choose to import the spreadsheet as a table or as text alone. By default, the spreadsheet is inserted into a table. You can leave this option as it is because this time you will have the linked spreadsheet placed inside a table.

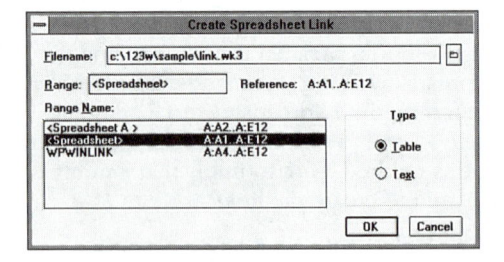

FIG. 7.8 *The Create Spreadsheet Link dialog box.*

5. In the Filename box, type the full path name for LINK.WK3. For example, if LINK.WK3 is stored in a directory named SAMPLE, type *c:\123w\sample\link.wk3*. You must include the full path in order for the link to work.

   Alternatively, you can click on the list button and scroll through the Select File dialog box to select LINK.WK3.

The full path name then is inserted into the Filename box. This method is the most fool-proof.

6. Click in the Range box.

   The Range and Range Name boxes are filled immediately with information. In the Range box, <Spreadsheet> is inserted, and to the right, the cell range for the entire spreadsheet is given. If you wanted to link the entire spreadsheet to the WordPerfect document, you would choose OK now. Because you want to link a named range, however, you must take one more step.

   The Range Name box shows all the range names in the current spreadsheet. Because you probably created only the one range name, WPWINLINK, you only see WPWINLINK in this box. Refer to figure 7.8 for an example of a Range Name box that displays several range names. Consider how helpful this information would be if you couldn't remember the exact name of the range you wanted to link. All you have to do is enter the file name and all of its range names are listed for you.

7. In the Range Name box, click WPWINLINK so that it is highlighted.

   Notice that the Range box now displays WPWINLINK instead of <Spreadsheet>. Also, the cell reference changes to represent those cells occupied only by the WPWINLINK range.

8. Choose OK.

   The spreadsheet is inserted into LINK.ME (see fig. 7.9).

Notice how different the new spreadsheet appears from the one above it. Link code bars border the top and bottom of the new spreadsheet. These code bars are very helpful if you have several linked spreadsheets in one file, not only because the bars quickly remind you that a spreadsheet is linked, but they also display the spreadsheet name, the range name, and the cell range.

Because you selected the Table option, the spreadsheet data rests inside a table. Note that this spreadsheet is quite a bit smaller than the top spreadsheet. When you use the Spreadsheet Link command, spreadsheets tend to take up less room when you use the Edit Link Create command.

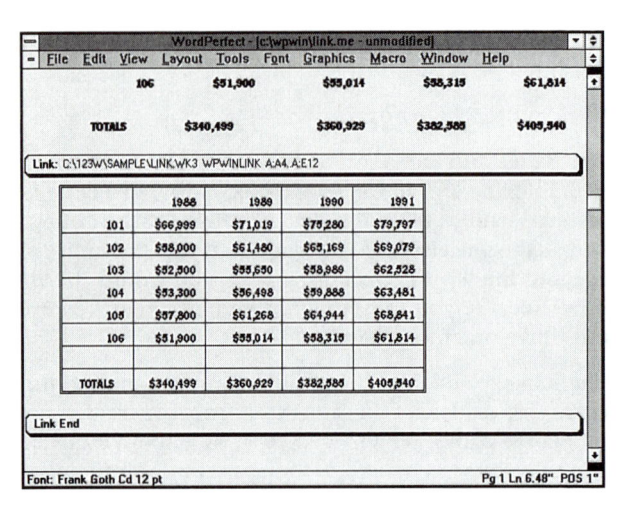

FIG. 7.9 *The spreadsheet linked using the Spreadsheet Link command.*

Setting Link Options

With WordPerfect, you can have all linked spreadsheets in the current document updated each time you retrieve the document. Keep in mind that this applies only to spreadsheets linked using the Spreadsheet Link command, not to those linked by the Edit Link Create command. WordPerfect also enables you to choose whether or not link codes are shown in the current document. You configure both of these options in the Link Options dialog box.

TASK: Remove link codes and configure the link to be updated automatically each time you open LINK.ME.

1. From the Tools menu, choose Spreadsheet and then choose Link Options.

    The Link Options dialog box appears (see fig. 7.10). By default, WordPerfect does not update spreadsheet links automatically when you open the document, but does display link codes.

Linking a Named Range in 1-2-3 to WordPerfect

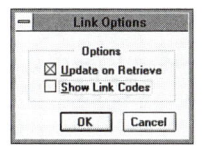

FIG. 7.10 *The Link Options dialog box.*

2. Choose Update On Retrieve.

   From now on, whenever you open LINK.ME, WordPerfect will automatically update all spreadsheet links created with the Spreadsheet Link command so that the most recent figures are shown.

3. Deselect Show Link Codes and then choose OK.

   As figure 7.11 displays, the link codes no longer appear in the document. You find it more difficult to distinguish between the two spreadsheets now. More often than not you will display the link codes—they give you more control over the document. Also, link codes help you distinguish spreadsheet links created with the Spreadsheet Link command from those created with the Edit Link Create command. Link codes also do not show up on a printout.

FIG. 7.11 *The spreadsheet with link codes hidden.*

Editing the Spreadsheet Link

After you have created a spreadsheet link, you can change a few of its properties. If the data resides in a table, you can remove the table so that only the text remains. You also can switch the range so that an entirely different group of cells displays in place of the old cells. To do this, simply select a new range name in the Range Name box.

You can even change the file name so that a completely different spreadsheet is used. The only time you would want to do this, however, is if you wanted to delete an existing linked spreadsheet in WordPerfect and in the same spot place a new spreadsheet from 1-2-3. Basically, this serves as a shortcut for deleting the old link and then using the Create Link command to insert a new linked spreadsheet.

TASK: Remove the table from the linked spreadsheet so that only text remains.

1. Place the insertion point anywhere inside the linked spreadsheet.

    This step becomes significant when you have more than one spreadsheet link in a document because the information shown in the Edit Spreadsheet Link dialog box depends on where the insertion point is located.

2. From the Tools menu, choose Spreadsheet and then choose Edit Link Create.

    The Edit Spreadsheet Link dialog box appears (see fig. 7.12). The dialog box shows the name of the linked file and range, and whether the spreadsheet is in table or text format.

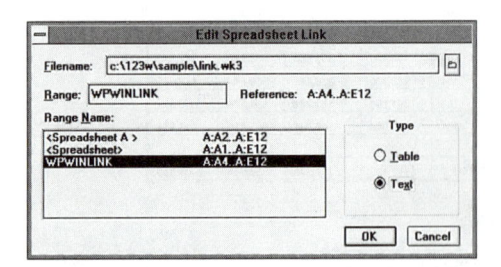

FIG. 7.12 The Edit Spreadsheet Link dialog box.

3. In the Type box, choose Text, and then choose OK.

   WordPerfect removes the table so that only the text remains, as shown in figure 7.13. Notice that the overall size of this spreadsheet is still smaller than the top spreadsheet. Keep this in mind when you can use either linking method.

Updating the Spreadsheet Link

As mentioned earlier, even if both the source and destination files are open and you make changes to the 1-2-3 spreadsheet, those changes are not reflected in the WordPerfect spreadsheet. This differs from spreadsheets created using the Edit Link Create command, which are updated instantaneously.

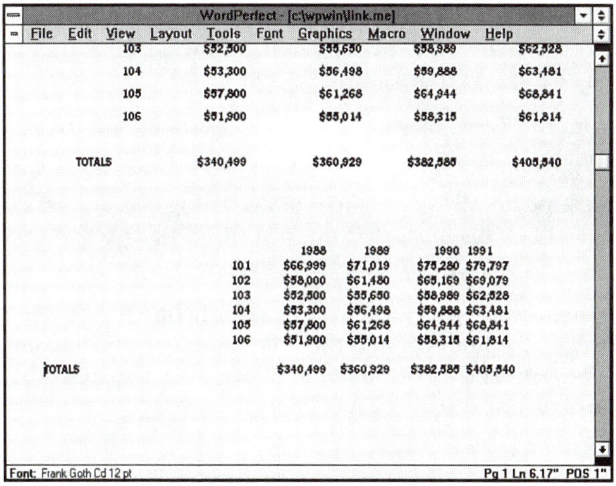

FIG. 7.13 *The edited linked spreadsheet.*

If changes are made to the 1-2-3 spreadsheet, those changes must be saved (using the 1-2-3 File Save command) before they can be incorporated into the WordPerfect spreadsheet. Even then, the changes are not reflected immediately in the WordPerfect spreadsheet. You must use WordPerfect's Update All Links command in order to receive the most recent 1-2-3 figures. One exception to this is when the changes are saved to the 1-2-3 spreadsheet while the linked WordPerfect document is closed. In this case, the next time you open the WordPerfect document, the linked spreadsheet will be updated automatically (so long as you have activated the Update On Retrieve option discussed earlier).

II — *Exploring Linking and Embedding Techniques*

When you have multiple spreadsheet links in a document, keep in mind that to update all linked spreadsheets created with the Spreadsheet Link command (versus those created with the Edit Link Create command), you need to make sure that the insertion point is not resting between any one spreadsheet's link codes; otherwise, only that particular spreadsheet will be updated. Remembering this can be helpful if you want only one spreadsheet updated, or if you don't want only one spreadsheet updated. For example, if you made formatting changes to one of the linked spreadsheets that you want to keep and you know the figures for that spreadsheet have not changed in the source spreadsheet, you update all other spreadsheets separately instead of updating them all.

TASK: Update the WPWINLINK link.

1. In WordPerfect, make a few changes to the linked spreadsheet so that when it is updated, you will notice it (because the changes you made will be lost!).

2. From the Tools menu, choose Spreadsheet and then choose Update All Links.

   The Update All Spreadsheet Links dialog box appears (see fig. 7.14). This box asks you to confirm that you want to update all of the linked spreadsheets.

   Remember, if you want to update only one link, place the insertion point between the link codes before choosing Tools Spreadsheet Update All Links. This way, only that particular spreadsheet will be updated.

FIG. 7.14 *The Update All Spreadsheet Links dialog box.*

3. Choose Yes.

   The WPWINLINK link is updated, and the changes you made to the spreadsheet are lost.

Linking a Named Range in 1-2-3 to WordPerfect **151**

Deleting the Spreadsheet Link

Removing a linked spreadsheet completely from a document is as simple as highlighting the entire spreadsheet and pressing the Delete key. The link is severed and the spreadsheet no longer appears in the document. (Incidentally, if you immediately change your mind, the Edit Undelete command will restore a deleted link.)

Deleting the link itself while leaving the spreadsheet intact, however, requires a different procedure. You probably will use this procedure frequently. Suppose that after a spreadsheet link has been in effect for several months, the project you were working on closes and you want to archive the file containing the link. Certainly, you would break the link but leave the spreadsheet intact in order to keep a clean copy of the document. Or, suppose that a spreadsheet link is active while you work on a draft for several weeks, and now you are ready to print the final copy. You could sever the link and make any formatting changes you wanted to the spreadsheet, knowing that those changes would be permanent.

For whatever reason, deleting a link while leaving the linked data is simple.

TASK: Delete the WPWINLINK link, leaving the spreadsheet intact in WordPerfect.

1. Place the insertion point just above the Link End code bar.

   To view the codes, ensure that Show Link Codes is selected on the Tools, Spreadsheet, Link Options dialog box.

2. From the WordPerfect View menu, choose Reveal Codes.

3. The [Link End] code should be highlighted, as shown in figure 7.15. If not, move the arrow keys until it is highlighted.

4. Press the Del key.

5. Again from the View menu, choose Reveal codes.

Now, only the spreadsheet appears in LINK.ME. The link codes have disappeared, letting you know that the link has been broken. If the data changes in the 1-2-3 LINK.WK3 file now, the WordPerfect link cannot be updated, short of starting from the very beginning and re-creating the link.

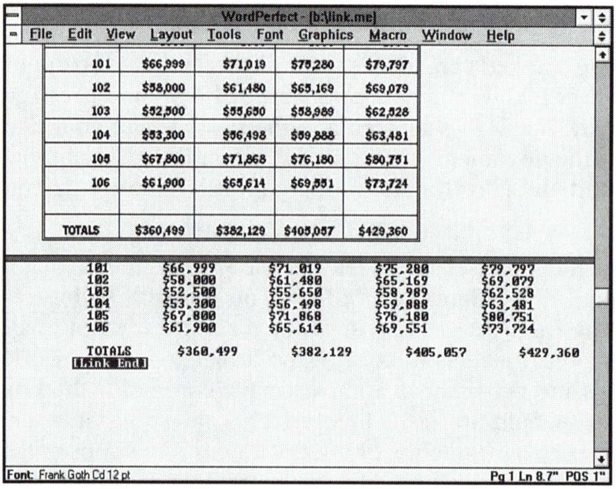

FIG. 7.15 *Deleting the link code.*

Summary

During this chapter you learned how to link a named range in 1-2-3 to a WordPerfect document using two separate methods, the Edit Link Create command and the Spreadsheet Create Link command. You probably will use both linking methods for different purposes in the future. Refer back to table 8.1 for help on which linking method to use for different situations.

For more information on using the programs 1-2-3 for Windows and WordPerfect for Windows, refer to Que's books *Using 1-2-3 for Windows*, Special Edition, and *Using WordPerfect for Windows*, Special Edition.

CHAPTER EIGHT

Linking between Ami Pro and WordPerfect

In each of the previous tutorials, you practiced linking Windows applications with DDE. Chapter 6 showed you how to link a spreadsheet in one application to a spreadsheet in a different application. In Chapter 7, you learned how to link a spreadsheet application to a word processor. Now you learn how to link data from one word processor to another word processor using DDE and OLE.

People sometimes have a difficult time understanding the difference between DDE and OLE linking (see Chapter 1). After awhile users come to understand the difference between linking and embedding, but DDE linking and OLE linking? Actually, you don't necessarily need to understand the technical differences between DDE and OLE; you simply need to know when to use one over the other. You can experiment by trial and error, but that will waste a lot of your time. If you attempt to link an object via the Object Packager to WordPerfect 5.1 for Windows, for example, you will go through several steps only to find out that the link can't be implemented because WordPerfect doesn't support OLE.

The type of software you use will determine whether you use DDE or OLE linking. Most newer applications designed for Windows 3.1 support OLE. Many of the earlier versions designed for Windows 3.0 support only DDE linking. Before you attempt to establish a link, find out if the application containing the source document supports OLE. Then find out if the destination application supports OLE. This information is important because if you want to link two or more documents and the source application doesn't support OLE, you must use DDE linking to connect the source document to every application that supports only DDE. However, you can use OLE linking even if the source application does not support OLE so long as the destination application does. For example, WordPerfect does not support OLE, but Ami Pro 2.0/3.0 for Windows does. This means that you can use OLE (via the Object Packager) to link a WordPerfect document to Ami Pro—as you will discover in the second part of this lesson—even though WordPerfect does not support OLE.

Remember, an application merely supporting OLE linking isn't enough. If a document is to be linked to another document using OLE, the source document's application must be a server. If a document is to accept a link, the application used to create this document must be a client. The reason this is significant is that some applications, such as Paintbrush, are only servers, while other applications, such as Write, are only clients. For example, you can OLE link from a Paintbrush drawing to a Write document, but you can't OLE link from a Write document to a Paintbrush drawing.

The following table may help you understand when to use OLE versus DDE linking:

Source application	Destination application	Type of linking to use
Does not support OLE	Does not support OLE	DDE linking
Does not support OLE	Supports OLE as a client	OLE linking
Supports OLE as a server	Does not support OLE	DDE linking
Supports OLE as a server	Supports OLE as a client	OLE linking

If you are still somewhat foggy about the differences between DDE and OLE linking (even after having read the conceptual portion of this book), you should understand those differences by the time you finish this chapter.

The goals of the lesson are as follows:

■ To link an agenda created in Ami Pro to a WordPerfect memo using DDE linking

- To link a table created in WordPerfect to an Ami Pro report using OLE linking

To achieve these goals, you perform the following tasks:

- Create an agenda in Ami Pro
- Copy the agenda to the Clipboard
- Paste link into a WordPerfect memo
- Edit the DDE link
- Update the DDE link
- Use the File Manager and Object Packager to embed a linked document into Ami Pro
- Associate a file extension to WordPerfect
- Edit the OLE link

Linking an Ami Pro Agenda to a WordPerfect Memo

Ami Pro supports DDE and OLE links, functioning as both a server and a client of OLE. WordPerfect, however, supports only DDE links. Therefore, all links you establish from Ami Pro to WordPerfect will be via DDE linking, even though Ami Pro supports both types of links. When you link from WordPerfect to Ami Pro, you will use OLE linking (see earlier table).

> **NOTE** Although you can link from Ami Pro to WordPerfect or from WordPerfect to Ami Pro, you can only embed a WordPerfect object into an Ami Pro document—an Ami Pro object cannot be embedded in WordPerfect because WordPerfect does not support OLE.
>
> In short, you can:
>
> - Link from WordPerfect to Ami Pro
> - Link from Ami Pro to WordPerfect
> - Embed a WordPerfect document in Ami Pro
>
> You cannot:
>
> - Embed an Ami Pro document in WordPerfect

Links from Ami Pro to WordPerfect can be created in two ways, both of which have their advantages and disadvantages. Copying the material from Ami Pro to the Clipboard and then paste-linking it into WordPerfect is the easiest way. This method is somewhat time-consuming, however, because you must switch back and forth between the two programs. The second method enables you to establish the link without leaving WordPerfect by using the Edit Link Create menu command. The drawback to this method is even greater because you must type in the name of the source file, and more significantly, the type of item you want to link (for example, a spreadsheet range or a bookmark number)—information that may not always be apparent to you.

This lesson teaches you how to use the first method (described in the preceding paragraph) because using the Clipboard is more convenient. You begin by creating an agenda in Ami Pro and then, after copying the agenda to the Clipboard, you paste-link it into a WordPerfect memo. After the link has been established, you edit and update it.

Using DDE Linking

Suppose that it's February and you're preparing a memo to send to all of the Marketing Managers in your company informing them of a conference to be held in the fall. The memo specifies the tentative dates and location for the conference (see fig. 8.1). You want the memo to include a tentative daily agenda so that the managers can review it and offer feedback if they have suggestions or comments about the schedule. Each time the proposed agenda changes in the future, you plan to update the memo and then send out revised copies to the managers.

You usually create all of your memos in WordPerfect. Because Ami Pro offers more sophisticated desktop publishing features, however, you generally create items such as agendas in Ami Pro. You want to avoid having to retype the agenda in the WordPerfect memo after you have created it in Ami Pro.

At first you think the solution is to simply cut and paste the agenda into WordPerfect after you have finished producing it in Ami Pro. The problem with this solution, however, is that the agenda will change regularly over the next few months. Because you intend to send out revised agendas to the Marketing Managers each time the data changes, you don't want to have to recut and repaste the agenda into the WordPerfect memo each time it changes in Ami Pro. What's worse, you plan to include updated copies of the agenda in other correspondence as well. This means that you would have to repaste over and over again in order to keep all copies of the agenda up to date. The perfect solution is DDE linking. By linking the original document to all other documents containing a copy of the agenda, you eliminate the need to revise each of these documents manually. Each time you change the information in the original agenda, all copies of the agenda are updated automatically at the time the documents are opened (unless you selected manual updating).

September Marketing Conference
Agenda

Wednesday, September 4, 1992

8:00	COFFEE AND DONUTS IN THE EMPRESS ROOM (EAST SIDE OF HOTEL)
8:30	LEE HONG: WHERE WE'RE HEADING
12:00	LUNCH
1:30	RON PRICE: POWER MARKETING
3:00	SMALL GROUPS: BRAINSTORMING SESSION
5:00	CLOSING REMARKS

FIG. 8.1 *The Ami Pro Agenda.*

Creating the Agenda and Copying It to the Clipboard

You don't need to format your agenda exactly as it appears in the figure just for the purposes of this tutorial. As you will discover, when you paste-link an item into WordPerfect, all of the formatting is lost anyway—in the WordPerfect document, not in the original Ami Pro document. If you want your agenda to look exactly as it does in the figure, however, use the Ami Pro ~OVERHD1.STY style sheet (without the contents selected). You will need to adjust some of the styles; for example, edit the Bullet style used for the time specifications so that lines no longer begin with a checkmark, and assign black text to the Headline style.

Task: Reproduce the agenda shown in figure 8.1 in Ami Pro and save it as SOURCE.SAM; then copy the agenda to the Clipboard.

1. Start Ami Pro if it is not already running.
2. From the File menu, choose New.
3. In the New dialog box, double-click ~OVERHD1.STY.
4. Type the text as it appears in figure 8.1, emulating the formatting styles if you want.

    For the purpose of this tutorial, the agenda covers only one day of the conference rather than all three days.

5. From the File menu, choose Save.

    You must save a document before you can link it.

6. In the Save dialog box, type *source.sam* and then click OK.
7. Select a portion of the agenda, beginning with Wednesday, September 4, 1992 to the end of the agenda.

    Note that you can link a partial document as well as an entire document with DDE.

8. From the Edit menu, choose Copy.
9. Click the Minimize button in the upper right corner of the application window to reduce Ami Pro to an icon at the bottom of your desktop.

    Do not close Ami Pro—in order for the link to be established, the source application must be running.

Opening and Preparing the WordPerfect Document

You have copied the source data to the Clipboard, so now you're ready to start the destination application—in this case WordPerfect. You will spend significantly less time on this task than you did on the previous one because you will use a WordPerfect Learn file to link the Ami Pro data to—in other words, the memo is already set up for you.

Task: Open the WordPerfect Learn file depicted in figure 10.2 and save it as DESTINAT.ION. Then add some text and place the insertion point in the proper location.

1. Start WordPerfect.
2. From the File menu, choose Retrieve.
3. In the Retrieve File dialog box, double-click [learn] to display LEARN subdirectory files.
4. Click LEARN07.WKB.
5. Click the Retrieve button.

   The document depicted in figure 8.2 now appears on your screen.

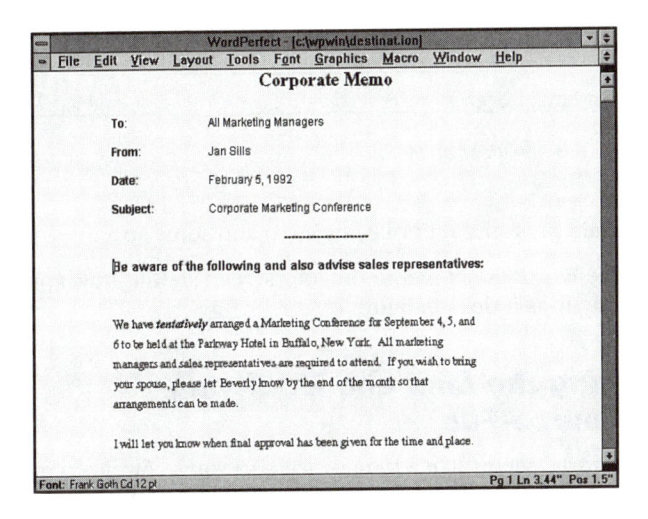

FIG. 8.2 *The WordPerfect memo.*

6. From the File menu, choose Save As.

7. In the Save As dialog box, type *c:\wpwin\destinat.ion* and then click Save.

8. Place the insertion point at the end of the first paragraph in the memo (after the word *made*).

9. Press the Enter key twice to add some space.

10. Without indenting, type the following sentence (see fig. 8.3):

    To date, the agenda is configured as follows:

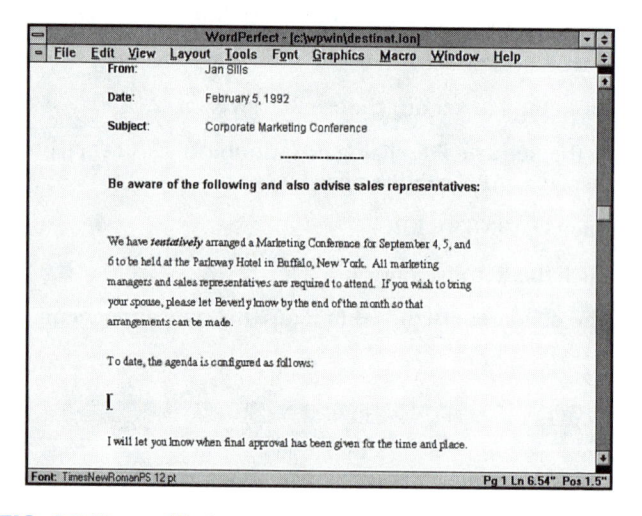

FIG. 8.3 *The modified memo.*

11. Again press the Enter key twice to add some space.

    The WordPerfect memo on your screen should now appear exactly as it does in figure 8.3.

Creating the Link and Modifying the Source File

If this tutorial seems like a long process to you so far, keep in mind that creating a link will save you from potentially hours of work spent later duplicating data had you not established the link. Also, the more experienced you get with linking, the faster it becomes.

Linking between Ami Pro and WordPerfect **161**

Task: Use the Paste Link command to create a link from the Ami Pro agenda to the WordPerfect memo. Then change the agenda in the Ami Pro document and watch as the changes are made simultaneously in the WordPerfect memo.

1. From the Edit menu, choose Link. From the cascading menu, choose Paste Link.

   The Link is now created between the two documents. The WordPerfect memo on your screen should now appear as in figure 8.4.

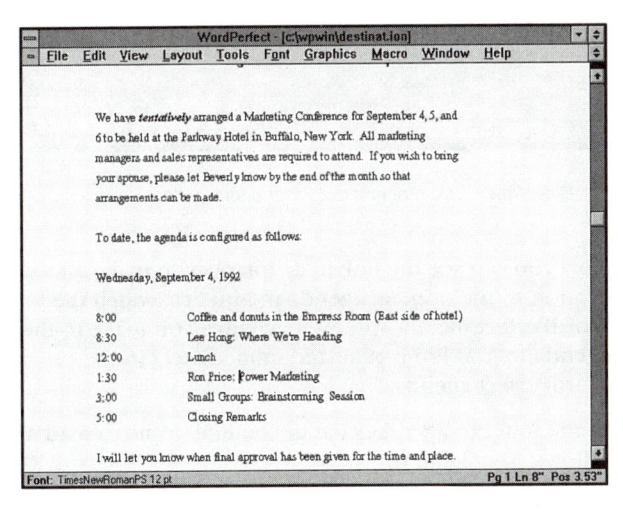

FIG. 8.4 *The linked memo.*

2. Click on the Sizing button at the upper right corner of the WordPerfect application window (this button has two arrows—one facing up, the other facing down).

3. Resize the WordPerfect application window to half its current size (use the sizing bar on the bottom edge of the application window), as shown in figure 8.5.

4. Restore Ami Pro by double-clicking its reduced icon at the bottom of your desktop.

5. Now resize the Ami Pro application window, following steps 2 and 3. Adjust both application windows so that you can view the 8:30 item in each window (refer to fig. 8.5).

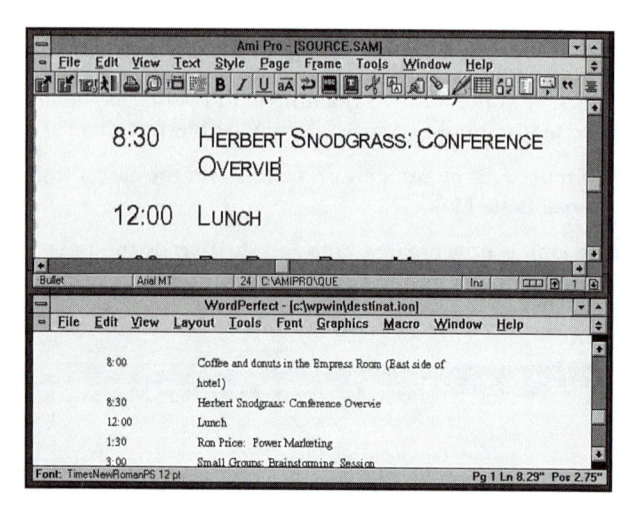

II — Exploring Linking and Embedding Techniques

FIG. 8.5 *Viewing both documents at the same time.*

Now you can see the link in action. As you make a modification to the original agenda in Ami Pro, watch the WordPerfect memo—the same change you make to the agenda in Ami Pro is reflected immediately in the WordPerfect agenda.

6. In the Ami Pro agenda, change the 8:30 topic to read as follows (see fig. 8.5):

    Herbert Snodgrass: Conference Overview.

    The 8:30 topic in the WordPerfect memo immediately changes to the new description.

Unwanted Coding

You may have noticed a bunch of little hearts, arrows, letters and other characters following the last line of the linked agenda in WordPerfect. These are formatting codes from the source file (the Ami Pro file). You can safely highlight these codes and delete them—they no longer serve any useful purpose.

Your WordPerfect formatting codes may be interrupted by the linked data, meaning that text following the imported data may lose its previous format style. If this occurs, choose Reveal Codes from the View menu and then reinsert the proper WordPerfect formatting codes directly after the [DDE Link End:*name*] code that appears after the last line of the imported (linked) data.

If you want to apply special formatting to the linked data, be sure to insert the appropriate WordPerfect formatting codes before the [DDE Link Begin:*name*] code. This is necessary because formatting codes and text are changed each time a link is updated. If the formatting codes are located after the [DDE Link Begin:*name*] code—and you apply italic to the linked data, make it bold, and change the font size to 24 points—all of these changes will be lost the next time the link is updated. You must specifically place formatting codes before the [DDE Link Begin:*name*] code.

Editing the Link

If you have several links in one document, managing those links may be rather challenging because their names may not aid you much in determining which link is which. In WordPerfect, all links are named according to this pattern: DDE_BOOKMARK1, DDE_BOOKMARK2, DDE_BOOKMARK3, and so on. Suppose that you want to delete a link. If the destination document has six links, will you easily remember that the one you want to remove is called DDE_BOOKMARK5? Probably not. Fortunately, you can make link names more meaningful so that instead of DDE_BOOKMARK5, a link is called FY91 SPREADSHEET. A name like this will quickly identify the link for you.

You may not always want a link to be updated automatically, as it would be by default. For example, did you notice how your system slowed down as you made changes to the Ami Pro agenda? Changes are reflected automatically in the WordPerfect document. Therefore, the speed at which you can enter text lags because your system divides its time between accepting the new data in Ami Pro and immediately inserting the same data into WordPerfect. If you have a lot of data to input, you may want to assign manual updating. Manual updating causes new data to be inserted into the WordPerfect document only when you tell it to, rather than automatically.

Normally when you open a destination document, any changes that have been made to the original (source) document since the destination document was last opened are now reflected automatically in the destination document. In other words, the link is updated automatically. Suppose that you make changes to the source application that you do not want reflected in the destination document. Unless you set the link to a manual update, the new data will be present when you open the destination document.

At times, therefore, you may want to edit a link so that it is updated manually.

In the following steps, you change the agenda link to manual updating so that you can update its contents at your command.

Task: Change the name of the link. Then edit the link so that it updates manually rather than automatically.

1. From the WordPerfect Edit menu, choose Link. Then from the cascading menu, choose Edit.

   The Edit DDE Link dialog box appears (see fig. 8.6). Notice that the name of the destination file, in this case DESTINAT.ION, appears at the top of the dialog box. Below the Link Name, the name of each link in the destination document is displayed. Because only one link is in this document, only one link name appears—DDE_BOOKMARK1.

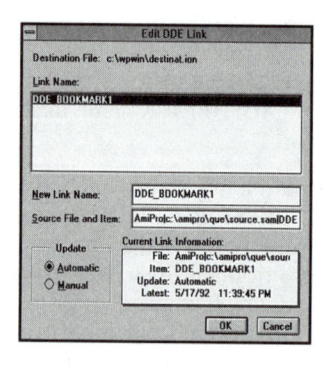

FIG. 8.6 *The Edit DDE Link dialog box.*

2. In the New Link Name box, select DDE_BOOKMARK1.
3. Type *AGENDA*.
4. In the Update box, click the Manual option button.
5. Click OK.

The link now has a new name and will be updated only when you execute the Link Update command, which is discussed in the next section.

Notice that information about the current link is displayed in the Current Link Information box at the lower right of the dialog box.

The name of the source file and the current link are given. A discrepancy seems to exist here: the link name is labeled as Item. This is no discrepancy; a link name also can be referred to as an *item*. Knowing this becomes significant when you establish a link using menu commands rather than the Clipboard. Every application will prompt you to enter the "item" before it will create a link. With WordPerfect, the item would be DDE_BOOKMARKX, where X is the number of the link. When linking from a spreadsheet application, the item may be a range name.

Updating the Link

As mentioned earlier, links are updated automatically by default. This means that if a destination document is open while you work on the source document, all modifications are made simultaneously to the destination document. If you modify the source document while the destination document is closed, the next time you open the destination document, its contents are updated to match the current data in the source document.

On the other hand, after you assign manual updating to a WordPerfect link, you can update the link only by executing the Link Update menu command. The following steps show you how this works.

Task: Change the agenda in Ami Pro and then use the WordPerfect Link Update command to update the link in WordPerfect.

1. Switch to Ami Pro.

2. Place the insertion point just before 12:00 in the Ami Pro agenda.

3. Press the Enter key twice.

4. Press the up-arrow key twice.

5. Type *10:30*.

   Notice how much faster Ami Pro works now that the link has been changed to manual updating.

6. Switch to WordPerfect.

   The agenda appears as it did before. Because you assigned manual updating, the change you just made to the Ami Pro agenda has not been duplicated in the WordPerfect agenda.

7. From the Edit menu, choose Link. Then from the cascading menu, choose Update.

   The Update DDE Link dialog box appears (see fig. 8.7).

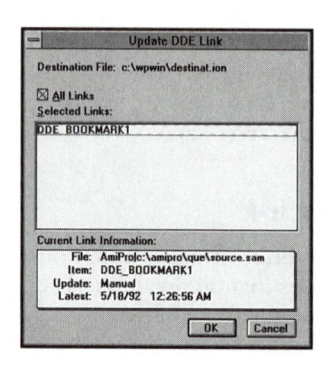

FIG. 8.7 *The Update DDE Link dialog box.*

8. In the Selected Links box, click DDE_BOOKMARK1 so that it is highlighted.

   You are taking this step only to familiarize yourself with it. Actually, this step is necessary only if you have more than one link and you do not want to update all links in the document. By default, the All Links checkbox is marked. If you're working with only one link or if you want to update all links, you need only click OK after opening the dialog box.

9. Click OK.

   The dialog box closes and the link data is updated. The agenda now shows the 10:30 item you added to the Ami Pro agenda.

Linking a WordPerfect Table to an Ami Pro Report

Now that you have had plenty of experience working with DDE linking, you are ready to see how OLE linking works. Although the link itself works like a DDE link, an OLE link from WordPerfect is established quite differently from a DDE link to WordPerfect and also looks dissimilar. Rather than copying the data directly to the

Clipboard, as you did in Ami Pro, you use the File Manager and Object Packager (a new Windows accessory) to create the link. The linked data is not displayed outright in Ami Pro; instead, an icon representing the linked data appears.

Using OLE Linking

Suppose that you're creating a financial report on the stock holdings of various companies. Your boss wants you to submit the report to him on disk. Part of your strategy for this report is to supply as much supporting documentation as possible, but without cluttering the text of the report. The perfect solution is object linking and embedding, otherwise known as OLE. When you embed an item—a spreadsheet, report, chart, and so on—in the report, the contents of that item do not appear on-screen. Instead, an icon representing the item appears. When you double-click this icon, the item then is displayed in its entirety. If you embed a linked WordPerfect table in an Ami Pro report, for example, that table is not visible—an icon with the name of the file containing the table appears instead. When you double-click the icon, WordPerfect starts and the table is displayed. Considering this, imagine how you can streamline a document using OLE embedding! What's more, the reader can decide whether he wants to review each piece of supporting documentation or only certain ones.

Under the Conclusions and Recommendations section of the report, you plan to include a WordPerfect table whose data supports one of the recommendations you make. Normally, the table would already exist as a WordPerfect file, so you wouldn't have to start WordPerfect in order to create the link. For this tutorial, however, you need to prepare the WordPerfect table before creating the link.

Preparing the WordPerfect Table

You will use a WordPerfect Learn file again to set up the link. You will not need to make any modifications—all you do is save the file under a new name. You may be wondering at this point: why not link the Learn file as it is if no modifications will be made? You will discover the answer a few sections later.

Task: View the table to be linked and save the WordPerfect learn file under a new name.

1. Start WordPerfect if it isn't already running.
2. From the File menu, choose Retrieve.

3. In the Retrieve File dialog box, double-click [learn] to display LEARN subdirectory files—if you aren't currently in the LEARN subdirectory.

4. Double-click SPREAD26.PLN.

   The document shown in figure 8.8 now appears on your screen. Notice that all of the dates end in '91. Later, you will compare the first and last figures in the Initial Investment column with the figures here to see the link in action.

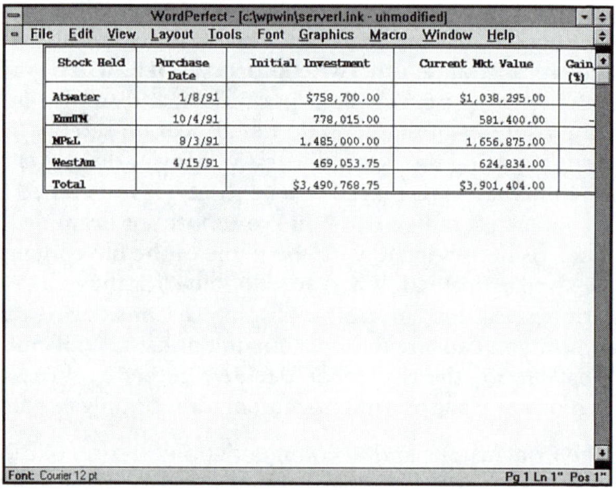

FIG. 8.8 *The WordPerfect Table.*

5. From the File menu, choose Save As.

6. In the Save As dialog box, type *c:\wpwin\serverl.ink* and then click OK.

   This file is named SERVERL.INK so that you can remember that the *server* application is the one containing the original data.

7. Exit completely from WordPerfect; don't just minimize it.

Using the File Manager and Object Packager

These steps should be new to you because the Object Packager is new to Windows 3.1. The Object Packager is simply a program that

Linking between Ami Pro and WordPerfect **169**

places the document to be linked into a tidy "package" so that it can be embedded in the destination document. Packages can contain links or embedded objects, but packages themselves always are embedded in the destination document. The Object Packager assigns icons and labels to an object (for example, a document, spreadsheet, drawing, and so on), which you have the option of changing. You learn how to change a package's icon and label in Chapter 10. For now, you will just learn how to package an object.

Task: Use the File Manager to copy the source document to the Clipboard. Then use the Object Packager to create a package for the file.

1. In the Main window, double-click the File Manager icon to start the File Manager.

2. Scroll through the directory tree until you locate the SERVERL.INK file.

   The file's path should be C:\WPWIN\SERVERL.INK.

3. Click SERVERL.INK so that it is highlighted.

4. From the File menu, choose Copy.

   The Copy dialog box appears (see fig. 8.9).

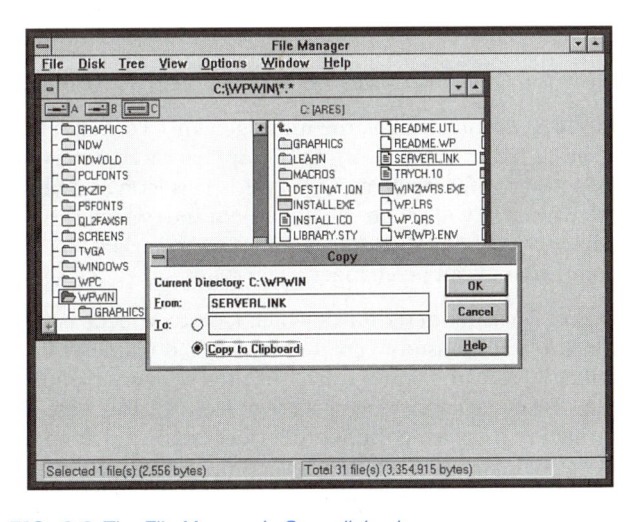

FIG. 8.9 *The File Manager's Copy dialog box.*

5. Click the Copy To Clipboard option button.
6. Click OK, and then close the File Manager.

   A copy of the file is now located on the Clipboard.

7. Double-click the Accessories group icon located at the bottom of the desktop.
8. Double-click the Object Packager icon.

   The Object Packager window appears, as shown in figure 8.10.

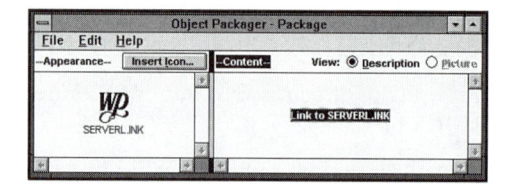

FIG. 8.10 *The Object Packager window.*

9. Click Content.

   The area around the word Content changes color; nothing else happens.

10. From the Object Packager's Edit menu, choose Paste Link.

    In the Content window, the message `Link to SERVERL.INK` appears (refer to fig. 8.10). In the Appearance window, an icon and the file name are displayed. This icon and file name are what you will see in the document into which the package will be embedded. As mentioned earlier, the icon and the label can be changed.

    Object Packager determines which icon to select based upon the application used to create the linked document. If the linked file's extension is not associated with an application, the Object Packager assigns its own icon. Chances are that instead of displaying the WordPerfect emblem that appears in figure 8.10, your screen shows the same graphic that belongs to the Object Packager icon (the opened box). This is because the extension INK is most likely not recognized by Windows as belonging to WordPerfect documents. Therefore, the Object Packager assigns its own icon. Later, you will associate INK with WordPerfect.

11. From the Edit menu, choose Copy Package.

    The package is now copied to the Clipboard and ready to be pasted into the destination document.

Pasting the Package into Ami Pro

The Ami Pro report you are going to paste the package into already exists, so again you don't have to enter any text. You do need to use your imagination here, however, because the report you're going to use is really only a conglomeration of headings—the report has no meat, or text. You can grasp the beauty of OLE linking in a skeletal report just as easily as you can in a meaty one.

Task: Complete the link by pasting the package into Ami Pro.

1. Switch to Ami Pro.

2. From the File menu, choose New.

3. In the New dialog box, double-click ~REPORT 4.STY. Make sure the With Contents check box is marked.

4. Click OK.

    The ~REPORT4.STY style sheet appears on-screen, similar to figure 8.11.

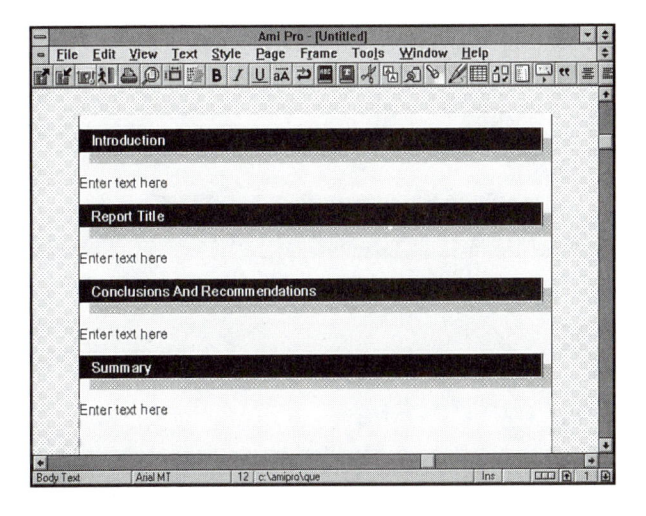

FIG. 8.11 *The Ami Pro report.*

II — *Exploring Linking and Embedding Techniques*

5. From the File menu, choose Save.

6. In the Save As dialog box, type *client.sam*.

   You're naming the document this way to help you remember that applications receiving embedded packages are called client applications.

7. Move the cursor to the Conclusions and Recommendations section, placing the insertion point just before the word `Enter`.

8. Delete the `Enter text here` phrase. Make sure that the insertion point rests at the beginning of the line.

9. From the Edit menu, choose Paste.

   The package, looking just as it did in the Object Packager window, is now inserted into the Ami Pro report (see fig. 8.12).

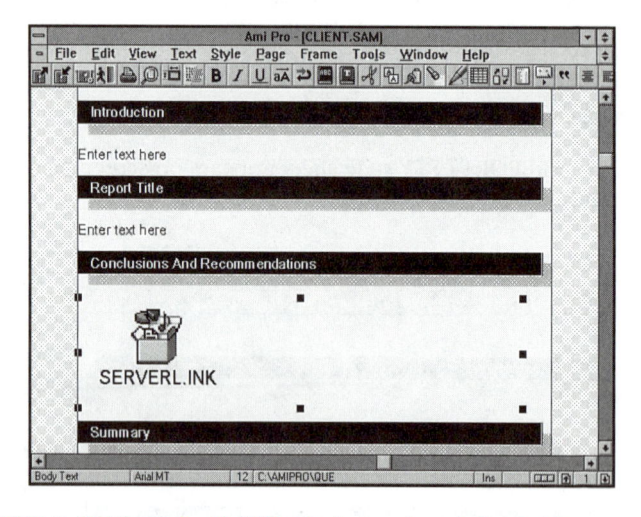

FIG. 8.12 *The embedded WordPerfect package in the Ami Pro report.*

Opening the Package

After a package has been embedded into a document, all you have to do to access the object contained in the package is double-click the icon. When you do, the application used to create the object, in this case WordPerfect, is started and the object, in this case, the

Linking between Ami Pro and WordPerfect **173**

WordPerfect table, is displayed. You then can modify the contents if you want, or simply review them.

Now you will find out why you named the WordPerfect Learn file SERVERL.INK.

Task: Open the packaged table.

1. Double-click the SERVERL.INK icon.

What happened? Shouldn't the object be displayed when you double-click the icon? Instead, you get a dialog box saying that no association exists for this file (see fig. 8.13). This is why you assigned the uncommon INK extension to the source file—to see what happens when you OLE link a WordPerfect document. WordPerfect is uncommon in that it does not automatically assign file extensions to its documents as do other applications. For example, all Ami Pro text files end in SAM and Word text files end in DOC. You can assign any extension you want, however, to a WordPerfect text file. When embedding objects from WordPerfect, you first have to associate the file extension used—in this case INK—before you can open the embedded package. This sounds complicated, but it's not.

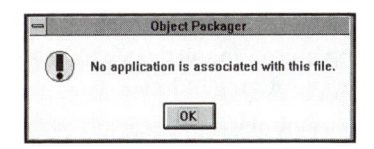

FIG. 8.13 *A warning that no file association exists.*

2. Click OK to remove the error message.
3. Click the Ami Pro Minimize button.
4. Open the File Manager.
5. From the File menu, choose Associate.

   The Associate dialog box appears (see fig. 8.14).

6. In the Files with Extension box, type *ink*, following the example in the figure.
7. Click the Browse button.
8. Move around your drive until you get to the WPWIN subdirectory, and then click it.

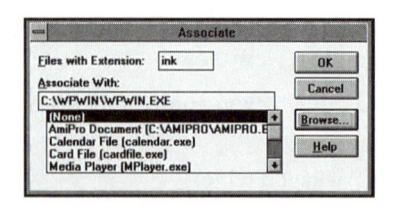

FIG. 8.14 *The Associate dialog box.*

9. Find and double-click the WordPerfect for Windows executable file, WPWIN.EXE.

   In the Associate With box, the WPWIN.EXE file name (including its path) appears.

10. Click OK.

11. Close File Manager.

12. Double-click the Ami Pro icon to restore the Ami Pro application window.

13. Now try double-clicking the package icon.

    WordPerfect starts and SERVERL.INK is opened.

14. Click the Sizing button in the upper right corner of the WordPerfect application window.

    The WordPerfect application window now takes up only a portion of the desktop so that you can see the Ami Pro report underneath (see fig. 8.15).

> **NOTE** If you create a new package now, the WordPerfect icon (see fig. 8.10) would be displayed in the Object Packager's Appearance window instead of the generic icon seen in figure 8.12.

Editing the Link

You can appreciate one thing about OLE linking: whenever you make a change to any client document, that change is reflected not only in the source document, but in all other client documents as well. Suppose that you link the WordPerfect table to twenty other documents. If you need to update the figures in all of those tables, you can do so from any one of the client documents or in the

Linking between Ami Pro and WordPerfect **175**

source document; all of the documents linked to the source document will be updated to include the new data. The following steps demonstrate how this works:

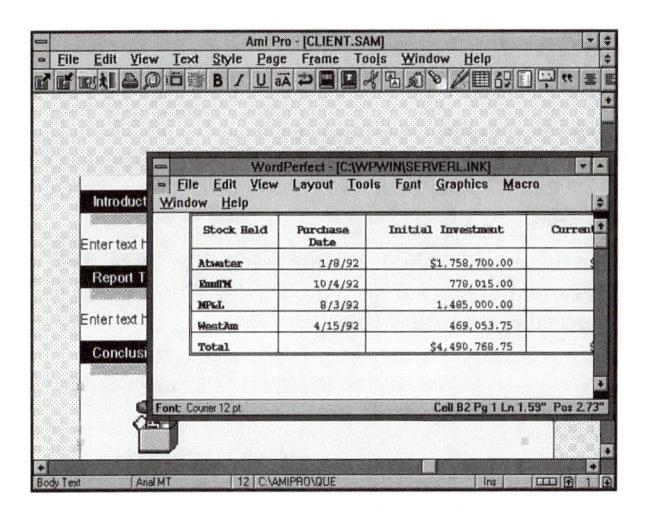

FIG. 8.15 *The linked table as it appears inside the Ami Pro report.*

Task: Modify the original WordPerfect table via the Ami Pro link.

1. In the Purchase Date column, change all of the dates from '91 to '92 (refer to fig. 8.15).

2. In the first row of the Initial Investment column, add a 1 and a comma after the dollar sign so that the number reads as follows: $1,758,700.00.

3. In the last row of the Initial Investment column, change the 3 to 4, so that the number reads as follows: $4,490,768.75.

4. From the WordPerfect File menu, choose Exit.

5. When asked whether you want to replace the existing file, click Yes.

6. Minimize Ami Pro.

7. Start WordPerfect.

8. From the bottom of the File menu, choose SERVERL.INK.

Look at the figures in the table. They now match the changes you just made in Ami Pro.

Summary

Both DDE and OLE linking make your work with WordPerfect for Windows and Ami Pro for Windows easier. In this chapter, you learned how to link from WordPerfect to Ami Pro using the Windows 3.1 Object Packager and from Ami Pro to WordPerfect using ordinary DDE linking.

For more information about the programs WordPerfect 5.1 for Windows and Ami Pro 2.0, see Que's *Using WordPerfect for Windows*, Special Edition, and *Using Ami Pro*.

CHAPTER NINE

Linking an Embedded Excel Chart to a Word Memo

A chart (or graph) is a pictorial presentation of numerical figures in a worksheet. You can create charts two different ways in Excel 4.0 for Windows. One way is to produce the chart in a document window of its own, saving the chart as a separate file apart from the worksheet data used to develop it. The second, more common way, is to embed the chart directly inside the worksheet containing the data used to generate the chart.

Linking an embedded Excel chart to Word for Windows is a bit different than linking a chart that already exists in its own file, which is called a chart file. A chart file, which always has an XLC extension, contains only the chart, not the worksheet figures used to produce the chart. You can link a chart located in a chart file in fewer steps than an embedded chart. This is because an embedded chart has been nested in an Excel worksheet and first must be saved on its own in a chart file before it can be linked to Word—a step obviously redundant for a chart that already exists in a chart file.

The goal of this lesson is as follows:

- ■ To link a chart embedded in an Excel worksheet to a memo in Word

To achieve this goal, you will perform the following tasks:

- Set up the data to be charted in a new worksheet file and then save it as LINK1.XLS.
- Create an embedded chart in the LINK1.XLS worksheet.
- Select the chart and then copy it to the Clipboard.
- Create a memo in Word that will receive the embedded chart link.
- Establish a link from the embedded chart in Excel to the Word memo.
- Change the link to manual updating, make a change to the original Excel chart, and then update the chart in MEMO.DOC.
- Reconnect a broken link by changing the source file name.
- Cancel the link to CHART1.XLC.
- Edit the background pattern and other features of the chart.

Linking a Chart Embedded in a Worksheet

Just when you have finally grasped the concept of embedding one application inside of another, you hear the phrase, "an embedded chart in Excel." If you're following along logically, you may wonder if this is referring to a 1-2-3 or Quattro Pro chart snuggled inside an Excel worksheet. This is a logical assumption, but an inaccurate conclusion. "Embedded chart" simply means that when you create a chart based on figures in a worksheet, that chart is placed inside the worksheet itself and saved as part of the worksheet file. Charts of this nature are labeled "embedded" to distinguish them from an ordinary chart stored in its own chart file, apart from the worksheet data used to generate the chart—meaning that when you open that chart file, you see only the graphic representation of the data, and not the worksheet figures themselves.

This is the situation for this tutorial: It's July, 1990 and your boss has just asked you to submit a chart each month that graphs the sales totals for Moby, Inc. by product for the previous month. She wants you to begin with June, 1990.

Linking an Embedded Excel Chart to a Word Memo **179**

The same Excel worksheet is used to store the sales figures for the most recent full month. When a new month's figures come in, the old data for the previous month is saved under a different file name.

You dread having to create a chart for each new month, copy it, and then paste it into a new memo. Your plan is to set up one memo in Word that is linked to the chart in Excel. Because the same Excel worksheet is used for each month's figures, each month the chart will be updated automatically to reflect the new month's data. When the chart is updated in Excel, the memo in Word also will be updated, thanks to the OLE link. All you have to do at the beginning of each month is print the Word memo and submit it to your boss. This way, after you set up the link, you don't have to open the Word file again!

Setting Up the Data To Be Charted

Fortunately, you don't have to develop a new worksheet for this tutorial. As in earlier lessons, you borrow data from the sample files included with Excel. (Rather than have you tamper with the Workbook file you will use to obtain the spreadsheet figures, you will place the chart in a new file.)

TASK: Set up the data to be charted in a new worksheet file called LINK1.XLS, and then save it as CHART1.XLC.

1. Start Excel if it isn't already running.

2. From the File menu, choose Open.

3. In the Open dialog box, double-click the EXAMPLES subdirectory.

4. Double-click SALETRAC.XLW to open it.

   The SALEANAL.XLS section of the SALETRAC.XLW file appears in the Excel application window (see fig. 9.1). SALETRAC.XLW is displayed in brackets because it is a Workbook file that contains three bound files, one of which is SALEANAL.XLS.

5. Select (highlight) cells 80C through 86G.

6. From the Edit menu, choose Copy to copy the data to the Clipboard.

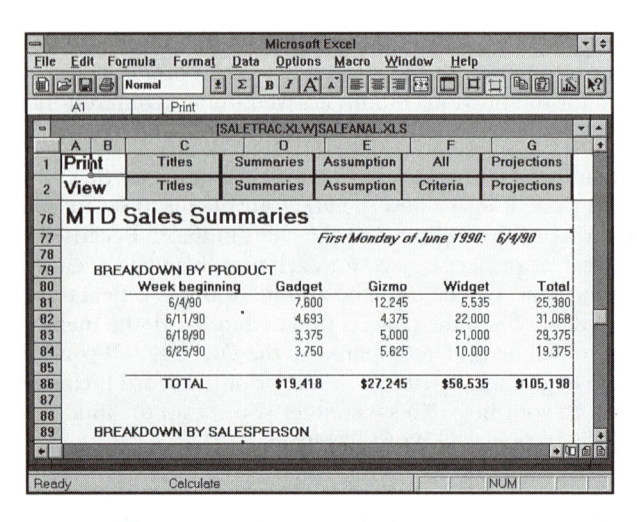

FIG. 9.1 *The SALEANAL.XLS document.*

7. From the File menu, choose Close Workbook to close SALETRAC.XLW. Choose No when asked if you want to save any changes.

   Sheet1 (or Sheet2, Sheet3, and so on) should now appear again inside Excel. If not, choose New from the File menu and open a new worksheet.

8. From the File menu, choose Save.

   This is an important step. Remember, you cannot link an object without first saving the file in which the object is located.

9. In the File Name box located in the Save As dialog box, type *link1.xls*, and then choose OK.

10. Place the pointer in cell A1. From the Edit menu, choose Paste.

11. Click once on cell A1 to deselect the pasted chart.

Creating an Embedded Chart

You now will perform a series of steps to create an embedded chart for the selected data. If you are an experienced chart maker, create a simple column chart with grid lines, include a legend, and title the chart: BREAKDOWN BY PRODUCT. Then skip to step 8 in the steps that follow.

Linking an Embedded Excel Chart to a Word Memo

TASK: Create an embedded chart in the LINK1.XLS worksheet.

1. On the Toolbar near the top of the screen, click on the ChartWizard tool icon (this is the second icon from the right).

   The first ChartWizard dialog box appears and asks you to define the range of cells to be used for the chart (see fig. 9.2).

2. Drag the mouse from cell A1 to cell E7 so that the entire table is surrounded by moving dotted lines.

   If you make a mistake, don't panic. You can select the range as many times as you need until you get it right. When you see =$A$1:$E$7 in the Range box, the range is correct. Sometimes the ChartWizard dialog box is in the way, making it difficult for you to select the right cells. If so, click on the dialog box title bar and drag the dialog box to a new location.

3. After =$A$1:$E$7 appears in the Range box, choose Next.

   The second ChartWizard dialog box appears (see fig. 9.3).

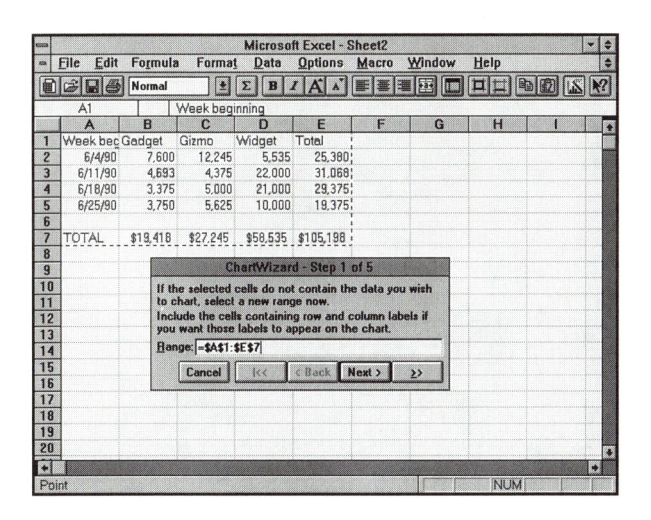

FIG. 9.2 *Step 1 in the ChartWizard process.*

4. Because the chart type you're going to use—a simple column chart—is highlighted by default, simply choose Next again.

182 II — *Exploring Linking and Embedding Techniques*

The third ChartWizard dialog box appears (see fig. 9.4).

FIG. 9.3 *Step 2 in the ChartWizard process.*

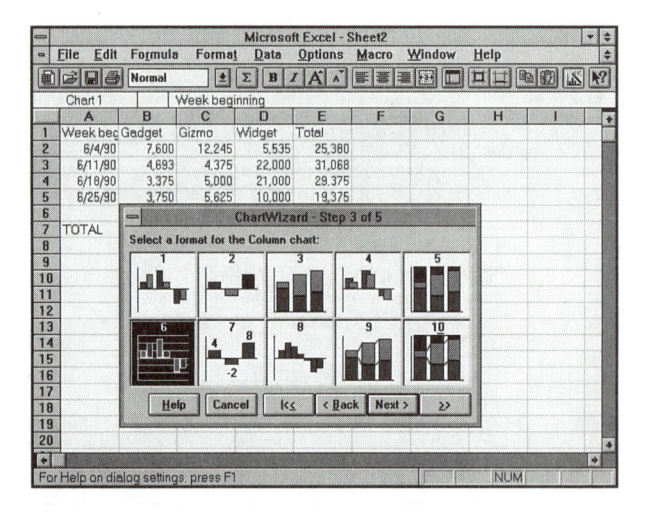

FIG. 9.4 *Step 3 in the ChartWizard process.*

Linking an Embedded Excel Chart to a Word Memo **183**

5. Click number 6. This causes grid lines to appear in the chart, which makes the figures easier to read.

6. Choose Next.

   The fourth ChartWizard dialog box appears, showing you an example of what the chart will look like. You don't need to make changes to this dialog box.

7. Choose Next.

   The last ChartWizard dialog box appears, asking you to provide a title for the chart, among other things (see fig. 9.5).

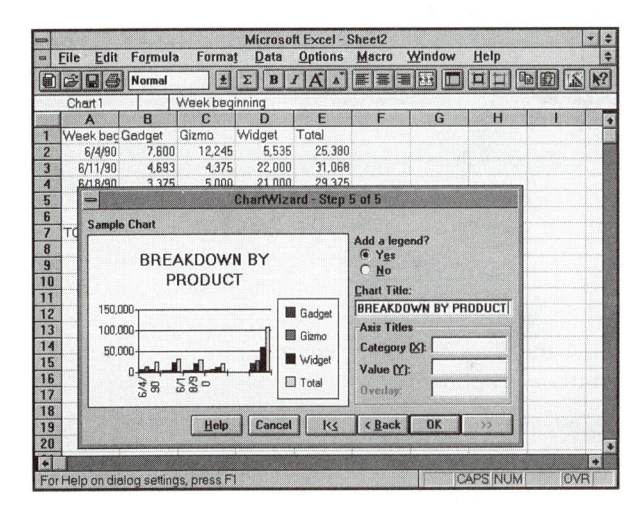

FIG. 9.5 *The Last step in the ChartWizard process.*

8. In the Chart Title box, type *BREAKDOWN BY PRODUCT*. Then choose OK.

   The chart is now embedded inside the LINK1.XLS worksheet. The frame holding the chart is so small, however, that you cannot see its contents.

9. Using the mouse, adjust the sizing handles and move the chart so that it fills cells A10 to H26, as shown in figure 9.6. The chart is now ready to be saved as a chart file.

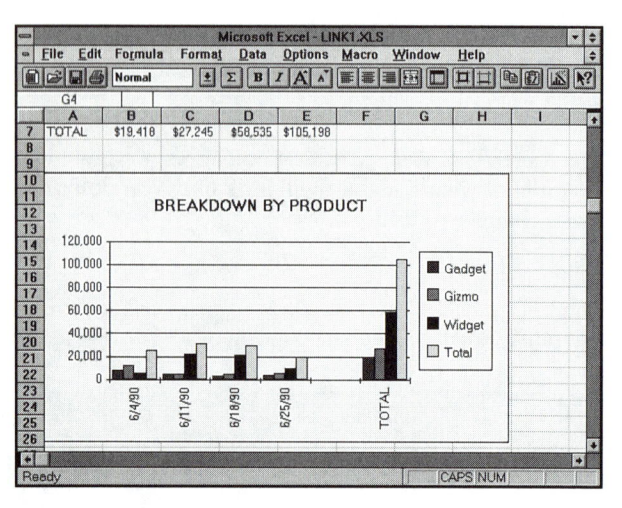

II — Exploring Linking and Embedding Techniques

FIG. 9.6 *The embedded chart.*

Saving the Chart and Copying It to the Clipboard

TASK: Save the chart as a chart file, select the chart, and then copy it to the Clipboard.

1. Double-click anywhere on the chart.

   The chart is placed in a new window labeled LINK1.XLS Chart 1, and the Chart menu is added to the Excel menu bar.

2. From the File menu, choose Save.

   The Save As dialog box appears and suggests that you save the chart as CHART1.XLC.

3. Choose OK.

4. From the File menu, choose Open.

5. Double-click CHART1.XLC.

   The chart appears in a new chart window, so three document windows are now open (see fig. 9.7). Also, the Chart menu now appears on the Excel menu bar.

Linking an Embedded Excel Chart to a Word Memo

6. From the Chart menu, choose Select Chart. Alternatively, you can click on a blank spot in the chart to select the entire chart, but unless you click the right place, you may end up choosing only part of the chart, such as the legend or title.

    Small boxes now outline the chart (see fig. 9.7).

> **NOTE** Double-clicking the chart does not select it.

7. From the Edit menu, choose Copy.

    Dotted lines move around the chart, letting you know it has been copied to the Clipboard (see fig. 9.7). You now are ready to paste-link the chart into Word.

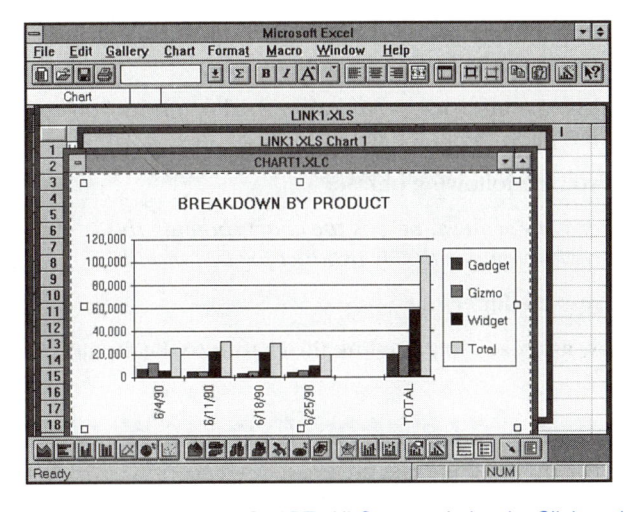

FIG. 9.7 *The contents of CHART1.XLC are copied to the Clipboard.*

Setting Up the Word Memo

Before paste linking the chart into Word, you need to create a simple memo. This will be quite an expedient process because you will use Word's macro-run MEMO2 template.

TASK: Create a memo in Word which will later receive the embedded chart link.

> **NOTE** Make sure that you do not copy anything to the Clipboard; otherwise, you will have to go back into Excel and copy the chart to the Clipboard again.

1. Start Word if it is not already running.
2. From the File menu, choose New.
3. Double-click the MEMO2 template.

   A dialog box now appears asking you to enter information that will be inserted into the memo. If you want to enter false data for the names and subject, follow the steps Word presents to you. If you want to use the memo as it is, choose Cancel, Yes, and then OK.

4. From the File menu, choose Save and type *memo.doc* in the Save As dialog box.
5. Place the insertion point below the line under Subject, and then press the Enter key.
6. Type the following phrase:

   Per your request, here is the chart showing the breakdown of sales by product for last month.

7. Press the Enter key.

You now are ready to paste-link the chart into the memo.

Creating the Link from Excel to Word

TASK: Establish a link from the embedded chart in Excel to the Word memo.

1. From the Edit menu, choose Paste Special.

   The Paste Special dialog box appears (see fig. 9.8). When the dialog box first appears, Microsoft Excel Chart Object is highlighted in the Data Type box. Notice, however, that the Paste Link option button is dimmed. In order to link the embedded chart to Word, you must choose the Picture data type.

2. Next to Source, the type of object to be linked or embedded is identified. Directly below this appears the name of the file containing the object.

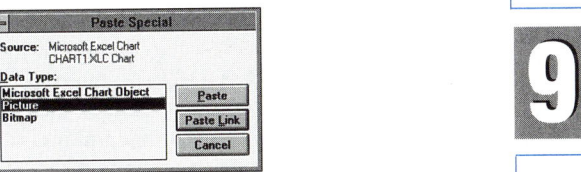

Linking an Embedded Excel Chart to a Word Memo **187**

FIG. 9.8 *The Paste Special dialog box.*

3. In the Data Type box, choose Picture.

    The Paste Link option button becomes active.

4. Choose Paste Link.

    After a short pause, the chart appears inside a frame just below the insertion point (see fig. 9.9).

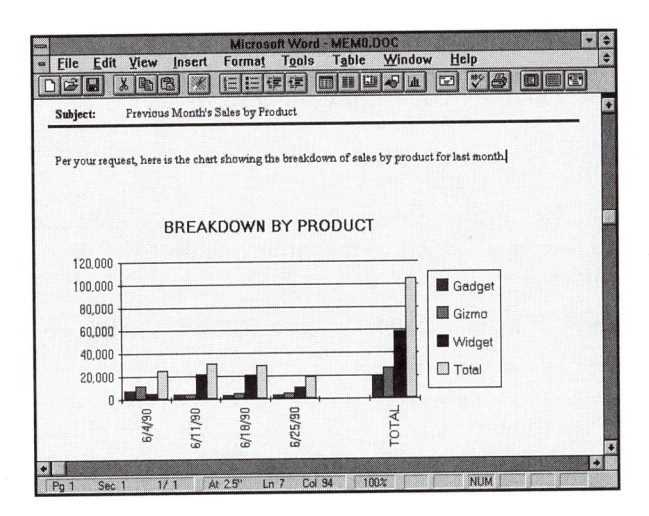

FIG. 9.9 *The embedded chart is now linked to the word memo.*

Choosing Manual Updating

By default, links are updated automatically while you have both the source and the destination files open. However, if you close the destination file—in this case MEMO.DOC—the next time you open it, you are given the option of updating the link. Figure 9.10

II — Exploring Linking and Embedding Techniques

shows the dialog box that appears just after you open the destination file. If you choose Yes, Excel starts (if it's not already running), and the chart in MEMO.DOC is updated. Choosing No leaves the chart in the same configuration as the last time you saved MEMO.DOC. Even with automatic linking in effect, you are given the choice to update or not when you reopen the linked file.

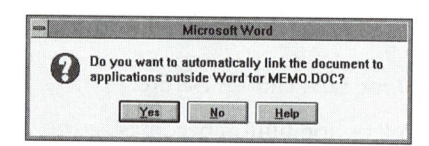

FIG. 9.10 *This dialog box appears immediately after you open a linked Word document.*

Having the option of linking automatically or manually is especially helpful when you have linked a document to several different sources. Some of the links may need to be updated regularly, while others may need updating only when you determine.

If you want to shut off automatic linking for a link, you can do so easily using the Links dialog box.

TASK: Change the link to manual updating. Next, make a change to the original Excel chart and then update the chart in MEMO.DOC.

1. With MEMO.DOC open, choose Links from the Edit menu.

    The Links dialog box appears (see fig. 9.11). If you selected a link in the document (by clicking the linked data once) before choosing Edit Link, that link is now highlighted in the Links box. When you're working in a document with several links, you can highlight multiple links in the Links dialog box by pressing the Ctrl key as you click each link.

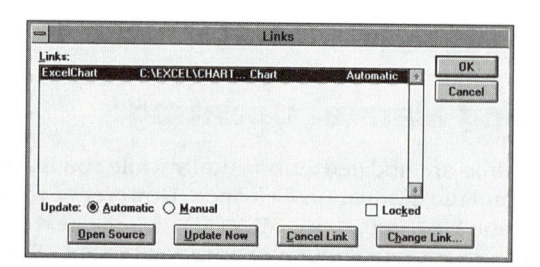

FIG. 9.11 *The Links dialog box.*

Linking an Embedded Excel Chart to a Word Memo **189**

2. Make sure that the ExcelChart chart is selected, and then choose the Manual option button. Choose OK.

3. Switch to Excel (leaving Word running) and open LINK1.XLS.

4. Change cell E7 to 95,198.

   The top figure in the chart changes from 120,000 to 100,000.

5. Switch back to Word.

   Normally, the change you just made to the chart would now show in the memo. Because you chose manual updating, however, the chart configuration still shows the old information.

6. From the Edit menu, choose Links.

   The Links dialog box appears (refer back to fig. 9.10).

7. Choose Update Now.

   The chart now shows 100,000 as the top number on the x-axis, matching the configuration of the original chart in Excel.

Reconnecting a Broken Link

Quite frequently, files are renamed or moved to a new directory. When this happens to a source file, all links to other files are broken. Suppose that the Excel source file name changes from CHART1.XLC to CHART20.XLC. When this happens, the link in the Word document will no longer be updated because Word no longer can find the source file under CHART1.XLC. Rather than remove the chart from the Word memo and start all over in Excel, you can simply change the name of the source file that Word searches for to CHART20.XLC—including the proper path.

You also can change the object that is being linked without changing the source file name. If you want to link to a new named range from the same source file, for example, you can enter the new range name in the Item box of the Change Link dialog box.

For practice, you will perform the following steps as if you were going to change the link, but you won't actually implement the change.

TASK: Reconnect a broken link by changing the source file name.

1. Click once on the link you want to change to select it.

2. From the Edit menu, choose Links.

3. In the Links dialog box (refer to fig. 9.11), choose Change Link.

   The Change Link dialog box appears (see fig. 9.12). Information for the current link is displayed in the dialog box. The application presently being linked from is displayed in the top box, the name of the source file is displayed in the File Name box, and the link object type is identified in the Item box.

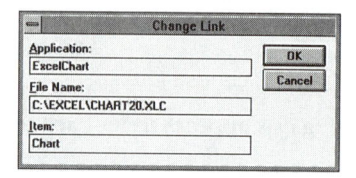

FIG. 9.12 *The Change Link dialog box.*

4. In the File Name box, change CHART1.XLC to CHART20.XLC.

5. Normally you would choose OK and the link would be reconnected, but for now choose Cancel.

Cancelling the Link

At times you may want to break a link intentionally. If you want the data from a link never to change from its present configuration, for example, you can cancel the link. When you do so, the linked data does not disappear. On the contrary, the linked information remains intact, but it no longer can be updated, which is what you want in this case.

> **NOTE** If you think that any chance exists that you may want to update the link in the future, lock the link rather than cancel it. When you lock a link, linked information does not change until you remove the lock. You can lock a link in the Links dialog box by selecting the link and then marking the Locked check box.

For practice, you will perform the following steps as if you were going to cancel the link, but you won't actually implement the cancellation.

TASK: Cancel the link to CHART1.XLC.

1. From the Edit menu, choose Links.
2. In the Links dialog box, select the ExcelChart Chart.
3. Choose Cancel Link.

   Word displays a dialog box asking you to confirm the cancellation.

4. Normally you would choose OK and the link would be cancelled, but for now choose No.

Editing the Appearance of the Chart

Editing a linked chart is quite different from editing a linked spreadsheet from Excel. Normally, you can edit a linked object directly from Word. After you double-click the linked object, Excel starts and the source file opens, which you then can edit. When you double-click a linked chart, however, only the chart itself opens, not the worksheet containing the figures the chart is based upon—the very figures you need to edit. Double-clicking on a linked chart within Word, therefore, does you no good if you want to change any of the chart's statistics; those numbers or labels can be modified only in the original worksheet in Excel.

Therefore, to edit a linked chart from Excel, you have to leave Word, start Excel, open the worksheet file containing the data used to generate the chart—in this case LINK1.XLS—and then edit the worksheet figures. After you modify the figures, the chart in Word will change to reflect the new information after it is updated either automatically or manually, depending on how you defined updating.

On the other hand, if you want to change the appearance of the chart—not numbers or labels—you can do this directly from Word. For example, if you want to change font styles and sizes, text orientation, the legend, the title, background patterns, and so on, you can do so without leaving Word. Figure 9.13 shows the changes that were made to the chart directly from Word.

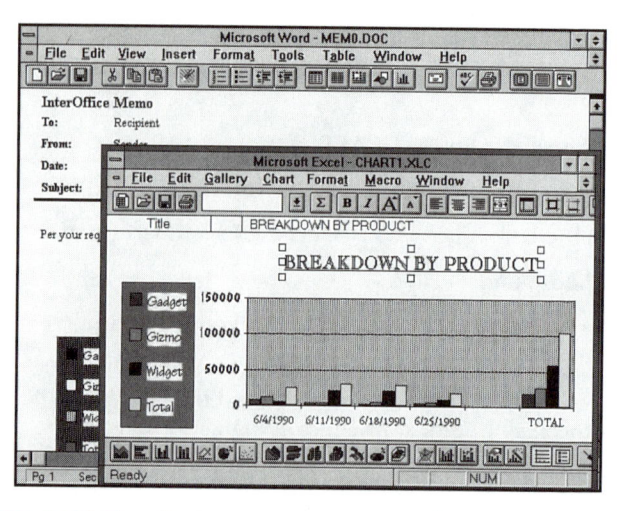

192 II — Exploring Linking and Embedding Techniques

FIG. 9.13 *The edited chart.*

TASK: Edit the background pattern and other features of the chart from within Word.

1. Double-click anywhere on the chart in Word.

   A pause occurs as Excel is started and the source file, CHART1.XLC, is opened. You may be asked whether you want to update remote references. If so, choose Yes. An Excel application window now appears on the upper right side of the screen, and then a document window containing CHART.XLC opens inside of the application window (see fig. 9.14).

2. Click on the middle of the chart so that the graph itself is selected (the graph will become outlined with small boxes).

3. Double-click on the selected graph.

   The Patterns dialog box appears on-screen (see fig. 9.15). From this dialog box, you can make changes to the text, title, legend, and background of the chart.

4. Click Background to display a drop-down list of choices (refer to fig. 9.15).

5. Choose the pattern you desire and then choose OK.

   The pattern you chose now fills the background of the graph.

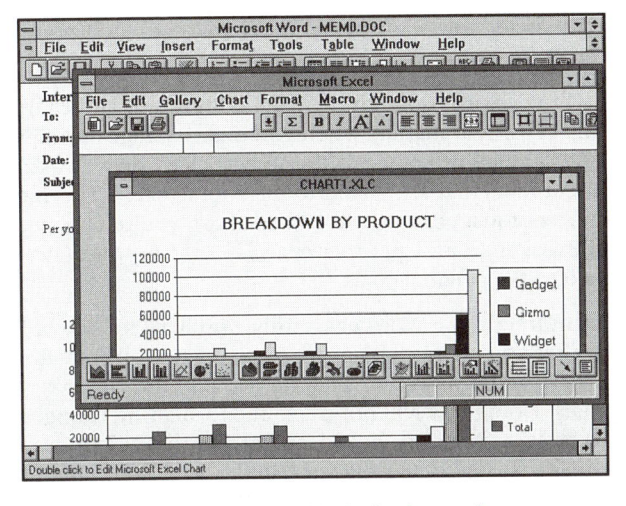

Linking an Embedded Excel Chart to a Word Memo **193**

FIG. 9.14 *Excel opens with Word in the background.*

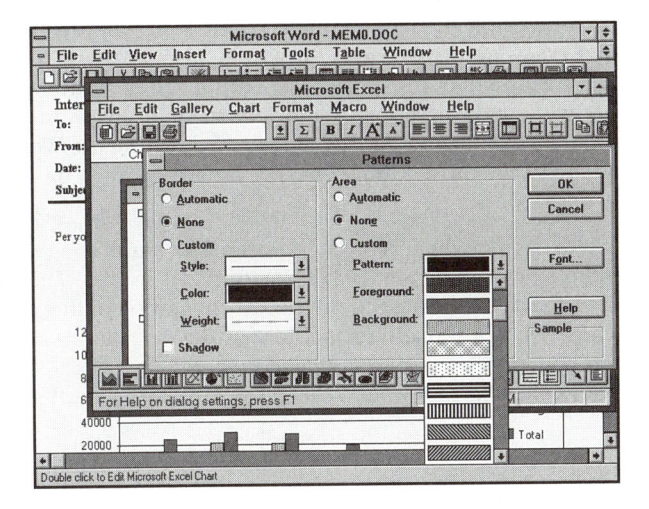

FIG. 9.15 *The Patterns dialog box.*

6. Make any other changes to the chart that you desire, following the examples in figure 9.15, if you want.

7. Click on the Minimize button in the Excel application window to exit Excel and return to the Word chart. Excel asks you whether you want to save changes to the chart. Choose Yes.

All changes you made to the Excel chart are incorporated in the Word chart.

You need to consider something when editing a linked chart, or other object for that matter. When you make changes from within Word, the changes are made to the source chart, as well as all other documents that are linked to the source chart. This means that you're not just changing the Word chart, you're changing the original Excel chart and all other charts in other applications that are linked to the original chart.

If you want to edit the Word chart only, you have to lock or break the link after you make changes to the Excel chart from within Word. Then, when you quit Excel, do not save the changes to the Excel chart. Doing this will not cause the formatting changes in Word to be lost. You also should realize that this will prevent statistical changes from being reflected in the Word chart because it is locked.

You should consider something else: if you do not break the link, and new formatting changes are made to the Excel chart within Excel that eradicate the previous formatting, the next time the Word chart is updated, the former formatting will be gone— replaced by the most recent modifications made in Excel. In other words, all of the time and effort you spent formatting the Word chart was in vain—those format changes are wiped away by the new changes.

You have to decide which is more important to you: having the latest figures or keeping the fancy formatting. Of course, if all of the linked charts can appear in the same format, no conflict occurs. When you want to add special formatting to only one chart, however, you sacrifice having the most recent figures because you have to lock the chart in order to keep the formatting in effect.

Summary

This tutorial taught you how to link a chart embedded in an Excel worksheet to a memo created in Word. Refer back to the steps presented in this chapter to establish, cancel, and edit links of this type until you can accomplish these tasks on your own.

For more information on using the programs Excel 4.0 for Windows and Word for Windows 2.0, refer to Que's *Using Excel 4 for Windows,* Special Edition, and *Using Word for Windows 2,* Special Edition.

CHAPTER TEN

Embedding Word in an Excel Worksheet

You worked with embedding briefly in Chapter 8 when you embedded a linked package from WordPerfect into Ami Pro via the Object Packager. You don't need to use the Object Packager each time you want to embed an object, however. You used the Object Packager to create a link from WordPerfect to Ami Pro because WordPerfect does not support OLE, and unless a server application supports OLE, the Object Packager must be used to create the link.

As you learned in Chapter 9, both Word and Excel support OLE—Excel as a server and Word as a client. During this lesson, you discover that the opposite also holds true—Excel serves as an OLE client, and Word as an OLE server. This makes linking and embedding trouble-free between Word and Excel because you don't have to figure out if the applications support OLE, and in the right role (as server and client).

You may find it helpful to briefly review the difference between OLE linking and OLE embedding. When you link an object, ties remain between the source document and the object in the destination document. If you change the source document, the destination document changes accordingly. Likewise, if you change the destination document, the source document changes accordingly. On the other hand, when you embed an object, no ties remain between the source document and the destination document. If you change the source document, no changes are made to the destination document. Likewise, if you change the destination document, no changes are made to the source document.

When you embed an object, the object's entire file is placed right into the destination document. The embedded object stands on its own as an editable file. Like a linked object, you can fully edit the information, but any changes you make will not affect the source document.

What is the point of embedding then? Doesn't ordinary copying from the Clipboard do as much? Not at all. You do get a copy of the object in the destination document when you use regular Clipboard methods, but you cannot edit this object the same way you can when you embed. In some situations, you cannot edit the imported object at all. The distinct difference is that when you edit an embedded object, you use the original application to make the modifications, not the application into which you've embedded the object. Just the opposite is true when you copy an object from the Clipboard in the ordinary fashion.

Suppose that you're working in Word and you embed an Excel worksheet into the current document. When you double-click on the worksheet to edit it, Excel starts and you can make full use of Excel's sophisticated spreadsheet functions and commands to edit the worksheet data (even though you're currently in Word). If you simply copy the worksheet into the Word document, however, you have to use Word's inferior table functions to edit the worksheet data.

Embedding gives you an object that you can edit using the powerful, specialized resources of the original (server) application. You can make any changes you want to the object without having those changes applied to the original object in the source document.

You can embed an object from two locations. If you have not yet created the object you want to embed into the current document, you should start from the destination (current) document. If the object you want to embed already exists, you should start from the source document. During this tutorial, you first will practice embedding an entire Word document starting from Excel. Later, you will embed only part of a Word document starting from Word.

You can embed a Word object in Excel in different ways. First of all, you can embed the object using Excel's Insert Object command. Second, you can start from Word, copy the material to be embedded, and then use Excel's Paste Special command to embed the data. Third, you can use the mouse to embed a packaged object. You make use of the first two methods during this lesson. In the next chapter, you will use the mouse to embed a packaged object.

Embedding Word in an Excel Worksheet **197**

The goals of this lesson are as follows:

- To embed an entire Word document into an Excel worksheet
- To embed part of a Word document into an Excel worksheet

To achieve these goals, you will perform the following tasks:

Goal 1

- Set up the Excel worksheet into which you will embed the two Word documents.
- Use the Insert Object command to embed the first document into Excel, and then type the document.
- Save and then close the Word document (leaving Word running) and return to Excel.
- Embed the second Word document into the Excel worksheet.
- Edit the second embedded Word document.
- Detach the first embedded object from the worksheet cells.
- Prevent the second embedded object from printing.
- Print the contents of the second embedded object in the Excel worksheet.
- Delete the second embedded object.

Goal 2

- Copy the data you want to embed into Excel from Word to the Clipboard.
- Prepare CHARD293.XLS to receive the copied data.
- Embed part of CONVINFO.DOC into CHARD293.XLS.

Embedding an Entire Word Document into an Excel Worksheet

Suppose that you work in the marketing department of a large winery. In your office, rough drafts are reviewed on disk in an effort to curb the escalating paper waste and to lessen the amount of time spent on file management. Your boss has asked you to submit a revised Chardonnay price list and a promotional letter that will accompany the price list and sample wine distributed to selected wine writers. You have come up with two distinct approaches for the letter and want to present them both to your boss so that she can determine which angle to take. Rather than send her three separate files, you send her the one Excel worksheet file containing the price list, and then embed the two Word letters below the worksheet data.

Setting Up the Excel Worksheet

As mentioned earlier, when you plan to embed a Word document that has not already been created, you should begin in Excel.

TASK: Set up the Excel worksheet into which you will embed the two Word documents.

1. Start Excel (if it is not already running) and open a new worksheet.

2. Set up a few rows of data similar to those in figure 10.1.

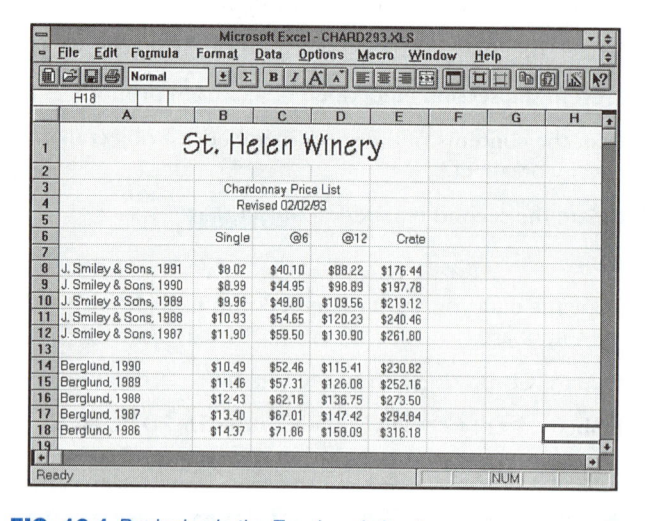

FIG. 10.1 *Beginning in the Excel worksheet.*

3. From the File menu, choose Save and save the file as CHARD293.XLS.

4. A few rows beneath the last row of data, type the following phrase in an A column cell (see fig. 10.2):

   Click this to read a conventional promotional letter...

Embedding Word in an Excel Worksheet **199**

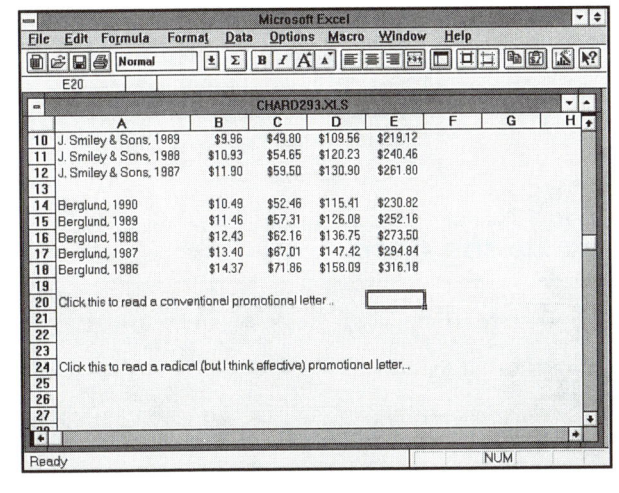

FIG. 10.2 *Introducing the embedded objects.*

5. Skip three rows and then type the following phrase in an A column cell:

    Click this to read a radical (but I think effective) promotional letter...

Embedding the First Document

TASK: Use the Insert Object command to embed the first document into Excel. Then type the document.

1. Place the cell pointer in the cell to the right of the first phrase you entered in the last task (refer to fig. 10.2).

2. From the Edit menu, choose Insert Object. The Insert Object dialog box appears (see fig. 10.3).

    This dialog box shows a list of all the applications installed on your system that support OLE as servers. The Windows accessories OLE servers, Package, Paintbrush Picture, and Sound, will always appear in this box.

3. Choose Word Document, and then choose OK.

    Word starts and Document1 opens (see fig. 10.4). You are now ready to begin typing the letter.

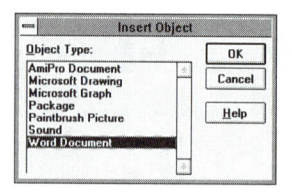

II — Exploring Linking and Embedding Techniques

FIG. 10.3 *The Insert Object dialog box.*

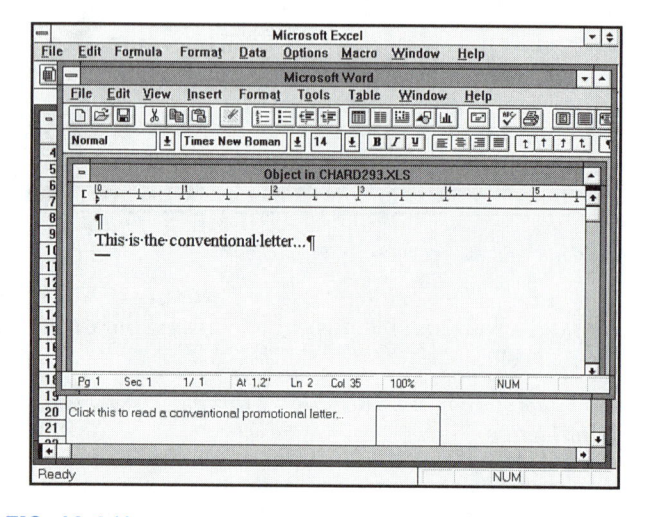

FIG. 10.4 *You now can create the document in Word.*

4. For the purposes of this lesson, type the following phrase (refer to fig. 10.4):

   This is the conventional letter...

Returning to the Excel Worksheet

After you finish creating the document in Word, you can exit back to Excel in three different ways:

- Choosing Exit from the Word File menu closes the document and Word. Windows asks you whether you want to update the embedded object. This method takes longer, and if you want to edit an embedded Word object again, accessing the embedded object takes longer because Windows has to start up Word all over again. Use this method if you know you will not edit an embedded Word object again during your work session.

- Choosing Close from the Word File menu closes the document only—Word continues to run. Windows asks you whether you want to update the embedded object. This method takes less time to return to Excel and to reopen an embedded Word object because Word is still running. Use this method if you aren't sure whether you will need to edit an embedded Word object during your work session, or if you will be editing more than one object.

- Clicking the Word Minimize button leaves the document open and Word running. You are not asked whether you want to update the embedded object because the document remains open (when you exit Excel, however, you are asked then whether you want to update the object). This is the fastest way to switch back and forth between Excel and Word. Use this method if you plan to edit the same embedded Word object frequently during your current work session.

TASK: Save and then close the Word document (leaving Word running) and return to Excel.

1. From the Word File menu, choose Save As.

   The Save As dialog box appears. If you want to save this document in a Word directory, move through the directory tree to select the desired Word directory.

   > **NOTE** You do not have to save the embedded object apart from the Excel worksheet. If you want a separate copy of the document in a Word directory that will not be changed when you make changes to the Excel embedded object, however, then you must use the File Save command now to retain a copy of the document in its current configuration in Word.

2. After you select the correct Word directory, type *embed1.doc* for the file name.

3. From the File menu, choose Close.

   A dialog box appears asking you whether you want to update the embedded object (see fig. 10.5). Your choice here is very significant. If you choose Yes, all the work you just performed in the Word document is saved to the embedded Excel object. If you choose No, nothing you have done is remembered by Excel, and if you didn't already save the object separately as a Word file, all your work is lost. By choosing Cancel, you return to the document where you can resume your work.

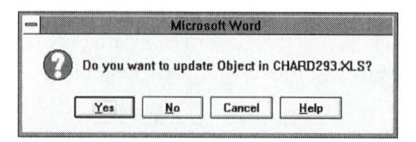

FIG. 10.5 *This box prompts you to update the embedded object.*

4. In the message box, choose Yes.

   The document closes, Word disappears (although it is still running in the background), and you are returned to the Excel worksheet, where an icon for the embedded object appears (see fig. 10.6).

FIG. 10.6 *The embedded object in CHARDXLS.DOC.*

Embedding the Second Document

Now that you have had some practice, embedding the second Word document should run more smoothly.

TASK: Embed the second Word document into the Excel worksheet.

1. In the Excel worksheet, move the cell pointer to the right of the phrase that introduces the second embedded object.
2. From the Edit menu, choose Insert Object.
3. In the Insert Object dialog box, choose Word Document, and then choose OK.
4. In Word Document1, type the following phrase:

   This is the radical letter...

5. From the Word File menu, choose Save.
6. In the Save As dialog box, select the appropriate Word directory, and then enter *embed2.doc* as the file name.
7. Click the Word Minimize button.

   You minimize Word rather than close the document because in a moment you're going to edit the embedded object.

8. Click the Excel Minimize button.

   Notice that both Word and Excel are represented by icons at the bottom of the desktop, letting you know that both programs currently are running. Had you chosen File Close, the Word application window would still be open, but hidden behind the Excel worksheet; had you chosen File Exit, Word would be shut down altogether.

9. Double-click the Word icon to restore Word, and then double-click the Excel icon to restore the Excel worksheet.

Editing an Embedded Object

An embedded object is not linked to any source document. If a source document does exist—remember, you can create an embedded object in Excel that is never saved as a Word file—any changes you make to the embedded object are not reflected in the source document.

You can edit an embedded object in two ways: You can double-click the object or click the object once with the right mouse button (keeping the button depressed) to display an Excel short menu, from which you choose Edit Object.

204 *II — Exploring Linking and Embedding Techniques*

TASK: Edit the second embedded Word document.

1. With the *right* (or nonprimary) mouse button, click the second object (named Picture 2 on the Excel status bar) to display the menu shown in figure 10.7.

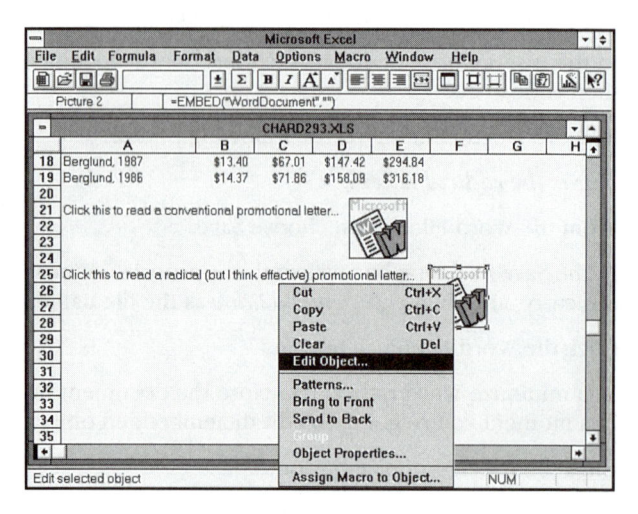

FIG. 10.7 *The Excel short menu for objects.*

2. Choose Edit Object.

   The embedded document is displayed inside the Word application window (see fig. 10.8).

3. Make any changes to the document you want.

4. From the Word File menu, choose Close.

5. When asked whether you want to update the embedded object, choose Yes.

   Word becomes hidden behind Excel, and you are returned to the Excel worksheet.

Setting Object Properties

You can move an object at any time just by dragging it to a new location. You also can change an object's size by clicking the object once and then dragging the sizing handles in different directions until you achieve the size you want. Neither of these changes affect the position of any cells in the worksheet. But the reverse might not hold true. If you change the position or size of certain cells in the worksheet, the object may change accordingly (depending on how the properties are configured). If you insert rows above an object, for example, by default that object will move down to make room for the inserted rows.

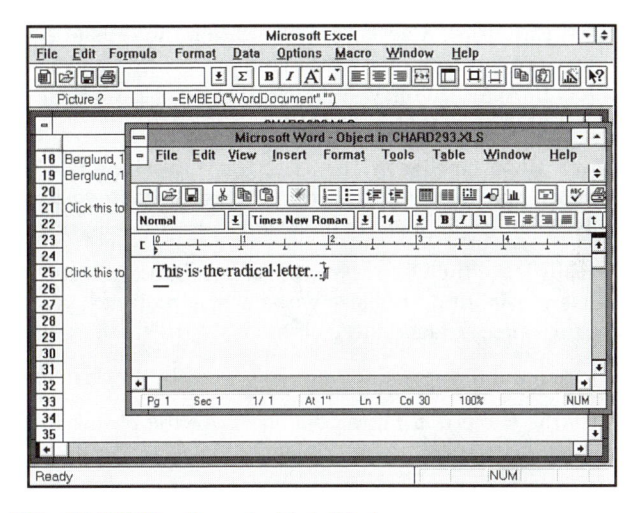

FIG. 10.8 *Editing the embedded object.*

However, you ensure that objects are completely unaffected by the changes that are made to cells. The Object Properties dialog box (see fig. 10.9) enables you to determine how objects are attached to cells, which becomes significant, of course, when you move or size cells. By default, objects move but do not size with cells. However, if you want to fix the object relative to the cells it occupies so that when the cells change size the object changes as well, you can attach an object to its underlying cells. Then, when you size the underlying cells, the object changes size accordingly.

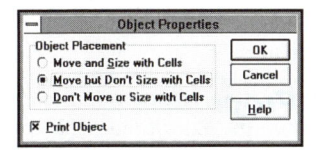

FIG. 10.9 *The Object Properties dialog box.*

The following list briefly explains each of the Object Placement options in the Object Properties dialog box:

- **Move And Size With Cells.** When the cells under the object's upper left and lower right corners change their position and size, the object changes along with the cells.

- **Move But Don't Size With Cells.** When the cells under the object's upper left corner change their position and size, the object moves with the cells under its upper left corner, but does not change size.

- **Don't Move Or Size With Cells.** The object maintains its position and size regardless of changes to the underlying cells because the object is detached from the cell grid.

You normally leave the Object Properties configuration as is so that objects move but do not size with cells. Sometimes, you may not want the object attached to cells at all.

TASK: Detach the first embedded object from the worksheet cells.

1. Place the cell pointer immediately above the phrase introducing the first embedded object.

2. From the Edit menu, choose Insert.

3. In the Insert dialog box, choose Entire Row, and then choose OK.

   Notice that when the row is added, both objects move down a row accordingly.

4. Click the right mouse button on the first embedded object to display the short menu.

5. Choose Object Properties.

   The Object Properties dialog box appears (refer back to fig. 10.9).

6. Choose Don't Move Or Size With Cells, and then choose OK.

7. Repeat steps 1 through 3.

This time the object doesn't move down a row (if you missed this, choose Repeat Insert from the Edit menu as many times as necessary until the object's lack of movement becomes apparent). Notice, however, that the second object continues to move with the cells. This reminds you that each object's properties are entirely independent from the properties of all other objects in the worksheet.

Preventing an Object from Printing

You may have noticed the Print Object option in the Object Properties dialog box. By default, objects print when the worksheet is printed. You can deselect the Print Object option, however, so that the objects do not show on the printout.

> **NOTE** Printing an object does not refer to printing an object's contents! It refers only to printing the icon which represents the object.

TASK: Prevent the second embedded object from printing.

1. Hold down the right mouse button on the second embedded object to display the short menu.

2. Choose Object Properties.

   The Object Properties dialog box appears (refer back to fig. 10.9).

3. Choose Print Object to deselect this option, and then choose OK.

4. Print the file.

   The icon representing the first embedded object does not appear on the printout; the icon for the second object does appear, as long as your printer can print graphics.

Printing an Embedded Object

You use Word, not Excel, print commands to print the contents of an embedded object.

TASK: Print the contents of the second embedded object in the Excel worksheet.

1. Double-click the second embedded object so that the document opens within Word.

2. From the Word File menu, choose Print.

   The Print dialog box appears. You can choose Current Page or print only a few of the object's pages, just as you would any normal Word document.

3. Choose OK.

A dialog box appears telling you that printing is in progress. Notice that this dialog box identifies the object as `Object in CHARD293.XLS`, reminding you that you're not printing an ordinary Word document.

Deleting an Embedded Object

You may assume that you can delete an embedded object simply by selecting it and then pressing the Del key. You assume correctly. This isn't the only way, however, that you can delete an object.

TASK: Delete the second embedded object.

1. Click once on the second embedded object to select it.
2. From the Edit menu, choose Clear.

   or

   Hold down the right mouse button on the second embedded object to display the short menu.

3. Choose Clear.

Embedding Part of a Word Document into an Excel Worksheet

Because the document you want to embed into Excel already exists this time, you will start the process from Word rather than Excel. You will discover that the process differs a bit from the one you just learned, starting from Excel.

Copying the Existing Data in Word

For the purpose of this lesson, you will copy part of a file that already exists in Word—CONVINFO.DOC. This way, you don't have to type any text.

TASK: Copy the data you want to embed into Excel from Word to the Clipboard.

1. Start Word if it is not already running.
2. From the File menu, choose Open.
3. In the Open dialog box, select CONVINFO.DOC.

4. Select the following part of the document, as in the example in figure 10.10:

   Highlight from the first word in the document to "WordPerfect versions 5.0 and 5.1," located in the middle of the bulleted list.

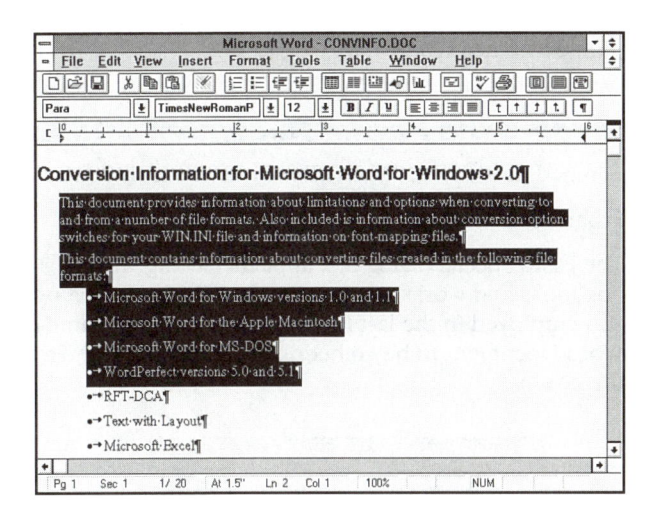

FIG. 10.10 *Copying part of CONVINFO.DOC.*

5. From the Edit menu, choose Copy.

   The selected data is copied to the Clipboard, ready to be embedded into Excel.

6. Click the Minimize button, but do not close Word.

Preparing the Excel Worksheet

When you embed beginning in Excel, you use the Insert Object command, as you learned earlier. Because the data you want to embed is located already on the Clipboard, you now use the Paste Special command to embed the data.

TASK: Prepare CHARD293.XLS to receive the copied data.

1. Start Excel if it's not already running.

2. Open the same file you used in the last tutorial: CHARD293.XLS.

II — Exploring Linking and Embedding Techniques

3. Place the cell pointer in the B column a few rows below the last embedded object and type the following phrase (refer to fig. 10.12):

   Here is part of the CONVINFO.DOC document embedded in the Excel worksheet.

4. Place the cell pointer in the A column to the left of the phrase you just typed.

Embedding the Partial Document into Excel

TASK: Embed part of CONVINFO.DOC into CHARD293.XLS.

1. From the Edit menu, choose Paste Special.

   The Paste Special dialog box appears (see fig. 10.11). This box looks and works similar to the Insert Object dialog box you employed in the last lesson. Notice that the name of the Word Document to be embedded is identified at the top of the box.

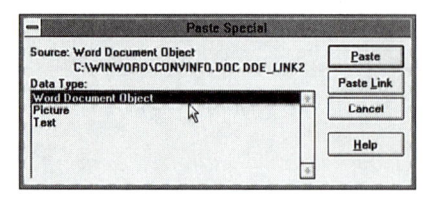

   FIG. 10.11 *The Paste Special dialog box.*

2. Because Word Document Object is highlighted already, simply choose OK.

   A new object appears in the Worksheet, containing the embedded data (see fig. 10.12).

3. To verify that the data was copied correctly, double-click the newly embedded object.

   Word is opened and Excel moves to the background. The data you copied from CONVINFO.DOC is placed inside Object in CHARD293.XLS in the Word application window (see fig. 10.13).

Embedding Word in an Excel Worksheet **211**

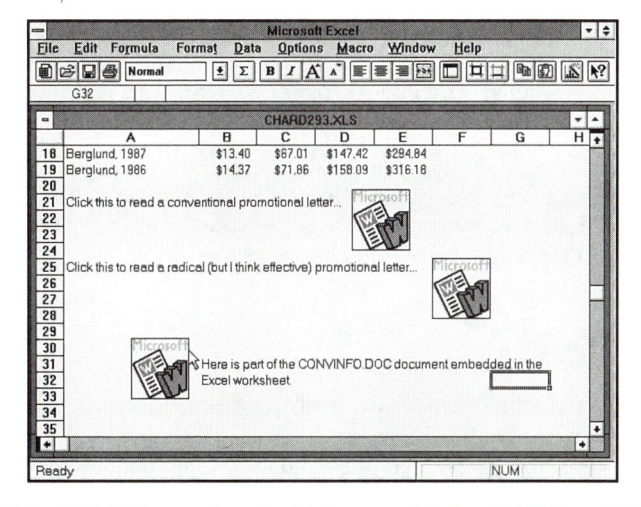

FIG. 10.12 *The data is embedded successfully into CHARD293.XLS.*

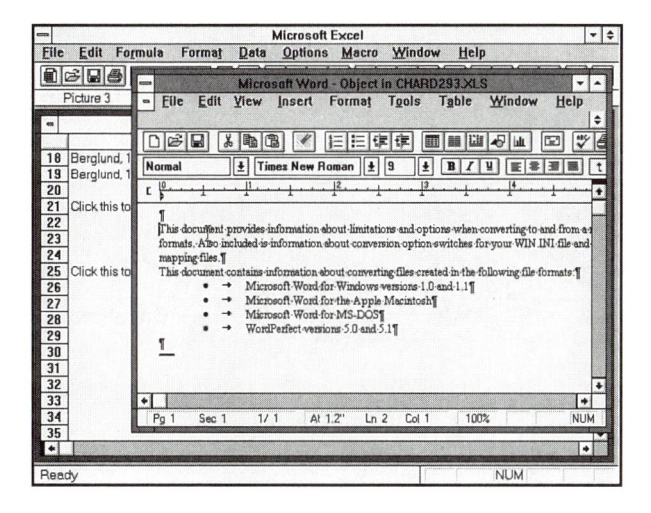

FIG. 10.13 *Viewing the embedded data.*

4. From the Word File menu, choose Exit.

5. You are asked whether you want to update the embedded object. Make sure that you choose Yes or else the data will not be embedded into the worksheet.

6. You are asked if you want to save changes to CONVINFO.DOC. Because all you did was highlight some data, whether you choose Yes or No makes no difference . If you had made changes to CONVINFO.DOC that you didn't want remembered, however, you would choose No here.

You can edit, set object properties for, print, and delete the embedded partial document following the same procedures outlined earlier for the embedded full documents.

Summary

This tutorial taught you how to embed a whole Word document and only part of a Word document into an Excel worksheet. Refer back to the steps presented in this chapter to embed, edit, and print Word objects in Excel until you can accomplish these tasks on your own.

For more information on using these programs, refer to Que's *Using Word for Windows 2*, Special Edition, and *Using Excel 4 for Windows*, Special Edition.

CHAPTER ELEVEN

Embedding a Harvard Graphics Presentation in Quattro Pro

Embedding objects is most useful when you are submitting reports as disk files rather than printouts. When you embed an object, you cannot print the embedded information as part of the document in which it is embedded. If you want to print the document and the embedded object, you have to print both separately. Additionally, an icon represents the embedded object in the document; in order to see the object in its entirety (for example, a spreadsheet, a slide presentation, another document), you must start the original application to do so. In other words, you cannot view the embedded object without opening the application used to create it.

What is the point of embedding then? Embedding enables you to open an object created with another application without having to leave the application in which you're currently working. In other words, you are launching another application on top of the one you are using. By double-clicking the embedded icon, you start the application used to create the embedded object. Embedding gives you access to the embedded object without having to leave the current application, start another application, and search for the object you want to edit. This can save a lot of time if you work with two or more related files in separate applications.

If you submit reports, proposals, presentations, and such on disk, using embedded objects can be helpful if the submission contains documents created in separate applications. Rather than submit separate files, you can send one main document with embedded subdocuments. Suppose that you're submitting a proposal created in Ami Pro that includes a Harvard Graphics 1.0 for Windows slide presentation and a Quattro Pro for Windows notebook. Rather than send three separate files, you can embed the slide presentation and the notebook into the main body of the proposal, introducing each embedded object with a sentence like "Double-click the film icon to view a slide presentation," or "Double-click the pie icon for a complete breakdown of product revenues." **You must keep in mind, however, that the person reviewing the proposal must have Harvard Graphics and Quattro Pro installed on his system in order to review the embedded objects.** You cannot open an embedded object unless the application used to create the object is installed on your system.

To embed an object in a document, that document's application must be an OLE client. An OLE client is simply an application that can receive OLE links and embedded objects. The application of the object you want to embed does not need to support OLE. Embedding is simpler if the application does support OLE as a server (meaning that it can send information to another application); however, you can still embed if it doesn't by using the Windows File Manager and Object Packager.

Harvard Graphics is not an OLE server, but Quattro Pro is an OLE client. This means that you can embed a Harvard Graphics document in a Quattro Pro notebook, but you have to use the File Manager and Object Packager to do so. If Harvard Graphics were an OLE server, you would not need to use the File Manager or Object Packager. (For more on embedding objects, refer to Chapter 10, "Embedding Word in an Excel Worksheet.")

The goal of this lesson is as follows:

- Embed a Harvard Graphics slide presentation in a Quattro Pro notebook.

To achieve this goal, you perform the following tasks:

- Prepare LESSON6.WB1 to receive the embedded object.
- Embed QSTART.PRS in the Quattro Pro file LESSON6.WB1.
- Assign a new icon to the embedded object.

Embedding a Harvard Graphics Presentation in Quattro Pro **215**

- Change the object's label to make the name more descriptive.
- Paste the object's icon and label into LESSON6.WB1. Then adjust the size of the icon and label, making the object larger.
- View the contents of the embedded object.
- Delete the embedded object.

Preparing the Quattro Pro Notebook

To save time, you use an existing Quattro Pro file for this exercise.

TASK: Prepare LESSON6.WB1 to receive the embedded object.

1. Start Quattro Pro if it isn't already running.
2. From the File menu, choose Open.
3. Select LESSON6.WB1 and then choose OK.

    LESSON6.WB1 opens, looking similar to figure 11.1.

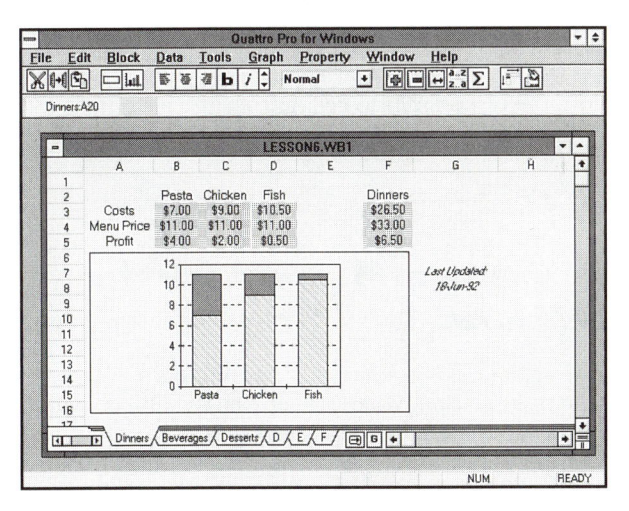

FIG. 11.1 *The LESSON6.WB1 notebook file.*

4. Move the cell pointer to cell A18.

5. Following the example in figure 11.2, enter the following phrase:

   Please double-click the icon below to view a slide presentation of our proposal.

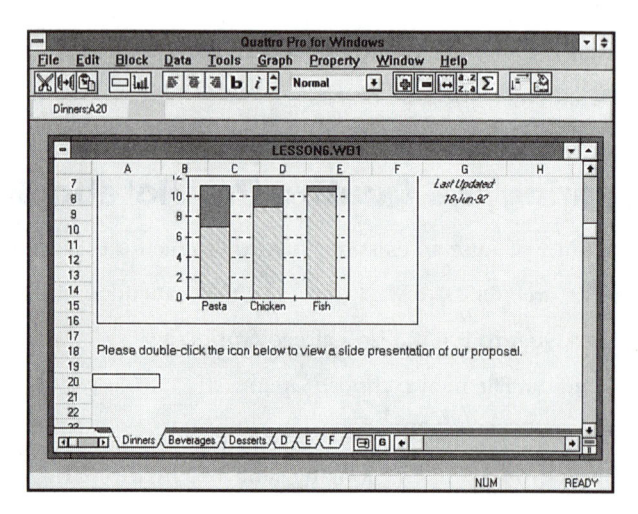

FIG. 11.2 *Introducing the embedded object.*

6. Move the cell pointer to cell A20.

   You are now ready to embed the Harvard Graphics document.

Embedding the Harvard Graphics Presentation

Harvard Graphics does not have to be running in order for you to embed the presentation. When you embed the object, Windows will start Harvard Graphics at that time.

Again to save time, you use an existing Harvard Graphics presentation for this exercise.

TASK: Embed QSTART.PRS in the Quattro Pro file LESSON6.WB1.

1. From the Edit menu, choose Insert Object.

   The Insert New Object dialog box appears (see fig. 11.3). The applications listed in the Object Type box depend upon what

Embedding a Harvard Graphics Presentation in Quattro Pro

applications are installed on your system. All applications on your system that are OLE servers are listed in the box. Because Harvard Graphics is not an OLE server, it is not listed in the Object Type box. Therefore, you must embed a package. If you were embedding an object from an OLE server application, such as Paintbrush, you could embed the object directly (without using the Object Packager).

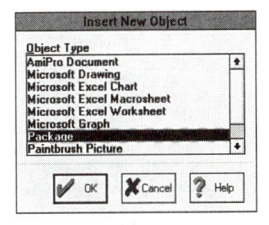

FIG. 11.3 *The Insert New Object dialog box.*

2. Select Package and then choose OK.

   Windows opens an Object Packager application window on top of the Quattro Pro application window (see fig. 11.4). Remember, the Object Packager application window consists of two sub-windows: an Appearance window on the left, and a Content window on the right. By default, the Content window is active when Object packager starts. A window is active when its title (Appearance or Content) is highlighted. Just click anywhere in a window to make that window active.

   The title bar at the top of the Object Packager application window displays the name of the application and file receiving the embedded object.

3. From the Object Packager File menu, choose Import.

   The Import dialog box appears (see fig. 11.5). Use this box to select the file you want to embed.

4. In the Directories scroll box, double-click the C:\ root directory, then the HGW directory, and finally the PRES subdirectory (refer to fig. 11.5).

   You may have to take an alternate path if your PRES subdirectory is located in a different location.

5. In the File Name scroll box, click QSTART.PRS, and then choose OK.

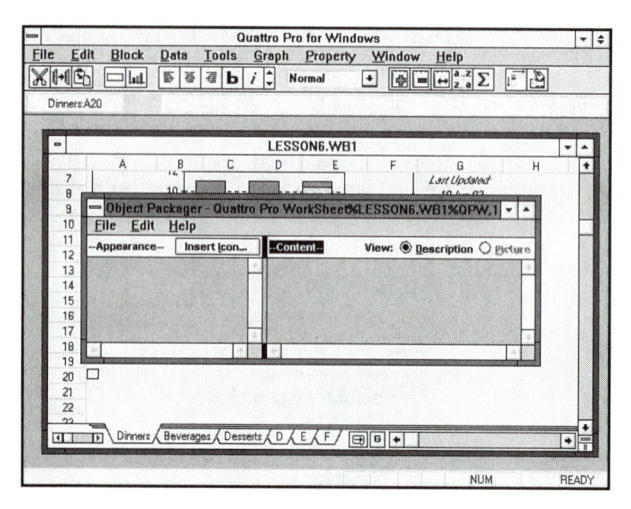

218 *II — Exploring Linking and Embedding Techniques*

FIG. 11.4 *The Object Packager application window.*

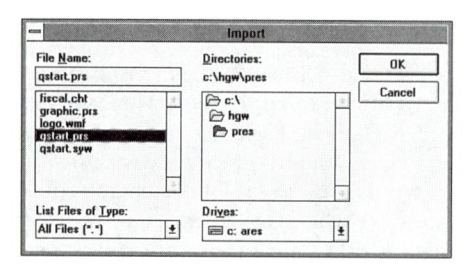

FIG. 11.5 *The Import dialog box.*

You are returned to the Object Packager (see fig. 11.6). The Content window displays the name of the file to be embedded. The Appearance window contains an icon and a label representing the embedded object. You can change both the icon and the label if you want.

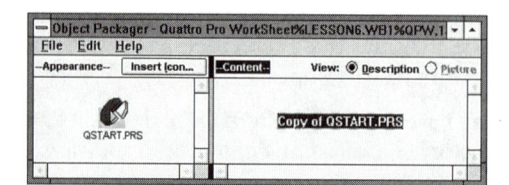

FIG. 11.6 *The file to be embedded is copied to the Object Packager window.*

Changing the Label

By default, the Object Packager labels the object with the name of the file to be embedded. You may want to make the label more descriptive. For example, if the slide presentation you are embedding is for a company named Restaurants Ltd., you can change the label so that it clearly identifies the contents of the object—such as "Restaurants Ltd. Slide Presentation."

TASK: Change the object's label to make the name more descriptive.

1. Click anywhere in the Appearance window.

   The Appearance window becomes active and the embedded icon and label are selected (see fig. 11.7).

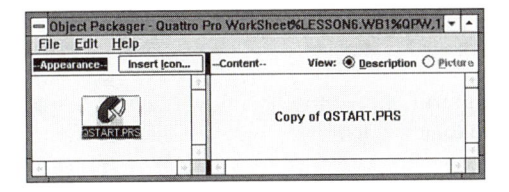

   FIG. 11.7 *The selected icon and label.*

2. From the Object Packager Edit menu, choose Label.

   The Label dialog box appears (see fig. 11.8). The Label box displays the name of the file to be embedded.

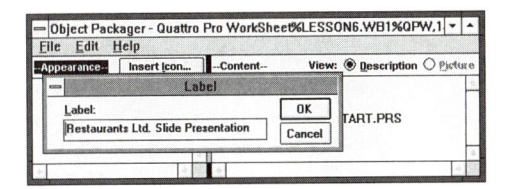

   FIG. 11.8 *The Label dialog box.*

3. In the Label box, type *Restaurants Ltd. Slide Presentation*, and then choose OK.

   You are returned to the Object Packager window. The new label appears in the Appearance window (see fig. 11.9).

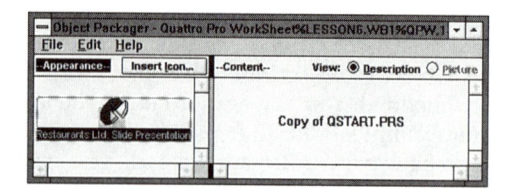

II — Exploring Linking and Embedding Techniques

FIG. 11.9 *The object's new label.*

Changing the Icon

By default, Object Packager assigns the icon associated with the application being embedded to the new object. Most executable files (EXE files) have an associated icon. You can assign any executable file's icon to the embedded object. For example, if you want an icon showing a printer, you can use the PRINTMAN.EXE icon.

Make sure that the Appearance window is active before you attempt to change the icon.

TASK: Assign a new icon to the embedded object.

1. In the Appearance window, choose the Insert Icon option button.

   The Insert Icon dialog box appears (see fig. 11.10). Because you are embedding a document from Harvard Graphics, the Harvard Graphics executable file (HGW.EXE) appears in the File Name box, and two icons associated with Harvard Graphics are displayed in the Current Icon box. Although only Harvard Graphics icons are showing now, you can use the icon(s) associated with any executable file. Most executable file's have only one icon (some don't have any). For the best selection of icons, choose the Program Manager's executable file (PROGMAN.EXE). You can choose from dozens of icons when you select this file. (If you're running Norton Desktop for Windows, choose NDW.DLL for a huge selection of icons.)

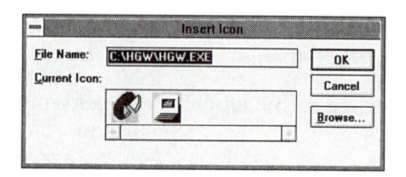

FIG. 11.10 *The Insert Icon dialog box.*

# Embedding a Harvard Graphics Presentation in Quattro Pro 221

2. Choose the Browse option button.

    The Browse dialog box appears (see fig. 11.11).

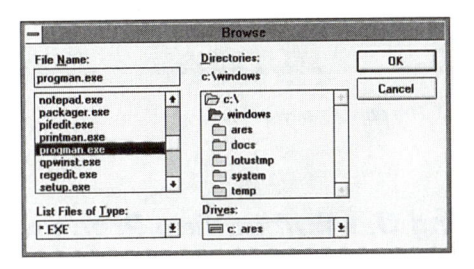

    FIG. 11.11 *The Browse dialog box.*

3. In the Directories scroll box, double-click the C:\ root directory and then the WINDOWS directory.

4. In the File Name scroll box, click PROGMAN.EXE, and then choose OK.

    Windows returns you to the Insert Icon dialog box (see fig. 11.12). The new file name, C:\WINDOWS\PROGMAN.EXE, appears in the File Name box. Also, a completely new selection of icons fills the Current Icon box.

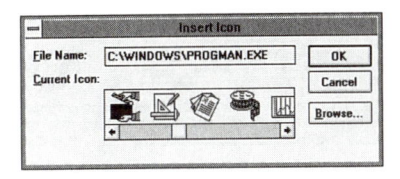

    FIG. 11.12 *The new selection of icons.*

5. In the Current Icon box, scroll though the selection of icons until you see the reel of film (second icon from the right in fig. 11.12), and then select this icon. The icon becomes highlighted.

6. Choose OK.

    The Object Packager now displays the new icon (see fig. 11.13).

You are now ready to paste the package into the Quattro Pro notebook.

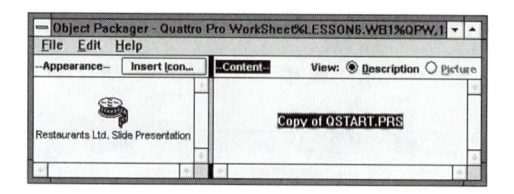

II — Exploring Linking and Embedding Techniques

FIG. 11.13 *The object's new icon.*

Completing the Embedding Process

At this point, all you need to do is paste the object into Quattro Pro and the job is done. At times you may want to adjust the size of the object so that it is smaller, larger, or located in a new place. Doing so is very easy.

TASK: Paste the object's icon and label into LESSON6.WB1. Then adjust the size of the icon and label, making the object larger.

1. From Quattro Pro's Edit menu, choose Paste.

    The Object Packager (still running) disappears behind the Quattro Pro application window. The object is embedded into the workbook (see fig. 11.14).

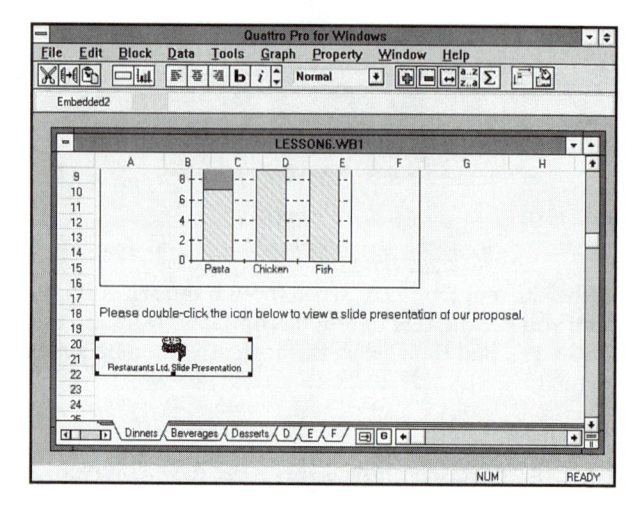

FIG. 11.14 *The embedded object.*

Embedding a Harvard Graphics Presentation in Quattro Pro   223

2. Drag the object's sizing handles to the right and down so that the object fills cells A20 to F24 (see fig. 11.15).

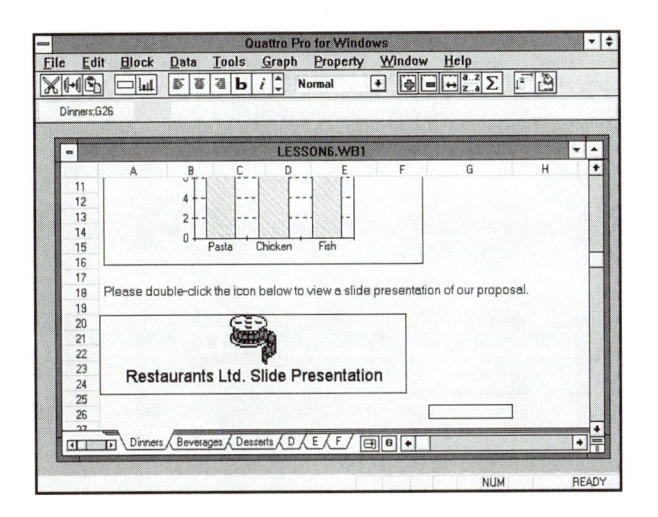

FIG. 11.15 *The new object size.*

Viewing the Embedded Object

So far you haven't even seen the file you embedded. This serves as a good reminder that you do not have to start the server application or open the source document before you can embed an object.

Viewing the contents of an object is as simple as double-clicking the object.

TASK: View the contents of the embedded object.

1. Double-click the embedded object.

Windows starts Harvard Graphics and opens a copy of the file you embedded (see fig. 11.16). Remember, this is a copy of the original (source) document; any changes you make to this embedded document will not be reflected in the original document. Likewise, if you make any changes to the original document, those modifications will not be incorporated in the embedded document. This is the difference between linking and embedding.

FIG. 11.16 *Viewing the embedded document.*

The Harvard Graphics application window sits on top of the Quattro Pro application window. You can return to the Quattro Pro window without closing the embedded document simply by clicking on a visible portion of the Quattro Pro application window. In figure 11.16, for example, a small portion of the Quattro Pro window shows just below the bottom edge of the Harvard Graphics window. If you click just below the Add Slide box, Harvard Graphics would disappear behind Quattro Pro. Then, when you wanted to return to Harvard Graphics, you could use the Control menu's Switch To command.

Also note that the name of the embedded object has been changed from the original file name. You see ~PKG3422.PRS in the document window title bar rather than QSTART.PRS, the original document name. This helps you remember that you are working with an embedded copy of the original file and not the source file itself.

 2. Next to Slide 1 of 5, click the right-arrow button four times.

    You reach the last slide (see fig. 11.17). Remember that when you view and work on an embedded object, you can do so just as freely as if you were viewing and working on a regular document that wasn't embedded.

Embedding a Harvard Graphics Presentation in Quattro Pro **225**

FIG. 11.17 *The last slide in the embedded object.*

Deleting the Embedded Object

Removing an embedded object from a document is simple. You cannot reestablish the connection, however, so make sure that you want an object removed permanently before you delete it. Otherwise, you have to start from scratch to restore the document. If you don't want an embedded object to show up in the workbook, and yet you're not sure you want to completely remove the object altogether, move the object to a remote location in the workbook temporarily (for example, to cell Q200). Then if you want the object back, you can quickly restore it to its original location.

TASK: Delete the embedded object.

1. Click the object once to select it.

    Sizing bars appear on all sides of the object, letting you know it has been selected.

2. Press the Delete key.

    The embedded object, ~PKG3422.PRS, is now permanently removed from the workbook.

Summary

Embedding a Harvard Graphics presentation in a Quattro Pro notebook is an ideal method to use to submit a very professional-looking proposal or report on disk to a client or to your boss. Additionally, you can work on both documents at once, saving you time and effort because you don't have to continually leave one program to enter the other. Refer to the steps in this chapter until you are able to embed a Harvard Graphics presentation in your Quattro Pro reports on your own.

For more information on using the programs discussed in this chapter—Harvard Graphics for Windows and Quattro Pro for Windows—refer to Que's *Using Quattro Pro for Windows*, Special Edition, and *Using Harvard Graphics for Windows*.

INDEX

Symbols

386 Enhanced mode, Windows, 85

A

absolute cell reference, 90
accessing
   bookmarks in word processing programs, 93-95
   databases, 95-98
   ranges in spreadsheet programs, 95
accessories
   Object Packager, 18
   Windows, Paintbrush, 23
activating packaged objects, 72
alert box, locating source document, 26
Ami Pro for Windows
   bookmarks, 11, 95, 113
   documents
      linking to 1-2-3 spreadsheets, 114-125
      linked to WordPerfect, 161
      linking to WordPerfect, 155-166
      preparing for linking, 115-117
      viewing simultaneously with embedded WordPerfect Package, 172
   packages, pasting, 171-172
   Version 2.0, 45

Appearance window (Object Packager), inserting custom icons, 77-78
applications
   client, *see* client applications
   communication between, with protocols, 91-92
   creating dynamic link between, 23-26
   data
      from two or more forming compound documents, 42-45
      sending to, 92
   DDE macro commands, 105-109
   DDE-capable, 20
      macros, 98-105
   embedding objects in, 14-16
   Equation Editor, 54
   Microsoft Draw, 54
   Microsoft Graph, 54
   Microsoft WordArt, 54-55
   Office Packager, 217-222
   OLE-capable, 11, 59
   requesting
      data from, 92
      update of data from, 92
   sending command strings to, 92
   server, *see* server applications
   stopping update of data from, 92
assigning icons, Object Packager, 170
Associate (File Manager) command, 173

A

Associate dialog box (File Manager), 173
associations (files), 173
automatic updating of links, 34-36

B

bit-mapped data type, 33
Bitmap format, 22
boilerplate text, 93
boilerplates, 114-115
bookmarks
    Ami Pro documents, 113
        creating, 122-124
        preparing for linking, 115-117
    linking, 115
        replacing links, 121-124
    saving text, 116-117
    word processing programs, 93-95
Bookmarks (Ami Pro) command, 117
Bookmarks dialog box (Ami Pro), 117
breaking linking, 36-37
broken links
    reconnecting, 189-190
    restoring, 37-38
business graphics program, 54

C

cancelling
    embedding procedure without deleting objects, 53
    links, 190-191
Cardfile, 11, 45
cell references, absolute cell, 90
Change Link dialog box, 190
channels for DDE
    conversion, opening, 92
    sending data through, 104
charting data for worksheet files, 179-180
charts, embedded
    copying to Clipboard, 184-185
    creating, 180-184
    saving, 184-185
    Excel, linking to Word memo, 186-187
    linked, editing, 191-194
ChartWizard, 181-183
choosing
    between embedding and linking, 16-17
    data types (formats), linked objects, 32-34
    embedding procedures, 45-46
client applications, 11, 21-23, 27-36
    embedding procedure, starting, 45, 49-58
    for embedding, 45
    initiating conversation with server applications, 87-91
    sizing for drag-and-drop packaging, 65-66
client documents, 14
Clipboard
    copying, 21-23
        from versus embedding, 196
        Quattro Pro for Windows document, 12
        source document, 169-171
    copying and pasting drawbacks, 10
    copying embedded charts to, 184-185
    copying method, 47, 49
    copying techniques versus linking and embedding, 17
    documents (Ami Pro), copying, 158
    objects
        linking via, 12-14
        packaging, 63-65
code bars, links, 145
    viewing, 151
codes, formatting
    deleting after link, 162-163
    interrupting in link, 162
    links, removing, 146-148

Index

Column/Row Size command, 129
columns, displaying linked spreadsheets, 129
command strings, sending to other applications, 92
commands
  DDE, 88, 97, 102-104
    accessing databases, 95-97
    accessing ranges in spreadsheet programs, 95
    executing, 104-105
    macros, 97-105
    message set, 91-92
    troubleshooting, 109-110
  dimmed, Paste Link, 134
  DOS, 79
    packaging, 78-80
  Edit Link Options Create (Lotus 1-2-3), 115-118
  Edit menu (Microsoft Word for Windows)
    Bookmarks, 117
    Copy, 125
    Insert Object, 45
    Link, 21-39, 161
    Link Create, 132-142
    Link Edit, 140
    Link Options, 127
    Link Update, 166
    Microsoft Excel Chart Link, 30
    Paste Link, 19, 126, 161
    Paste Special, 13, 19-21, 24-39
  File Links (Microsoft Excel), 23
  File menu
    Associate, 173
    Links, 35
    Open, 116-118
    Save, 137
    Save As, 118
  Options Workplace (Microsoft Excel), 87
  Range menu, Name Create, 136
  Spreadsheet Link, 142-151
  Tables menu, Column/Row size, 129
  Tools menu
    Spreadsheet Create Link, 132-133, 144
    Spreadsheet Update All Links, 150
  Update All Links, 149
  View menu, Reveal Codes, 151
  WM_DDE_ACK, 92
  WM_DDE_ADVISE, 92
  WM_DDE_EXECUTE, 92
  WM_DDE_INITIATE, 92
  WM_DDE_INITIATEACK, 92
  WM_DDE_POKE, 92
  WM_DDE_REQUEST, 92
  WM_DDE_TERMINATE, 92
  WM_DDE_UNADVISE, 92
  see also macro commands
Command Line dialog box (Object Packager), 79
communications
  between applications with protocols, 91-92
  interprocess, 85-87
compound documents, 14, 42-45
controlling update frequency linked objects, 34-36
conversation, DDE, ending, 92
Copy command, 125
Copy dialog box (File Manager), 64
copying
  documents
    Quattro Pro for Windows, 12
    Ami Pro to Clipboard, 158
  embedded charts to Clipboard, 184-185
  from Clipboard, versus embedding, 196
  source documents, Clipboard, 169-171
  spreadsheets, for linking, 125-126

copying (continued)
  with Clipboard, 21-23
  Word data to Clipboard, 208-209
Create DDE Link dialog box (WordPerfect), 134, 137-138
Create Spreadsheet Link dialog box (WordPerfect), 144
creating
  bookmarks, 122-124
  documents, Ami Pro, copying to Clipboard, 158
  dynamic link between applications, 23-26
  embedded charts, 180-184
  embedded objects
    from client applications, 49-51
    from server applications, 47-49
  icons for packages, 76-78
  links, 21-23, 126, 160-162
    Ami Pro to Lotus 1-2-3, 118
    DDE, 137-138
    spreadsheets (Lotus 1-2-3), 144-145
  Microsoft Word for Windows memos, 185-186
custom icons, inserting into Appearance window, 76-77
Custom package icons, (Quattro Pro for Windows), 78

D

data
  cancelling links, 190-191
  charting for worksheet file, 179-180
  creating embedded chart for, 180-184
  embedded charts
    copying to Clipboard, 184-185
    saving, 184-185
  from two or more applications forming compound documents, 42-45
  linked, changing format, 139-140
  location, item, 93-95
  Microsoft Word for Windows, copying to Clipboard, 208-209
  paste-linking, 91
  requesting from other applications, 92
  sending
    to other applications, 92
    to server applications, 102-104
    to server applications through DDE channels, 104-105
data exchange architecture for Windows and OS/2, DDE, 19-20
data types (format), 22
  choosing, 32-34
database programs, accessing ranges, 95-97
database queries, database management programs, 93
databases, accessing, 95-97
DDE, 85-87
  applications, macro commands, 105-109
  bookmarks, 93-95
  channels, sending data to server applications, 104-105
  commands, 88, 97, 102-104
    accessing databases, 95-97
    accessing ranges in spreadsheet programs, 95
  conversation
    acknowledging, 92
    ending, 92
  data exchange architecture for Windows and OS/2, 19-20
  executing, 104-105
  linking, 156-157
  links, 27
    creating, 137-138
    editing, 140-142

macros, 19, 97-105
message set, 91-92, 102-104
messages, structure, 87-91
opening channels, 92
standards, 83
troubleshooting, 109-110
versus OLE linking, 153-155
DDE-capable applications, 20
    macros, 98-105
DDELINK formula, 90-91
deactivating
    links, 129
    text, 124-125
default settings, data type and update frequency, linked objects, 31-36
deleting
    embedded objects, 208
    formatting codes after linking, 162-163
    link codes, 146-148
    links, spreadsheets, 151
    objects, embedded, 52-53, 225
    text, 124-125
destination documents, 11, 42-45
Device-Independent Bitmap data type, 33
dialog boxes
    Associate, 173
    Associate (File Manager), 174
    Bookmarks (Ami Pro), 117
    Change Link, 190
    Command Line (Object Packager), 79
    Copy (File Manager), 64
    Create DDE, 137
    Create DDE Link (WordPerfect), 134, 138
    Create Spreadsheet Link (WordPerfect), 144
    Edit DDE Link (WordPerfect), 140-141, 164
    Edit Link Options (Ami Pro), 124-125
    Edit Link Options Create (Lotus 1-2-3), 119-120
    Edit Link Options Edit (Ami Pro), 124
    Edit Spreadsheet Link (WordPerfect), 148
    File Save As, 118
    Import (Object Packager), 68, 218
    Insert Icon (Object Packager), 220
    Insert New Object (Quattro Pro), 217
    Insert Object (Excel for Windows), 200
    Insert Object (Quattro Pro for Windows), 46
    Label (Object Packager), 73
    Link (Ami Pro), 128
    link list (Word for Windows), 34
    link list (WordPerfect for Windows), 35
    Link Options (Ami Pro), 127
    Link Options (WordPerfect), 147
    linked Word documents, 188
    Links, 188
    Links (Object Packager), 76
    Object Properties (Excel for Windows), 205
    Paste Special (Word for Windows), 25, 32, 48
    Patterns (Excel), 193
    Range Name Create, 136
    Save As, 137
    Update All Spreadsheet Links (WordPerfect), 150
    Update DDE Link (WordPerfect) 166
    warning, 173
    with user-supplied values, 107
    WordBasic, 107
dimmed commands, Paste Link, 134
display type, 55
displaying columns, linked spreadsheets, 129

documents
    activating packaged objects, 72
    Ami Pro
        copying to Clipboard, 158
        linking to 1-2-3 spreadsheets, 114-125
        linking to WordPerfect, 155-166
        preparing for linking, 115-117
        with WordPerfect packages, 172
    containing links, opening, 30
    destination, *see* destination documents
    embedding into Excel, 210-212
    Harvard Graphics, 216, embedding into Quattro Pro document, 216-225
    icons, 70
    interactive, 59, 80-81
    linked, editing, 27-30
    linking, 87-91
        WordPerfect, 137
    multiple links, editing, 31
    packaging, 63-70
        part of, 70-72
    Quattro Pro for Windows, copying, 12
    source, 11
        copying to Clipboard, 169-171
    updating with hidden information, 21
    values paste-linked into, 89
    viewing Ami Pro and WordPerfect, 162
    Word for Windows, linked to Excel worksheet, 31
    WordPerfect
        linked from Ami Pro, 161
        preparing for linking, 159-160
        setting up for linking, 137

    see also compound documents; objects
DOS commands, 79
    File Manager menu commands, 83
    packaging, 78-80
drag-and-drop
    editing, 63
    method, packaging documents, 65-66
drawbacks, copying and pasting via Clipboard, 10
Dynamic Data Exchange (DDE), *see* DDE
dynamic linking, 26-27
    breaking, 36-37
    operations, menu commands, OLE, 83
    troubleshooting, 38-40
dynamic links, creating between applications, 23-26

E

Edit DDE Link dialog box (WordPerfect), 140-141, 164
Edit Insert Object command, 45
Edit Link Create command versus Spreadsheet Link command, 132
Edit Link Options Create (Lotus 1-2-3) command, 115-118
Edit Link Options Create dialog box, (Lotus 1-2-3) 119-121
Edit Link Options dialog box (Ami Pro), 123-125
Edit Link Options Edit dialog box (Ami Pro), 124
Edit Links (Microsoft Word for Windows) command, 23-39
Edit menu commands
    Bookmarks, 117
    Copy, 125
    Link, 161
    Link Create, 132-142
    Link Edit, 140
    Link Options, 127
    Link Update, 166

Paste Link, 19-24, 126
Paste Special command, 13, 21, 24-39
Edit Microsoft Excel Chart Link command, (Microsoft Word for Windows), 30
Edit Paste Special command, 19
Edit Spreadsheet Link dialog box (WordPerfect), 148
editing
   charts, linked, 191-194
   drag-and-drop, 63
   embedded objects, 203-204
   links, 126-128, 163-165, 174-176
      DDE, 140-142
      manual update, 164
      spreadsheets, 148-149
   objects
      embedded, 52
      linked, 27-30
      multiple links, 31
   packaged objects with Object Packager, 72-74
embedded charts
   copying to Clipboard, 184-185
   creating, 180-184
   saving, 184-185
embedded object properties, setting, 204-206
embedded objects, 216
   changing icons, 220-222
   changing labels, 219-220
   creating
      from client applications, 49-51
      from server applications, 47-49
   deleting, 52-53, 208, 225
   editing, 52, 203-204
   icons, 220-222
   printing, 207-208
      preventing, 207
   viewing, 223-225
embedded packages, 70-72
embedded WordPerfect package in Ami Pro document, 172

embedding, 9-10, 84, 167
   documents (Ami Pro) in WordPerfect, 155
   objects, 42-45
      completing process, 222-223
      in other applications, 14-16
   OLE, 195
   procedures
      cancelling without deleting objects, 53
      choosing, 45-46
      client applicartions, starting, 49-58
      server applicartions, starting, 47-49
      troubleshooting, 56-58
   versus copying from Clipboard, 196
   Word documents into Excel, 199-203, 210-212
   see also OLE
embedding and linking
   choosing between, 16-17
   using Object Packager, 18
   versus Clipboard copying techniques, 17
Equation Editor, 20, 54-55
error messages, 22
event-driven programs, 86
Excel 4.0, 20
Excel Chart object embedded in Word for Windows document, 47-48
Excel charts
   editing, 191-194
   inserted in Word for Windows documents, 27
Excel documents,
   embedding Word document into, 199-203, 210-212
   Excel documents with Word document in background, 193
Excel short menu, 204
Excel worksheets
   returning to, 200-202
   setting up, 198-199

{EXEC} macro command, 99
{EXECUTE} macro command, 99
executing DDE commands, 104-105

F

File Links (Microsoft Excel) command, 23
File Links command, 35
File Manager, 63, 168-171
    menu commands for DOS commands, 83
    packaging documents, 63-65
    sizing for drag-and-drop packaging, 66
    source document, copying to Clipboard, 169-171
File menu commands
        Associate, 173
        Open, 116, 118
        Save, 137
        Save As, 118
file names, Object Packager, 68-69
    paths, 138
File Save As dialog box, 118
files
    associations, 173
    Quattro Pro notebook, 215-216
    source, modifying, 160-162
    worksheet, charting data for, 179-180
format, changing linked data, 139-140
formats, 22
    data types, choosing, 32-34
    Picture, 32
    Rich Text Format (FTF), 32
    spreadsheets, linked, 139-140
Formats macro, 102
Formats SYSTEM topics, 102
formatted
    spreadsheets, 139-140
    text, 32
    text data type, 33

formatting
    changing linked spreadsheets, 129
    codes
        deleting after link, 162-163
        interrupting in link, 162

G-H

graphics, linked, inserted in Word for Windows document, 25
graphics programs, 54
Harvard Graphics documents, 216
    embedding into Quattro Pro documents, 216-225
hidden information
    objects, 26
    updating documents, 21

I-K

icon names, Object Packager, 69
icons
    assigning, Object Packager, 170
    creating for packages, 76-78
    Custom package, (Quattro Pro for Windows), 78
    documents, 70
    embedded objects, changing, 220-222
    Object Packager, 18, 60
illustrations created in Paintbrush, 24
Import dialog box (Object Packager), 68, 218
{INITIATE} macro command, 99
initiating conversation with server applications by client applications, 87-91
Insert Icon dialog box (Object Packager), 220
Insert New Object dialog box (Quattro Pro), 217

Insert Object command, 45
Insert Object dialog box
    Excel for Windows, 200
    Quattro Pro for Windows, 46
interactive documents, 59
    creating, 80-81
interactive letters containing package icons, 60
interprocess communications, 85-87
item
    location of data, 88, 93-95
    link name, 165

L

Label dialog box (Object Packager), 73
labels
    embedded objects, changing, 219-220
Link (Edit menu) command, 161
link codes, hidden in spreadsheets, 147
Link Create (Edit menu) command, 132-142
Link dialog box (Ami Pro), 128
Link Edit (Edit menu) command, 140
link list (Word for Windows), 34
link list (WordPerfect for Windows), 35
Link Options command, 127
Link Options dialog box (WordPerfect), 127, 147
Link Options dialog box (Ami Pro), 127
Link Update (Edit menu) command, 166
linked charts, editing, 191-194
linked documents, WordPerfect from Ami Pro, 161
linked objects
    editing, 27-30
    hidden information, 26
linked packages, 70-72
linked spreadsheets, edited, 127-128

linked text, 120-122
linking, 9-10, 26-27
    Ami Pro documents
        to 1-2-3 spreadsheets, 114-125
        to WordPerfect, 155-166
    breaking, 36-37
    copied objects, using Paste Special command, 13
    DDE, 156-157
    DDE vs. OLE, 153-155
    documents, 87-91, 115-117
        WordPerfect, 137
    embedded Excel chart to Word memo, 186-187
    File Manager, 168-171
    manual, 74-76
    Object Packager, 168-171
    objects, 21-23
        via Clipboard, 12-14
    OLE, 166-176, 195
    OLE vs. DDE, 153-155
    programs, spreadsheet, 90
    spreadsheets
        copying, 125-126
        preparing, 117-118
    spreadsheets (Lotus 1-2-3)
        named ranges, 135-136
        to Ami Pro documents, 125-129
        to WordPerfect, 131
    tables (WordPerfect)
        preparation, 167-168
        to reports (Ami Pro), 166-176
    trouble shooting, 38-40
linking and embedding
    choosing between, 16-17
    using Object Packager, 18
    versus Clipboard copying techniques, 17
linking operations, menu commands, OLE, 83
links
    bookmarks, replacing, 121-124
    broken
        reconnecting, 189-190
        restoring, 37-38

links (continued)
  cancelling, 190-191
  code bars, 145
    viewing, 151
  codes, removing, 146-148
  creating, 21-23, 126, 160-162
    Ami Pro to Lotus 1-2-3, 118
  data, changing format, 139-140
  DDE
    creating, 137-138
    editing, 140-142
  deactivating, 129
  editing, 126-128, 163-165, 174-176
    manual update, 164
  formatting codes, deleting, 162-163
  managing, 21-23
  manual updating, 36
  multiple, editing, 31
  names, 119
  naming
    item, 165
    WordPerfect, 163
  options, selecting, 146-147
  packages, pasting, 171-172
  renaming, 164
  replacing, 121
  spreadsheets
    creating, 144-145
    deleting, 151
    deleting tables, 148-149
    editing, 148-149
    multiple, 150
    updating, 149-150
  sustaining, with hidden information, 26-27
  updating, 165-166
    manually, 164, 187-189
    WordPerfect, 165-166
  WordPerfect, setting up before link, 134
Links dialog box, 188
Links dialog box (Object Packager), 76
lists of SYSTEM topics, 101
Lotus 1-2-3 for Windows, 93
  commands, Edit Link Options Create, 115-118
  spreadsheets
    files, 118
    linking to Ami Pro documents, 125-129
    preparing for linking, 117-118

M

macro commands
  DDE, 98-99
  DDE applications, 105-109
  DDE (Quattro Pro for Windows), 99
macros
  DDE commands, 97-105
  Formats, 102
  including DDE commands, 19
  WordBasic, 108
  WordBasic dialog box, 107
managing links, 21-23
manual linking, 74-76
  of objects, updating, 75-76
manually updating links, 34-36, 164, 187-189
mathematical equations, constructing, 54
memos
  creating in Microsoft Word for Windows, 185-186
  Word for Windows, linking Excel chart to, 186-187
menu commands
  dynamic linking operations, OLE, 83
  for DOS commands, File Manager, 83
menus, Excel short, 204
message sets, DDE, 91-92, 102-104
Microsoft Draw, 20, 54

Microsoft Excel for Windows, 45
    charts embedded in worksheets, linking to Microsoft Word for Windows, 178-187
Microsoft Graph, 20, 54
Microsoft Graph object, embedded in Quattro Pro for Windows document, 44
Microsoft Q&E
    copying data, 96
    data manager, 20
    DDE-capable, 96
Microsoft Windows
    DDE message set of commands, 91-92
    Version 2.0, 86
    Version 3.1, 45, 86
    see also Windows
Microsoft Word for Windows, 45
    bookmarks, 93-95
    charts embedded in worksheets, linking to Microsoft Excel 4.0 for Windows, 178-187
    commands, Edit Microsoft Excel Chart Link, 30
    data
        copying to Clipboard, 208-209
        copying to Clipboard, 209
    documents
        values paste-linked into, 88,
        embedding into Excel, 210-212
        in background of Excel document, 192-193
        memos, creating, 185-186
    Version 2.0, 22
Microsoft WordArt, 54-56
modifying source files, 160-162
mouse, packaging documents, 65
multiple links, editing, 31
multitasking, 85-87

N

Name Create (Range menu) command, 136
named ranges
    linking, 135-136
    programs, spreadsheet, 93
names, links, 119
naming links
    item, 165
    WordPerfect, 163
notebook files, Quattro Pro, 215-216

O

object data type, embedding, 33
Object Linking and Embedding (OLE), *see* OLE
Object Packager, 18, 59, 63, 67, 214-222
    application window, 218
    icon and file names, 69
    icons, assigning, 170
    linking, 168-171
    manual linking, 74-76
    packaged objects, editing, 72
    packages, creating, 169-171
    packaging documents, 67-82
object packager icon, 60
Object Packager window, 170
Object Properties dialog box (Excel for Windows), 205
object type list, (Word for Windows), 50
object-oriented graphics programs, 54
objects
    embedding, 42-45
        completing process, 222-223
        in other applications, 14-16
    Excel Chart, embedded in Word for Windows document, 48

objects (continued)
  linked
    editing, 27-30
    hidden information, 26
  linking, 21-23
    via Clipboard, 12-14
  linking copied, using Paste Special command, 13
  Microsoft Graph, embedded in Quattro Pro for Windows, 44
  multiple links, editing, 31
  packaged
    activating, 72
    editing, 73
  packages,creating, 169-171
  packaging with File Manager and Clipboard, 63-65
  WordArt, embedded in Quattro Pro for Windows documents, 44
  WordArt, embedded in Word for Windows documents, 43
objects, created in server application, 50
objects, embedded, 216
  canceling procedure without deleting, 53
  changing
    icons, 220-222
    labels, 219-220
  deleting, 52-53, 208, 225
  editing, 52, 203-204, 219
  icons, 220-222
  preventing printing, 207
  printing, 207-208
  setting properties, 204-206
  viewing, 223-225
OLE, 63-70, 70-72
  linking, 166-176, 167
  menu commands, dynamic linking operations, 83
  standard, 41
  versus DDE linking, 153-155
OLE embedding, 195
OLE linking, 195
OLE menu, data units not accessible, 93-97

OLE standards, 83
OLE-capable
  accessories, 45
  applications, 11, 45, 59
Open (File menu) command, 116-118
opening
  documents containing links, 30
  packages, 172-174
options,
  links, selecting, 146-147
  workspace, Microsoft Excel, 88
Options Workplace (Microsoft Excel) command, 87
OS/2, DDE, data exchange architecture, 19-20

P

package icons containing interactive letters, 60
packaged objects
  activating, 72
  editing with Object Packager, 72-74
packages, 59
  manually linked, updating, 75-76
  objects, creating 169-171
  opening, 172-174
  pasting Ami Pro, 171-172
  WordPerfect embedded in Ami Pro document, 172
packaging, 84
  documents, 63-70
    part of, 70-72
  DOS commands, 78-80
Paintbrush, 11, 23, 45
Paste Link command, 126, 161
  dimmed, 134
Paste Special dialog box, (Word for Windows), 25, 32, 48
paste-linking data, 90
pasting
  packages, Ami Pro, 171-172
  via Clipboard, drawbacks, 10

Index 239

paths, file names, 138
Patterns dialog box (Excel), 193
Picture data type, 33
Picture format, 22, 32
{POKE} macro command, 99
printing
  embedded objects, 207-208
    preventing, 207
process of embedding objects, completing, 222-223
programs
  business graphics, 54
  database management, database queries, 93
  databases, accessing, 95-97
  event-driven, 86
  graphics, 54
  spreadsheet
    accessing ranges, 95
    linking, 90
    named ranges, 93
  word processing, bookmarks, 93-95
  WordBasic, 107
properties, embedded objects, setting, 204-206
protocols, communication between applications, 91-92
  DDE, 86

Q

Quattro Pro for Windows documents
    copying, 12
    embedding Harvard Graphics documents into, 216-225
  notebook files, 215-216
  Version 1.0, 45
queries, database, database management programs, 93

R

Range menu commands, Name Create, 136
Range Name Create dialog box, 136

ranges
  accessing in spreadsheet programs, 95
  named, linking, 135-136
ready loop, 86
reconnecting broken links, 189-190
renaming links, 164
{REQUEST} macro command, 99
requesting
  data from other applications, 92
  update of data from other applications, 92
requests, acknowledging, 92
restoring links, broken, 37-38
returning to worksheets, Excel, 200-202
Reveal Codes (View menu) command, 151
Rich Text Format (RTF) format, 22, 32
Rich Text Format (RTF) text, 22
rows, decreasing, linked spreadsheets, 127-129

S

Save (File menu) command, 137
Save As command, 118
Save As dialog box, 137
saving
  embedded charts, 184-185
  text as bookmark, 116-117
selecting options, links, 146-147
Selection SYSTEM topics, 102
sending
  command strings to other applications, 92
  data
    to other applications, 92
    to server applications, 102-104
    to server applications through DDE channels, 104-105

server applications, 11, 15, 23, 31-36
 embedding procedure, starting, 45-49
 initiated into conversation by client applications, 87-91
 objects created in, 49-50
 sending data to, 102-104
  through DDE channels, 104-105
 source document in, 27
setting embedded object properties, 204-206
setting up
 links, WordPerfect, 134
 worksheets, Excel, 198-199
sizing File Manager and client application for drag-and-drop packaging, 66
Sound Recorder, 11, 45
source documents, 11, 14, 21, 27-30, 42-45
 copying to Clipboard, 169-171
 in server application, 27
source files
 formatting codes, deleting after link, 162-163
 modifying, 160-162
Spreadsheet Create Link (Tools menu) command, 132-133, 144
Spreadsheet Link command, 142-151
 versus Edit Link Create command, 132
spreadsheet programs
 accessing ranges, 95
 linking, 90
 named ranges, 93
Spreadsheet Update All Links (Tools menu) command, 150
spreadsheets
 copying for linking, 125-126
 edited linked, 148-149
 formatted, 139-140
 link code bars, 145
 linked
  changing format, 129
  decreasing rows, 127-129
  deleting tables, 148-149
  displaying columns, 129
  format changing, 139-140
 linking, preparing, 117-118
 links
  deleting, 151
  editing, 148-149
  multiple, 150
 tables, 145
 with link codes hidden, 147
spreadsheets (Lotus 1-2-3)
 linking
  named ranges, 135-136
  to Ami Pro documents, 125-129
  to WordPerfect, 131
 links
  creating, 144-145
  updating, 149-150
Standard Enhanced mode, Windows, 85
Status SYSTEM topic, 101
stopping update of data from other applications, 92
strings, command, sending to other applications, 92
structure, DDE messages, 87-91
SysItems macro, 102
SysItems SYSTEM topic, 101
SYSTEM topic, 100-102
SYSTEM topics generated by Sysitems macro, 101

T

tables
 linked spreadsheets, deleting, 148-149
 spreadsheets, 145
 WordPerfect, 167, 168
tables (WordPerfect)
 linking
  preparation, 167-168
  to reports (Ami Pro), 166-176
 Tables menu commands
  Column/Row Size, 129
{TERMINATE} macro command, 99

text
  boilerplate, 93
  deactivating, 124-125
  deleting, 124-125
  formatted, 32
  linked, 120-122
  Rich Text Format (RTF), 22
  saving as bookmark, 116-117
  unformatted, 22
Tools menu commands
  Spreadsheet Create Link, 132-133, 144
  Spreadsheet Update All Links, 150
topic, name of files, 88
Topics SYSTEM topic, 100-102
troubleshooting
  DDE commands, 109-110
  embedding procedures, 56-58
  linking, 38-40

U

unformatted text, 22
unformatted text data type, 33
Update All Links command, 149
Update All Spreadsheet Links dialog box (WordPerfect), 150
Update DDE Link dialog box (WordPerfect), 166
update frequency, linked objects, 34-36
updating
  data
    requesting from other applications, 92
    stopping, 92
  documents with hidden information, 21
  embedded objects, 202
  links, 165-166
    in documents, 30
    manual, 36
    manually, 164, 187-189
    WordPerfect, 165-166

V

values,
  paste-linked into a Word document, 88
  user-supplied dialog boxes, 107
vector graphics programs, 54
View menu commands, Reveal Codes, 151
viewing
  link code bars, 151
  objects, embedded, 223-225

W

Windows
  386 Enhanced mode, 85
  DDE, data exchange architecture, 19-20
  Standard Enhanced mode, 85
  see also Microsoft Windows
windows
  Object Packager, 170
  Object Packager application, 218
Windows File Manager, 214
WM_DDE_ACK command, 92
WM_DDE_ADVISE command, 92
WM_DDE_EXECUTE command, 92
WM_DDE_INITIATE command, 92
WM_DDE_INITIATEACK command, 92
WM_DDE_POKE command, 92
WM_DDE_REQUEST command, 92
WM_DDE_TERMINATE command, 92
WM_DDE_UNADVISE command, 92
Word documents, embedding into Excel, 199-203
word processing programs, bookmarks, 93-95
WordArt, 20

WordArt object
  embedded in Quattro Pro for Window document, 44
  embedded in Word for Window doucment, 43
WordBasic macro, 108
WordBasic program, 107
WordPerfect for Windows, 22, 93
  documents, 159-160
    linked from Ami Pro, 161
    preparing for linking, 159-160
    setting up for linking, 137
    viewing simultaneously, 162
  links
    naming, 163
    setting up before link, 134
    updating, 165-166
  tables, linking to reports (Ami Pro), 166-176
WordPerfect package embedded in Ami Pro document, 172
worksheet files, charting data for, 179-180
worksheets, Excel
  returning to, 200-202
  setting up, 198-199
workspace options, Microsoft Excel, 88
Write, 11, 45